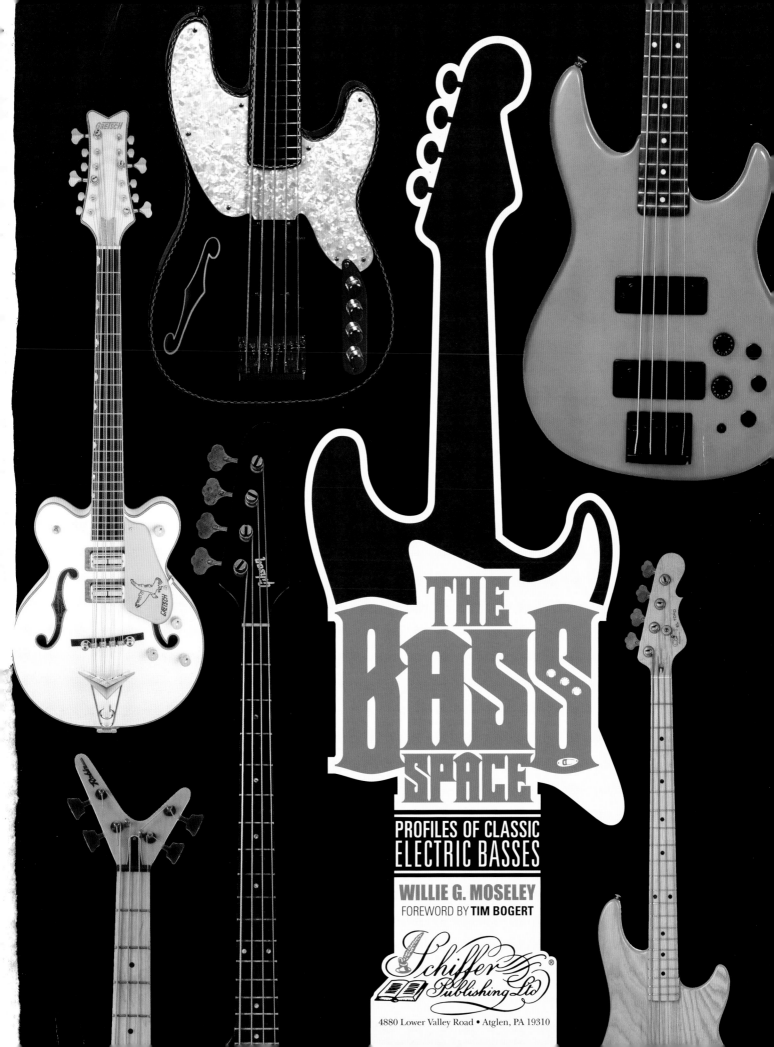

THE BASS SPACE

PROFILES OF CLASSIC ELECTRIC BASSES

WILLIE G. MOSELEY

FOREWORD BY **TIM BOGERT**

Schiffer Publishing Ltd

4880 Lower Valley Road • Atglen, PA 19310

Other Schiffer Books on Related Subjects:
Ball's Manual of Gretsch Guitars: 1950s
   by Edward Ball (978-0-7643-4643-9)
Gretsch 6120: The History of a Legendary Guitar
   by Edward Ball (978-0-7643-3484-9)
The Ultimate: An Illustrated History of Hamer Guitars
   by Steve Matthes and Joe Moffett (978-0-7643-4352-0)

Designed by Justin Watkinson
Type set in Crown Title/Univers LT Std/Minion Pro

ISBN: 978-0-7643-5522-6
Printed in China

Published by Schiffer Publishing, Ltd.
4880 Lower Valley Road
Atglen, PA 19310
Phone: (610) 593-1777; Fax: (610) 593-2002
E-mail: Info@schifferbooks.com

For our complete selection of fine books on this and related subjects,
please visit our website at www.schifferbooks.com. You may also
write for a free catalog.

This book may be purchased from the publisher.
Please try your bookstore first.

We are always looking for people to write books on new and related
subjects. If you have an idea for a book, please contact us at
proposals@schifferbooks.com.

Schiffer Publishing's titles are available at special discounts for
bulk purchases for sales promotions or premiums. Special editions,
including personalized covers, corporate imprints, and excerpts can
be created in large quantities for special needs. For more information,
contact the publisher.

This is for my father
The most honorable man I've ever known

There was one song, Ray Charles' "What'd I Say," that made me want to play in a band. I actually started out on saxophone, and once I switched to bass, I tried to play with a "horn" style, like Jack Bruce did in Cream. Other bassists that influenced me included Paul McCartney and James Jamerson, of course, but that great Memphis sax of King Curtis also figured into my development.

Since it's a fairly new item in musical ensembles, the electric bass is still evolving, and maybe I evolved as a player—I worked my way up from a four-string through a five-string, and I now concentrate on a six-string. The electric bass is a unique instrument, and its sonic possibilities are still being explored . . . and thank goodness for that.

And even though I've taught some lessons and conducted some seminars on bass playing at times, I'm still learning, myself . . . and thank goodness for that, as well. Discovering something new that the bass can do is always a fulfilling experience, and it never gets tiresome.

I've known Willie Moseley for more than twenty years (as this is being written), and he's still going strong with *Vintage Guitar Magazine.* He does his homework when he's preparing for interviews, and delves through lots of old catalog pages when he's researching the history of a particular brand and model of instrument.

Willie's compiled a great assortment of interesting and important basses for the contents of this book. Some of them are collector's items, some are historic, some are just interesting oddballs in the chronology and evolution of the electric bass. He even managed to dig out that old Frankenstein warhorse P-Bass I used earlier in my career!

Mr. Moseley tells me he's a bass player himself, but I get the feeling he prefers, whenever possible, to "perform" on the "keyboard" of a word processor. Check out the instruments he's profiled herein, and enjoy the ride.

Tim Bogert

Photo: Michael Angelo Garcia

INTRO

I think Gregg Allman nailed it when he opined that a drummer's right foot and a bass player's right hand are the backbone of a band . . . presuming, of course, said drummer and bassist are right-handed.

Allman's comments were heard in a documentary film called *Rising Low*, directed by Phish bassist Mike Gordon. The 2002 movie chronicled the recording of a memorial album by a band called Gov't Mule. The album was dedicated to Gov't Mule's late bassist, Allen Woody (1955–2000), and the sessions brought in famous bassists such as Jack Bruce, Chris Squire, Phil Lesh, and others as participants on individual songs. Woody and guitarist Warren Haynes had been members of the Allman Brothers Band before pursuing their off-shoot project full-time (and the perpetually-active Haynes would re-up with the Allman Brothers after Woody's death, but would also continue to helm the Mule, and would be involved with other musical affiliations as well).

While guitars and drum-style percussion instruments are centuries old, the (usually-electric) bass instrument that is encountered in most modern musical aggregations was introduced in the middle of the twentieth century, and did indeed seem to carve out its own sonic niche between percussion and instruments that were carrying the melody of a song.

And perhaps this writer gravitated towards basses because yours truly may have been, at different points in my amateurish musical aspirations, a frustrated guitar player and a frustrated drummer . . . plus, there was a bass player in one of the bands I was playing with who developed a habit of not showing up, so he was sacked, and I parked my rhythm guitar and took over his slot (which meant that the income, such as it was, would be divided in bigger proportions among band members). At the time, I didn't even know about the differences in scale length on certain bass models.

Playing bass does indeed mean that while a bassist needs to be in sync with a kick drum, he/she is also playing an instrument that emits (low-end) musical notes, so he/she has to be aware of tunings, tone, and riffs as well. And the more I played bass, the more fascinating the instrument became.

That being said, my musical abilities didn't necessarily improve dramatically. Nevertheless, I believe that musicianship as well as writing skills, whether formally taught or self-taught through long hours of concentration and practice,

should each have a sense of integrity as their respective foundations, and that's what I've always tried to convey as either a player or a scribe.

The basses profiled herein will be, for the most part, standard four-string instruments that are usually tuned (low-to-high) E-A-D-G. Five-string basses of two types (a lower B string and a higher C string) will also be encountered, as will true "bass guitars" with six strings.

Most instruments on display are American-made, but a few imported basses have been included because of a particular "cool" factor, be it innovative and/or nostalgic. Moreover, in some cases I've opted to feature a unique (and possibly short-lived) variant or custom-made example of a particular model if a decent example was available—early 1960s Gibson EB-0 and EB-3 basses being exemplary—instead of a "standard" item.

Ditto celebrity-associated models taking precedent, even if they were stock or highly modified examples.

We even managed to sneak a few guitars into this effort, on accounta they figured into the story lines of certain profiles.

It was also decided that this anthology would concentrate a bit more on "everyman" instruments instead of high-end, exquisitely-crafted creations, but a few custom-made/one-of-a-kind basses will indeed be found herein as well.

My thanks go out to Alan Greenwood and Doug Yellow Bird of *Vintage Guitar Magazine* for their efforts in supplying many of the images herein, most of which were photographed at guitar shows for the *VG* archive.

I've had a courteous and professional relationship with photographer Bill Ingalls Jr. since 1991, and his ongoing friendship and work ethic is inspiring, as exemplified by his help with this project.

And in more recent times, Mike Gutierrez of Heritage Auctions enthusiastically got involved in supplying a slew of instrument images (for the magazine and for this book), so I need to single out his support, too.

The approvals for re-use by Alan, Bill, Mike, other photographers, and other persons, businesses, or organizations that own the rights to certain images are deeply appreciated (they're listed in the Photo Credits at the other end of the book).

A tip of the headstock for input also goes to (alphabetical order): Paul Bechtoldt, Steve Brown, Susan Carson, Walter Carter, Jol Dantzig, George Gruhn, Tom Petersson, John Shanley, Kevin Wright, and Michael Wright.

Thanks also go out to Alan Greenwood, again, for ongoing writing opportunities, and here's another sincere "read-between-the-lines" salute to the Messrs. Spilman for encouraging me to become a full-time writer.

Last but not least, thanks to the following individuals and businesses/photographers (in alphabetical order) for supplying the instruments to be photographed, or ready-to-go images, as well as images of catalog pages, brochures, etc.:

Randy Anderson, Bass Emporium, Wes Bentley, Kevin Borden, Jonathan Bouquet, Charlie Bowen, Steve Brown, Jay Bruce, Buffalo Brothers Guitars, Ricardo Cabeza, Tom Callins, Jeff Carlisi, Capitol Music Center, Walter Carter, Guido Ciardetti, Randy Cooper, Russ DaShiell, Davy Davis, Jim "Flex" DeStafney, E.J. Devokaitis, Mark Egan, Barry Ehrlich, Elderly Instruments, Steve Evans, Charles Farley, John Files, Arnold Finkelstein, Ryland Fitchett, Bill Flippo, Allan and Terry Franklin, Fretted Americana, Sid Green, Don Greenwald, Gruhn Guitars, Guitar Center, Guitar Emporium, Guitars and More, Mike Gutierrez, Bruce Hall, Headless USA, Heritage Auctions, Gregg Hopkins, Bob Hynosky, Bill Ingalls Jr., Nan Jacobs, Doug Johnson, Dawn Jones-Garcia, Bill Kaman, Will Kelly, Michael Law, Dallas Lowndes, Mark Luciani, Marty's Music, Maverick Music, Debbie McDurmin, Dean Moody, Music City Pickers, Music Magic, The Music Shoppe, National Music Museum, Olivia's Vintage, Tom Petersson, Ricky Phillips, Jay Pilzer, Greg Platzer, Carl Ponder, Rockahaulix, Randy Pratt, Rudy's Music Shop, Rumble Seat Music, Judith Schiller, Bob Shade, Donnie Sheehan, Arian Sheets, Naffaz Skota, Gil Southworth, Michael G. Stewart, Frank Tanton, Fiona Taylor, Robert Tompkins, *Vintage Guitar Magazine*, The Vermont Collection, Dale Wagler, Darlene Ward, Steve Wariner, Dave Wintz, Bart Wittrock, Tom Wittrock, Kevin Wright, Richard Lee Young.

As Tim Bogert averred, the electric bass always seems to be in transition, as musicians seek to develop new sounds and new styles. The instruments profiled herein aren't all of the examples of the classic and/or unique low-end items that are around, so hopefully this presentation will merit a sequel sometime down the road; i.e., maybe this is volume one.

In the meantime, let's take a look at some cool basses.

W.G.M.

This battered and worn photograph, taken with a Polaroid "Swinger" camera ($19.95 list) dates from October 27, 1968. It shows the iconic British trio Cream in concert at Chastain Park, Atlanta, Georgia, during their final tour. The band's innovative music has held up over the ensuing half-century, as has the interest in their instruments. Left to right: Jack Bruce, who's playing an example of the bass with which he was usually associated, the Gibson EB-3; Ginger Baker is on drums, and Eric Clapton wields an early 1960s Gibson "reverse" Firebird I guitar. All things considered, the photo has held up pretty well too. *Willie G. Moseley*

LEXICON

ACTIVE CIRCUITRY: Solid-state circuitry built into certain instruments, which provides additional sonic options beyond standard/passive volume and tone controls. Such selections can include volume boost, tone enhancement, compression, etc. Active circuitry is usually powered by one or two 9-volt batteries installed in the instrument body.

ARCH-TOP: Self-explanatory; some instruments have a curved top that is sometimes carved. The term is usually associated with guitars rather than basses.

BINDING: Material that is usually made from flexible plastic; "binds" edges of wood together, but sometimes its use is strictly cosmetic.

BRIDGE: Metal, wood, or plastic part on the top of a bass where strings "transmit" vibrations to the body of the instrument for sonic reproduction. A bridge usually has small grooves in it to accommodate each string. Most bridges on electric basses allow adjustment of string height, and many also have adjustable "saddles" for individual strings, to allow intonation/fine tuning.

BOLT-ON: Refers to a type of attachment of a neck to a body (as found on most Fender basses).

BOUT: Upper and lower portions of a bass or guitar body, separated by an indention/"waist." The sections have a connotation that implies viewing an instrument that is on display vertically—"upper bout" refers to the part of the body nearer to the neck joint (and where cutaways are found), "lower bout" refers to the portion nearer the end of the body, where the bridge, controls on electric instruments, etc. are usually found.

CARVED TOP: This term usually describes a contoured top found on some basses. The carve may be part of the same wood as the body, or may be a different wood that is attached.

CENTER DETENT: A middle/halfway "stopping point" for reference on a rotary control.

COIL TAP SWITCH: Cuts out one of two coils in a humbucking-type pickup (see "PICKUP").

CONTOUR: Beveling on solid body basses to enhance comfort, as pioneered by the second-generation Fender Precision Bass of the mid-1950s. Usually such contouring consists of a "belly cut" on the back, and a "forearm bevel" on the top—and both of those terms are self-explanatory. As noted earlier, contouring can also be found on the top of an instrument body.

CONTRABASS: A six-string bass, with a lower-tuned and higher-tuned string in addition to the normal four strings on a standard bass. Regular tuning for a contrabass is B-E-A-D-G-C.

CUTAWAY: Portion of bass near neck/body joint that appears to have been "cut out" to allow access to higher area of the neck. Such shaping creates a "horn" on the body silhouette. Instruments may be single-cutaway (1950s budget instruments by Kay and Danelectro), symmetrical double-cutaway (Gibson EB-2), or offset double-cutaway (almost all solid body basses).

F-HOLE: F-shaped soundhole (as seen on cellos and other classical instruments). Usually found on arch-top instruments, but sometimes, fake/cosmetic f-holes are simply painted or applied (as decals or stickers) to the tops of certain basses (and guitars).

FLAT-TOP: Another self-explanatory term, this is the classic configuration of an acoustic guitar, and some bass models have a similar construction style.

FRET: A "space" on a bass fingerboard/fretboard that serves the same function as a piano key by changing the pitch of a string by one note. The small metal strips that delineate each fret are usually made of "fret wire," an alloy.

FRET MARKERS: Also known as "position markers." Decorative dots, blocks, or other inlay on the fretboard playing surface and/or side of the neck for visual reference.

FRETBOARD: Also known as a fingerboard. Top surface of a bass neck where notes are selected and played. Many times, a maple fretboard is actually part of the neck itself instead of being a laminated part. Rosewood and ebony are the most popular fretboard woods laminated to the top of a neck.

GERMAN CARVE: A contoured portion around the top edge of a guitar body; often seen on Mosrite instruments.

HEADSTOCK: Top of instrument where the tuning keys and brand name are (usually) found.

HOUSE BRANDS: Private label instruments that were marketed by larger retailers such as Sears (Silvertone), or wholesale distributors such as St. Louis Music (Custom Kraft). American-made house brand basses were usually made by budget manufacturers such as Harmony, Kay, Valco, and Danelectro.

JACK: Receptacle for guitar cord.

LUTHIER: Guitar builder; a person who handcrafts stringed instruments.

NECK-THROUGH: Construction style that utilizes a long piece of wood (sometimes made of several laminated layers) that runs the entire length of the instrument, as pioneered by the Rickenbacker 4000 in the mid-1950s. On a solid body instrument, the sides of the body are glued onto the neck/center portion.

NEW OLD STOCK: ("N.O.S."): Indicates an instrument that may be decades old, but was never sold at retail, for one or more anomalous reasons. The story behind the 1981 G&L L-1000 (serial number B003861) seen in this book is exemplary. Such instruments, by definition, are usually very clean for their age.

NUT: Small grooved part between headstock and fingerboard, usually made of bone, plastic, metal, or, in more recent times, space-age composite material.

PAN KNOB: A more-recent variant of pickup selection on basses. Rotary control that allows a player to gradually blend one pickup with another, instead of abrupt changes (see TOGGLE SWITCH).

PASSIVE ELECTRONICS: Standard/"non-active" electronics in an instrument; no battery required.

PHASE SWITCH: Reverses polarity of pickups to evoke unique sounds.

PICKGUARD: Somewhat self-defined item, usually made of plastic or metal, that shields the bass body from pick damage (if the player happens to use a pick); also known as a "scratchplate." Pickguards are usually mounted on brackets in an elevated position on arch-top or carved top basses, or flush on the body of most solid body or flat-top basses.

PICKUP: Microphone-like device consisting of magnet(s) and wiring that "picks up" string vibrations. "Single-coil" pickups have a self-explanatory designation, while "humbucking" pickups have two coils, wired in opposition to each other to cancel out annoying electrical noise. If an instrument has a coil-tap switch, one coil of a "humbucker" can be turned off to evoke a single-coil sound. While most pickups are mounted under the strings on the top of a bass body, some transducer-type pickups are built into a bass's bridge (and usually aren't visible). Many pickups have individual "polepieces" (one for each string at a minimum) for more efficient reception of the string's vibration signal, and some threaded polepieces are adjustable for height.

P/J PICKUP CONFIGURATION: A pickup arrangement on a bass that consists of one Precision Bass-style pickup (split offset) and one Jazz Bass-style pickup (straight rectangular).

POTENTIOMETERS: "Pots" aren't visible, but are critical to the function of an electric bass—they're the electronic controls underneath a volume or tone knob. Many potentiometers have an Electronic Industries Association (EIA) code stamped into their casing (if they were made in the US) that notes the date they were manufactured. If an instrument has no serial number—or the serial number has been removed—its pots, if original, can be useful in dating the instrument itself.

RADIUS: Curvature of fretboard. 12-inch and 7½-inch radii are often cited in guitar/bass construction. The lower the number, the more pronounced the curvature of the fretboard will be.

SCALE: Distance from nut to bridge. Fender's 34-inch scale on the original Precision Bass of the early 1950s has become the industry standard for basses, and is also known as "full scale" or "long scale." Some instruments have a short scale (30–30½ inches), a medium scale (32 inches), or an extra-long 35-inch scale.

SEMI-HOLLOW: Certain instruments, as exemplified by the groundbreaking Gibson EB-2 of the late 1950s, may look like a hollow body instrument on the outside, but have a center block inside, running from the neck joint to the end of the body.

SET-NECK: Refers to the glued-in neck style found on some basses (most Gibson models, for example).

STRING TREE: Hardware attached to headstock to stabilize strings between nut and tuning keys.

TAILPIECE: Anchor point for "ball end" of string. Independent tailpieces are usually "stop"-type (attached to the top of the bass) or "trapeze"-type (usually found on arch-top/semi-hollow basses, attached to end of the body). Many basses feature a bridge and tailpiece that are combined into one unit.

THINLINE: A hollow or semi-hollow guitar or bass configuration with a body that has a shorter depth (usually around two inches) than most acoustic stringed instrument bodies.

TOGGLE SWITCH: Turns individual pickups off and on. The most common configuration is found on a two-pickup bass, with a three-position toggle switch that works either pickup individually or both at the same time. Toggle switches are also used to control other funcations of a bass, particularly on active instruments.

TRANSDUCER: A type of pickup that fits under, or is built into, the bridge of an acoustic instrument.

TRUSS ROD (and TRUSS ROD COVER): Most modern basses have a metal truss rod inside the neck to alleviate string tension (which, if not controlled, could cause the neck to warp). The truss rod is usually adjustable, and on some brands, a small plate located on the headstock (just behind the nut/headstock juncture) covers the access point. On many bolt-on instruments, the truss rod can be adjusted by removing the neck.

VIBRATO: While the ability to change the pitch of a note or a chord on stringed instruments using a device with an "arm" that is manipulated by a player's hand is usually associated with electric guitars rather than basses, bass vibratos do exist.

VOLUTE: Thicker, hump-like portion of the back of the neck at the headstock juncture. Reportedly adds strength to help prevent cracking or damage at that location, but a volute isn't found on too many instruments.

ZERO FRET: An extra piece of fret wire positioned where the neck joins the headstock; utilized with a string guide placed where a nut would normally be to facilitate better-sounding chords . . . although chords generally aren't played on basses. Nevertheless, a zero fret might help smooth out multiple string bass riffs. Often found on Mosrites, Hallmarks, and Standels.

THE ONES THAT STARTED IT ALL

The ol' upright/"doghouse"/"bull fiddle" bass was a real pain for most combos or bands in the first half of the twentieth century, regardless of what musical genre such aggregations purveyed. The instrument was a critical sonic component in almost any outfit, but it was large and cumbersome. Countless smaller groups could be seen traveling from performance to performance in a station wagon, with the bass, ensconced in a canvas bag, strapped on top of the vehicle. The musicians could only hope and pray that the instrument had been fastened to the car in a secure manner, and that the canvas container didn't leak if they happened to encounter a rainstorm between gigs.

Accordingly, the idea of a louder and/or amplified bass interested many working musicians. The venerable Gibson company of Kalamazoo, Michigan, had built and marketed a large acoustic fretted bass instrument, the Style J Mando-bass, starting in 1912. It sported four strings that were tuned an octave below a guitar, and could be played standing or seated. It still had a standard-for-an-upright scale of forty-two inches.

By the mid-1930s, most forward-looking stringed instrument manufacturers had realized that electric amplification was the path to louder (and hopefully more compact) basses, and an obscure Washington state inventor and a California manufacturer were on parallel paths in designing and marketing an instrument that didn't look quite like a traditional upright bass, but was supposed to emulate its sound.

The earliest documentation of a modern-style bass with an electromagnetic pickup cites a Pacific Northwest musician/tinkerer named Paul Tutmarc, who appeared in an article titled "Pity Him No More—New Type Bull Fiddle Devised" in a 1935 edition of the *Seattle Post-Intelligencer*. Tutmarc was displaying what appeared to be a solid wood model of an upright bass. The item was actually a working instrument, however, and the article sang its praises as replacing the traditional bull fiddle.

A musical jack-of-all-trades, Tutmarc was a retailer, radio performer, and teacher, but his passion was experimenting with methods to improve the sound of instruments. He founded a company called the Audiovox Manufacturing Company, which concentrated on making amplifiers and lap steel guitars.

Tutmarc would ultimately disassemble his experimental instrument, trashing the body and retaining the neck and pickup in storage. However, his subsequent bass instrument—again, a solid body—was even more revolutionary regarding its construction, aesthetics, and playability.

The Audiovox 736 Bass Fiddle, first offered in 1936, was a small, four-string bass that had frets and was designed to be played horizontally, just like a guitar. Its body silhouette was similar to one of Tutmarc's lap steel designs, and its pickup and volume knob were installed in a mirror steel plate that mounted on the top of the instrument.

The body and neck were made of black walnut, and the ebony fretboard had sixteen (usable) frets, joining the body at the twelfth fret. Its scale was a comfortable 30 5/16 inches.

One ad for the 736 offered with a matching (and loud for the times) amplifier called the 936. The ad copy intimated that the volume produced by the pair, " . . . will take the place of three double basses."

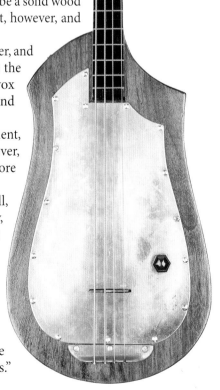

Audiovox 736 Bass Fiddle, mid-1930s.
John Vicory

Gibson upright electric bass, late 1930s. *Gruhn Guitars*

Historian/author Peter Blecha owns the 736 seen on page 11. For years, he served as the senior curator of the Experience Music Project museum in Seattle, and did the bulk of research in digging out the history of Paul Tutmarc and the Audiovox company.

"I first heard rumors about an early Seattle-based guitar and amp company back in the late 1970s," he recounted. "I saw the first photos of the Tutmarc family playing them in 1983. Soon after, I began buying lap steels and amps for $25 dollars, $50 dollars, and $75 dollars each because the shops did not know their history or significance. For years, area guitar shops would hold them for me because nobody wanted them. I have bought over forty various units over the years. Audiovox remains an abiding research topic of interest, as does the life and life's work of the self-described 'inventor' Paul Tutmarc. Along the way I have also acquired the cast-aluminum volume pedal he made in the 1930s and his brass telescope."

Blecha opined that musicians who heard the 736 when it was introduced in the mid-1930s would have probably found its sound to be " ... impressive and mind-blowingly solid."

As for the sound of the instrument through modern-day amplification, Blecha said, "It's not a boomer, but has good, distinct articulation. The famed Chilean solo bassist Igor Saavedras visited me in 2015; we got the bass out of storage, he played it, was delighted, and duly inspired, wrote a new song on the spot in dedication to it and its fine tone. I believe he has since recorded that song."

Gibson upright electric bass, late 1930s. *Jonathan Santa Maria Bouquet/ National Music Museum*

Electro Bass Viol, mid-1930s. *Gruhn Guitars*

The 736 may look somewhat homemade to some observers, but like better-grade Audiovox lap steels, it has a professional-quality finish and details, according to Blecha.

The 736 was not successful, and to vintage guitar aficionados, it would be considered an example of something that was ahead of the curve regarding traditional bass players. Another line called Serenader was marketed by Tutmarc's son Paul Jr. ("Bud") in the late 1940s. That brand also marketed a solid body fretted bass, but was also less than successful.

The primitive styling of the Audiovox 736 Bass Fiddle might mean that antique stores or flea markets may be unaware that they have some iconic rough diamonds in inventory, as only three 736s have ever been found.

Around the same time Paul Tutmarc was toiling in obscurity in Washington, California's Electro company was developing an electric bass with a decidedly more traditional playing style but a definitely-different look.

Electro's frontline brand was Rickenbacker, and that brand had already garnered notice for its early electric lap steel guitars. The company's Bass Viol, introduced in 1936, was basically the neck of an upright bass mounted on an aluminum frame, which was in turn mounted on top of an amplified speaker cabinet. The pickup for this instrument is the legendary "horseshoe" style, seen just above the bottom of the upright bass portion of this primitive "rig." Owing to the lack of a sonically-adequate amplifier, the Bass Viol was discontinued in 1941.

Gibson made several electric upright basses in the late Thirties; the existence of at least three has been documented, and two are shown here. They had all-maple bodies that were shaped like a guitar rather than a doghouse bass, and their 42¾-inch scale necks had lines on the fingerboard where metal frets would normally be on a guitar (if

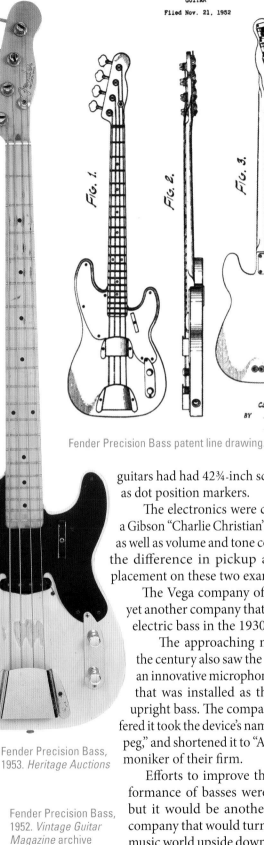

March 24, 1953   C. L. FENDER   Des. 169,062
GUITAR
Filed Nov. 21, 1952

FIG. 1.   FIG. 2.   FIG. 3.   FIG. 4.

INVENTOR.
CLARENCE L. FENDER
BY
Lyon + Lyon
ATTORNEYS

Fender Precision Bass patent line drawing.

guitars had had 42¾-inch scales), as well as dot position markers.

The electronics were comprised of a Gibson "Charlie Christian"-style pickup as well as volume and tone controls. Note the difference in pickup and control placement on these two examples.

The Vega company of Boston was yet another company that designed an electric bass in the 1930s.

The approaching mid-point of the century also saw the introduction an innovative microphone-like gizmo that was installed as the peg of an upright bass. The company that proffered it took the device's name, "amplified peg," and shortened it to "Ampeg" as the moniker of their firm.

Efforts to improve the sonic performance of basses were numerous, but it would be another California company that would turn the popular music world upside down in late 1951, with the introduction of an instrument that would revolutionize the sound and playability of low-end stringed instruments.

Fender Precision Bass, 1953. *Heritage Auctions*

Fender Precision Bass, 1952. *Vintage Guitar Magazine* archive

A decade and a half after Paul Tutmarc's primeval solid body fretted bass failed to garner any notice in the musical instrument marketplace, the Fender company of Fullerton, California, announced the introduction of its Precision Bass in November of 1951. The upstart Orange County manufacturer had already garnered a considerable amount of notice among musicians the previous year, when it had introduced a solid body, plank-like electric guitar with a bolt-on neck. The guitar would ultimately become known as the Telecaster, but the Precision Bass was a radically different item that quickly excited bass players in all types of musical aggregations.

Leo Fender (1909–1991) and his long-time right-hand man, George Fullerton (1923–2009) had labored long and hard to design a bass instrument that would not only appeal to upright bass players, but to guitarists who might be considering bass as an alternate instrument.

Accordingly, the Precision Bass looked and played like a solid body electric guitar, but was supposed to sound like an amplified bull fiddle. Fender and Fullerton tried more than one scale length on their experimental/workshop models, and settled on thirty-four inches, which is still the industry standard.

The instrument designs of Leo Fender and his associates were always more concerned with practicality rather than aesthetics, yet the original Precision Bass also turned some musicians' heads due to its cutting-edge (for the time) cosmetics. True, it had the same headstock silhouette, plank/slab-like body, butterscotch finish, and black Bakelite pickguard as found on the company's first electric guitar, but the Precision Bass was the company's first instrument with two cutaways. What's more, the chrome handrest in the middle of the body and the bridge cover both had a swept-back profile that might have been a subliminal and/or unintentional allusion to the Jet Age, which was also in its infancy (the handrest is missing from the 1953 example, exposing the primitive-looking pickup). Fender's new solid body bass was actually sleeker-looking than the solid body guitar that preceded it.

Controls were simple volume and tone knobs, mounted in a chrome plate on the surface of the body. With flatwound strings (which installed through the rear of the body) and a mute on the underside of the bridge cover, the Precision Bass sounded much like the doghouse bass it sought to supplant, but a brighter tone could be evoked if a player used a pick instead of fingers, and/or removed the mute. Capable of more than the stereotypical "thump" of an upright, the "P-Bass" quickly gained favor in musical genres such as country & western, as Fender's other products were already well-known among pickers in that segment of music.

Indeed, on page 166 of *Hank Williams: Snapshots From The Lost Highway* (Da Capo), a 1952 concert photo shows Williams introducing his new bride, Billie Jean, to an audience during a "Louisiana Hayride" tour. In addition to several "TV-front" Fender amplifiers onstage, the band's bespectacled bass player is seen holding a newfangled Fender Precision Bass just like the ones seen on page 13.

Word also rapidly spread among players of other musical styles about the new solid body stringed instrument that played low notes and was easy to transport.

The Fender Precision Bass was such a unique instrument that for a time, "Fender Bass" became a generic term in studio recording logs for any solid body fretted electric bass, in order to differentiate it from an upright bass.

In 1954, the Precision Bass underwent several significant changes, and while changes to the Telecaster guitar occurred around the same time, some of the transmogrifications to the P-Bass also owed a tip of the headstock to Fender's newer solid body electric guitar, the double-cutaway Stratocaster, introduced the same year.

Perhaps the most important change to the P-Bass was the conversion of its body to a contoured configuration for better ergonomics. The Precision acquired a forearm bevel on the front and a "belly cut" on the back, just like the body profile of the new Stratocaster. It needs to be pointed out, however, that some "slab" Precision Bass bodies were reportedly used by the company as late as 1957.

There were cosmetic changes to the second generation P-Bass as well: The standard finish became a yellow-and-brown/two-tone sunburst finish, which was also the standard finish on the Stratocaster. The standard pickguard for the P-Bass was changed to white, which was also the pickguard color for the Strat, but the P-Bass pickguard maintained the same large silhouette as its black predecessor. Blond became an optional finish, and also became a lighter shade, à la the color change for Telecasters around the same time (such a finish is often dubbed "Tele blond"). Pickguards on blond, contoured mid-1950s P-Basses were also eventually changed to white.

While the overall aesthetics of the mid-1950s P-Bass tilted more towards the Stratocaster instead of the Telecaster, its peghead retained the original Tele-type profile instead of the larger, curved-and-pointed/upside-down surf wave silhouette as seen on the Strat's headstock.

Other transitional actions on these transitional basses took place in 1955, and were "under the covers," so to speak. Steel bridge saddles replaced pressed fiber saddles, and the pickup got staggered-height polepieces to balance the output of the strings.

Yet another facet regarding mid-1950s Precision Basses was the official introduction of a special order custom color program in 1956. Standard Dupont ("Duco") colors were available for an extra charge, although this had apparently been an unofficial policy all along. Such an option was supplanted by an official list of standardized, factory-available custom colors later in the 1950s.

The difference in comfort between the original early 1950s P-Basses and the "in-between" mid-1950s P-Basses is immediately obvious to any player, thanks to the contouring on the latter, but many mid-1950s Precisions also have the reputation of being surprisingly lightweight, and that's the case for both examples seen here.

In 1957, the Precision Bass assumed the silhouette and electronics layout that have been with the standard version of the model ever since. Such items included a split/offset humbucking-type pickup with two polepieces for each string, a smaller pickguard (a lower extension of which housed the control knobs, eliminating the separate control plate), and a headstock silhouette that matched the Stratocaster. Strings now installed through the end of the bridge/tailpiece instead of through the body, and the chrome pickup cover/handrest and bridge cover had been restyled to a less-aerodynamic look.

The pickguard on the ultimate version of the standard P-Bass was originally a gold anodized aluminum item, but was soon replaced with a plastic tortoiseshell 'guard. Likewise, the fretboard originally stayed maple, but switched to rosewood late in the decade. The new fretboard sported flat white "clay dot" markers, which would change to pearl dot markers in the mid-1960s. The standard finish of the body became a three-tone sunburst, with a reddish color found between the yellow and dark brown finishes. Compare the differences in the two classic configurations seen here.

Moreover, this particular 1960 P-Bass is also historically significant, as it was owned by bassist Bill Black, the original bassist for Elvis Presley (but Black had parted ways with Presley when he acquired this instrument).

Black was a Memphis musician whose biggest claim to fame was backing Elvis Presley, along with guitarist Scotty Moore, at the outset of the King's career. Black's exuberant and percusive "slap" style on the upright bass was a critical part of the advent of rockabilly, but once drummer D.J. Fontana became a member of Presley's backing band, Black ultimately moved over to a mid-1950s "in-between" sunburst Fender Precision Bass with a white pickguard (and photos exist of Presley himself playing around with Black's P-Bass).

Black and Moore left Presley in September of 1957, and the bassist would organize Bill Black's Combo, in which he used newer-style P-Basses, including this one. That band garnered a major instrumental hit with "Smokie, Part 2," and had eight tunes in the Top 40 between 1959 and 1962. Bill Black's Combo opened for the Beatles on the English band's first tour of the United States (following their appearance on "The Ed Sullivan Show"), but Black himself did not participate. He was already battling a brain tumor, and would pass away during surgery in 1965, shortly before his fortieth birthday.

The cosmetic configuration of Black's 1960 P-Bass—sunburst finish, tortoiseshell pickguard, rosewood fretboard—would be seen in the hands of innumerable bassists during the "guitar boom" of the 1960s.

Of course, the Precision's hardware and electronics have been improved over the decades, and there have been other adjustments to such facets as string loading, but a standard P-Bass—regardless of where it's manufactured—looks pretty much like the version that was introduced in the year the Space Race began (the Soviet Union launched Sputnik, the first successful earth satellite, in October of 1957).

The Fender Precision Bass has been through many different variants over the decades—two-pickup models, active circuitry models, signature models, and other styles, but the standard P-Bass is a dependable and definitive example of "if it ain't broke, don't fix it" when it comes to musical instrument design.

CHAPTER TWO

ALEMBIC

The Alembic company of Santa Rosa, California, has been lauded for decades by professional musicians for its finely-crafted instruments using exotic woods and its cutting-edge innovations in electric bass and guitar luthiery.

Alembic's history began in the late 1960s, in a collaborative effort with some of the original San Francisco "psychedelic" bands such as the Grateful Dead. The Alembic founders were recording engineer Ron Wickersham and his wife Susan, soon to be joined by Bob Matthews, also a recording engineer, and luthier/guitarist Rick Turner.

The concept of installing active electronics into the body of a guitar or bass in an effort to improve its sonic capabilities had cranked up soon after solid body instruments had established their turf in the marketplace, but it wasn't until 1969 that active electronics came into prominence among notable musicians, when Alembic began hot-rodding guitars and basses.

While the earliest Alembic instruments were indeed one-of-a-kind items built to the specifications of a "Who's Who" of pro players (their first custom-made instrument was a medium-scale, neck-through bass built for Jefferson Airplane's Jack Casady), practical innovations would ultimately become a trait of the company's production instruments.

This 1975/first-year Series I bass was originally owned by Carl Radle (1942–1980), bassist for Derek & the Dominoes and other bands that also featured Eric Clapton as the guitarist. Radle had first hooked up with Clapton when the bassist was playing with Delaney & Bonnie and Friends, the band that opened for Blind Faith, the supergroup in which Clapton was a member, during Blind Faith's only tour.

Radle was also the bassist on Joe Cocker's "Mad Dogs and Englishmen" tour in 1970, and performed on Clapton's first solo album, which was released the same year.

The bass features a walnut top and back over a mahogany core, and has laminated maple and purpleheart neck-through construction. Its rosewood fretboard has abalone inlay, and the scale is thirty-four inches. A brass nut and brass bridge offer increased sustain, which was part of Alembic instruments' huge-and-resonant sound.

The headstock features a stainless steel Alembic logo, which shows a hand reaching down from a cloud, gripping a teardrop-shaped object.

Alembic Series I.
Steve Evans

The instrument's active circuitry controls include separate volume and tone controls for its two pickups (that's a "dummy" pickup, designed to cancel out electronic hum, between the two real ones), as well as "Q" switches for each (real) pickup. Alembic's "Q" circuitry provides the tone knob an extreme tone sweep capability that evokes a wah-wah pedal-like effect when the knob is manipulated. A pickup selector switch is found on the treble cutaway. There are two jacks on this bass—one is a standard ¼-inch type, while the other is a five-pin stereo cannon jack.

Of particular aesthetic and functional interest is what the company terms its "Standard Point" body silhouette. The pointed tail end at the bottom of the body is not there simply for esoteric reasons—it's also a reminder to a player that the instrument must be placed on a guitar stand when it's not in use, as the bass cannot be leaned up against a speaker cabinet by itself.

Alembic's records don't offer much information about the bass, other than its construction.

"We've never had it back here," said Alembic spokesperson Mica Wickersham, "so it's had a quiet life, from our perspective. But it seems more interesting things may have happened to it."

Former Clapton guitar tech Willie Spears recalled stenciling the information on this Alembic's flight case, and believes Radle might have used the bass on Clapton's *No Reason To Cry* album, released in 1976.

Rick Turner would depart Alembic in the late 1970s, and would go on to make his own guitars and basses. Before Turner left, however, the company began incorporating efficient production techniques into the creation of new models, in an effort to hit a lower price point.

The Distillate, introduced in 1981, was one of the earliest of the more-financially-accessible Alembic basses, and was the first standard Alembic model to be available in mono only. The first 1981 examples were single-pickup models with top-mounted brass control plates, made for the Japanese market.

Two-pickup Distillates, designated for the United States, came along in 1982, and the one seen here is a first-year example.

Standard features on the Distillate included a five-layer laminated maple and purpleheart neck-through design, and a Honduras mahogany body topped by an exotic wood.

Choices of such exotic woods, according to an Alembic price list, included Maple, Flame Maple, Quilted Maple, Burl Maple, Bird's Eye Maple, Walnut, Burl Walnut, Figured Walnut, Bubinga, Bocate, Coco Bola, Pinstripe Zebra-wood, Erratic Zebrawood, Flame Koa, Tulipwood, Lacewood, Rosewood, Maccassar Ebony, or Vemillion. This example has Flame Koa.

This early Distillate has a multiple-layer headstock in the original/standard Alembic silhouette. It's topped off with a koa laminate, and the neck has an ebony fretboard with standard oval-shaped inlays.

The nut, bridge, and tailpiece are all made of brass. The scale is thirty-two inches, which was more common with Alembic than most other manufacturers.

Two hum-canceling active circuitry pickups were controlled by a rotary switch, and the model had a master volume and master tone knob. Earlier examples had the rotary pickup switch on the treble cutaway, as seen here, while later Distillates' pickup switches were located just in front of three mini-toggle switches.

The first two of the three mini-toggle switches are each three-way, for bass boost/cut and treble boost/cut (the middle position is considered "neutral"). The third mini-toggle is two-way, and is a "Q" switch.

The small whitish item near the jack is an LED, which illuminates in red when the cord is inserted, to indicate that the battery is on. This LED wasn't seen on later Distillates.

For comparison, note the body silhouette, location of the pickup control, and absence of an LED on the Distillate, topped with a Zebrawood cap, shown in a 1989 catalog.

While the Distillate was a production instrument, some special-order options were available. On this one, which was ordered by a Florida music store, such custom features included neck width, pickup location, and a deeper-than-standard treble-side cutaway.

Other listed options for the Distillate included scale length, side position LED markers, fingerboard LED markers, laser LED fret markers, and custom fingerboard inlay. It was available in four-string, five-string, six-string, and eight-string variants, and could also be ordered in a left-handed configuration.

The Alembic Distillate was discontinued as a regular production instrument in 1990, but continued to be offered as a special-order bass.

As is the case with many, if not most, Alembic instruments, this 1982 Distillate is a one-of-a-kind item. While it was designed as a proportionally lower-priced model, it still has plenty of the unique and laudable facets that made the Golden State builder a legend in high-end luthiery.

Alembic Distillate, 1982. *Bill Ingalls Jr.*

DISTILLATE

I f near-perfect isn't near enough then the answer may just be a Distillate bass. Creating this "10" has been accomplished by incorporating several of the most requested features of Alembic's custom basses into a single, production instrument. The result is an instrument with an uncompromising look, sound and feel that will satisfy the perfectionistic player while simultaneously impressing even the most discriminating listener.

Alembic's hum cancelling active circuitry including unique bass and treble cut and boost controls, bookmatched hardwood top and five-piece laminated neck are among the many standard features of the Distillate Series.

Pickup Selector
Bass Cut/Boost
Treble Cut/Boost
Volume
"Q" Switch
1/4" Phone Jack   Tone Filter

From a 1989 Alembic catalog.

THREE

AMPEG/DAN ARMSTRONG

How's this for a paradox? One of the most eye-catching instruments to hit the market during the latter days of the fabled 1960s' guitar boom was actually colorless.

The Ampeg company was known primarily for its amplifiers, and by the end of the 1960s, the company had already made and marketed a "Baby Bass" upright bass and had imported English instruments made by the Burns company (re-branded as Ampegs).

Ampeg had also made several models of domestic-made fretted and unfretted solid body basses (some of which had holes that went all the way through the instrument's body; see catalog page from 1967), but nothing in the American market compared to the clear lucite/plexiglas guitars and basses that the Linden, New Jersey, firm debuted at the

National Association of Music Merchandisers (NAMM) show in June of 1969.

Fender had made a one-off all-plexiglas Stratocaster in 1957 (to be used as an educational tool), but the Ampeg instruments that premiered some twelve years later were bona fide production instruments. Produced in a collaboration with retailer/consultant Dan Armstrong, the "see-throughs," as the instruments were quickly dubbed, became instant favorites of notable rock stars.

Of particular note was the use of a guitar and bass, respectively, by Keith Richards and Bill Wyman of the Rolling Stones, during that band's infamous 1969 US tour, which culminated at a disastrous free concert at the Altamont Speedway in California. Other players who would ultimately play "plexi" Ampeg/Dan Armstrong basses included Jack Bruce of the Cream, as well as the Mahavishnu Orchestra's Rick Laird.

ASB-1 Fretted & Fretless Basses

AEB-1 Freted Bass

AUB-1 Fretless Bass

SSB Short Scale (Compact) Bass with Magnetic Pickup

The instruments featured a maple neck with a faux rosewood laminate on the headstock, and Grover tuners. The instrument had a 30½-inch short scale. The fretboard was (real) rosewood with tiny dot position markers. It had twenty-four frets, all of which were, er, clear of the body. The pickups on the see-through guitars were interchangeable, but the bass had a permanent and powerful stacked humbucking pickup, with a treble coil on top and bass coil on the bottom.

Surprisingly, the bridge/tailpiece was very no-frills, apparently having been (subliminally?) inspired by the Danelectro company's cheapo instruments (see "Danelectro/ Silvertone"). Strings anchored in the tailpiece, and the bridge was a small piece of rosewood that could be manipulated to evoke a bit of fine-tuning.

There were two strap buttons on the body, to allow a player a choice regarding how to balance the instrument when a strap was attached, but the redundant components also provided a more stable resting position if an instrument was leaned against a speaker cabinet.

Controls were a simple volume control, and a not-quite-simple tone control. On the first 1,000 or so instruments produced, the tone knob functioned as a type of mixer between the two coils of the pickup. Subsequent examples offered a two-way toggle switch (seen on this example) to bypass the treble coil and cut in an additional capacitor for even more bass tone.

Sonic deficiencies in their electronics troubled the see-through series, to the extent that a notice was distributed by the factory in 1971, concerning modifications (capacitors, rewiring, etc.) to improve the instruments' sound. Production ceased around the end of that year.

In addition to the solitary fretted plexi bass shown here, a trio of combo instruments seen on the next page—an Ampeg see-through guitar, a set of clear Ludwig drums, and a fretless Ampeg see-through bass (of which around 150 were made) exemplify why such instruments looked incredibly cool.

In terms of playability, Ampeg's see-through basses fit the stereotype of short scale instruments being easy to plunk. While a bass with a shorter-than-standard scale can be considered sonically-challenged, the Ampeg/ Dan Armstrong's unique controls and dense body evoke a sound that was more vibrant than most other 30½-inch scale basses. However, "dense" = "weight": These are among the heaviest short-scale basses ever produced.

The Ampeg brand is now owned by St. Louis Music, a wholesale distributor that also owns other instrument and amplifier companies. An imported re-issue series of lucite guitars and basses was marketed in the late 1990s, featuring an improved bridge.

Accordingly, any time something is (re-) introduced as a "retro" product, the original item must have had something going for it, which was definitely the case for Ampeg/Dan Armstrong See-throughs. Say the phrase "cool and clear" to any knowledgeable guitar fan, and he/ she will most likely immediately know what brand and model you're talking about.

See-through bass, circa 1970.
Vintage Guitar Magazine archive

See-through guitar, drums, and fretless bass. *Steve Evans*

FOUR

BALDWIN BY BURNS

An average observer of the musical instrument marketplace would probably surmise that any time a famous maker of pianos wants to get involved in the electric guitar market, the latter instrument genre must be pretty active, and such was the case when the Baldwin Piano & Organ Company bought the Burns company of London, England.

Jim Burns had been building instruments in England since the early 1950s, and his guitars and basses had been gaining in popularity there in the first half of the 1960s. Reportedly, Baldwin had been one of the contenders to purchase California's Fender guitar company when the innovative Golden State manufacturer was sold to CBS in 1965, so the legendary piano company turned around and purchased Burns of London the same year.

Burns instruments had actually appeared in America earlier in the decade under their own name, and as noted in the previous chapter, had also showed up briefly in the US sporting the Ampeg brand. With Baldwin, however, a full-blown attempt to compete with Gibson, Fender, et. al. was in the offing.

About all Baldwin had to do to its newly-acquired line was change the brand name on the pickguards of instruments (and for that matter, such a move had also been the case when Ampeg had sold Burns-made guitars and basses). Endorsers in the latter half of the 1960s would include the American Breed, of "Bend Me, Shape Me" fame.

Exemplary basses from the Baldwin-Burns era, which lasted a bit more than half a decade, included the Jazz Bass, which had no connection to the Fender model of the same name.

The Jazz Bass was a short-scale instrument with twenty-two frets. Curiously, the scale on the Baldwin variant was thirty inches, while the original Burns model had a scale of 31½ inches (close to medium scale's standard length of thirty-two inches).

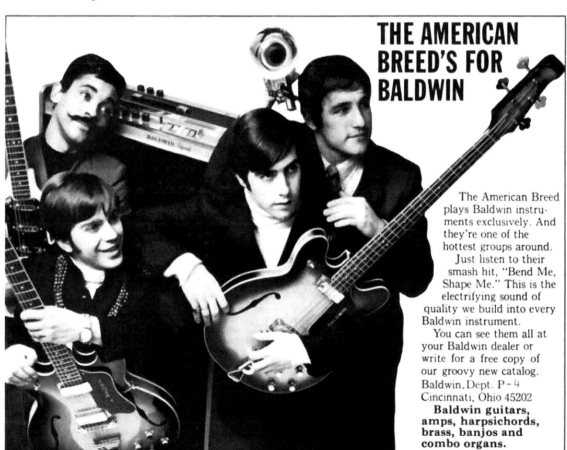

American Breed endorsement ad.

The model was sort of a rare bird, electronics-wise, in that it was a three-pickup bass (Burns Tri-Sonic units). It had a companion guitar, the "Jazz Split Sound," so named because of the unique circuitry that proffered a four-position rotary selector knob (closest to the logo on the pickguard). The four sonic designations for the Jazz Bass were "Contra Bass," "Bass," "Treble," and "Wild Dog" (and that latter setting is a nostalgic favorite for many aging guitarists). The middle knob was the tone control, while the rear knob was the volume control.

Finishes included red sunburst (shown), green sunburst, white, black, or red; the guitar was available in the same colors. The headstock configuration would be changed later in the model's history.

One "new" Baldwin model that was introduced soon after the piano company acquired Burns was the Baby Bison, its name indicating that it was a less-fancy/budget model based on another Burns bass. Again, there was also a matching Baby Bison guitar.

Proffered from 1966–1970, the Baby Bison had actually been created by Burns just prior to its sale to Baldwin. The English company wanted to market this model for export only, and such a scenario happened, albeit not in the manner some Burns employees might have expected.

The Baby Bison also had a thirty-inch scale and twenty-two frets, with a slightly-scrolled headstock style (and this is the same headstock profile that the Jazz Bass would ultimately acquire).

Note the four pieces of plastic attached to the top of the body—while the control plate and (clear) pickguard are functional, the two pieces on the cutaway horns are purely cosmetic, and may have been placed there to reinforce the model name.

The pickups were two "Bar Magnet" bass units. Controls consisted of volume, tone and "density" knobs, plus a three-way pickup toggle switch. The bridge/tailpiece was a relatively-short-lived item called a Reso-Tube unit.

Finishes (for both the guitar and the bass) included red (shown), white, black, and golden sunburst.

Baldwin lacquired the Gretsch brand later in the 1960s, and dropped Burns-made instruments from its lineup in favor of the better-known American brand.

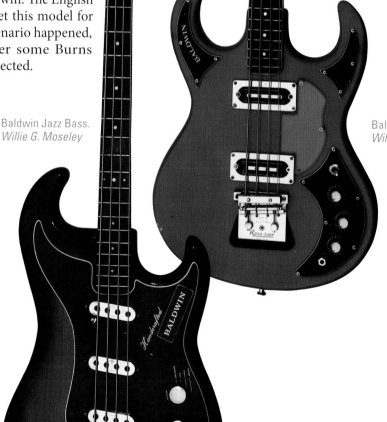

Baldwin Jazz Bass.
Willie G. Moseley

Baldwin Baby Bison.
Willie G. Moseley

BARRINGTON

In the mid-1980s, Peter LaPlaca, who already had years of experience as the head of sales and marketing for Gibson during its Norlin ownership era, and who had been a principle in the early days of the Kramer company, was itching to get back into the guitar business. He had left Kramer in 1981, but was still involved with other musical instruments besides guitars (saxophones in particular).

"With Kramer losing ground, there was a 'hole' in the market for something new or different," he said of the middle of the 'Me Decade,' "as long as I could get old or reliable contacts to support design concepts and production availability in both Japan and Korea."

As it turned out, two factories in Japan would manufacture the instruments for LaPlaca's new venture. The music industry veteran chose the brand name for the line due to his company's location in Barrington, Illinois.

LaPlaca recruited Ron Lukowski, who was adept at guitar design and production, as vice president and general manager, and the Barrington Guitar Werks launched its effort at the NAMM show in Anaheim in 1987.

Some Barringtons were labeled as the "U.S.A. Pro Series," and LaPlaca explained that those instruments were so named because of the input of professional American musicians. Many instruments were shipped to Illinois to have upgrade electronics, bridges, and tuners installed.

"Ron was a bit uncomfortable with the 'U.S.A.' identification," LaPlaca recounted. "but the bottom line is that these were made exclusively for us, for U.S.A. distribution, and were all designs by U.S.A. artists and our team here."

Players who were associated with Barrington on their U.S.A. Pro Series included bassist T.M. Stevens, who was involved with the design of the bass models that bore his initials.

"T.M. was a great friend of mine since the Kramer days," LaPlaca recalled, "and he contacted me about us doing something special for him . . . he visited with us for several days as we worked out a custom design model."

At the time, Stevens was the bassist for the Joe Cocker Band, and he would quickly recruit that band's guitarist, Phil Grande, as another Barrington endorser.

The TMS-5 featured a bolt-on maple neck with a contoured heel. A brass nut was standard, as well as a striped ebony fretboard, which had twenty-four frets. The alder body had a unique silhouette with more-offset-than-usual cutaway horns, as well as a carved top. Gold hardware was also standard.

Electronics were two single-coil pickups, one of which was wound in reverse to evoke a humbucking effect when both pickups were on. TMS basses had active circuitry, and the four in-line control knobs had a sensible layout—master volume, a pickup pan knob, and master bass and treble controls.

Finishes included Jet Black (JB), Gold Flake White (GW, seen on this example), Candy Red (CR), True Metallic Blue (TMB), Nile Blue (NB), and Magenta (MG). The model was also available with an ash body and a Transparent Walnut (TW) finish.

The TMS-5 listed for $1,599.50, while a four-string (TMS-4) and a four-string fretless version (TMS-4/F) each listed for $1,499.50. The four-string models had the same construction features and came in the same finishes as the five-string model.

A Candy Red TMS-5 and several photos of Stevens with a white example graced the cover of the 1989 Barrington bass catalog, along with images of bassist Randy Coven, who endorsed Barrington's NTB-332 Newport bass.

Barrington Guitar Werks would also market a Korean-made sub-brand called Foxxe, and that effort would figure into the end of the company's brief existence, as LaPlaca recalled: "Our demise was a matter of too much, too soon, with inadequate financial control. Banks came to lend us money, but we wasted too much with promotions that did not pay off. We also launched Foxxe as a lower end line of electric solid bodies too early in the game, which ate up a lot of cash. We started with a new Korean factory for

Barrington TMS-5, late 1980s. *Willie G. Moseley*

CHAPTER FIVE

Foxxe, and had enormous quality control issues. At one point, we discovered almost 600 pieces of Foxxe models that we could not sell due to neck pocket problems. In addition, Barrington Guitar Werks was in competition with our own successful line of saxophones. We sacrificed the guitar business in exchange for keeping the sax business moving ahead. All of this came down in 1990–91. Tragic as it was, I still receive many inquiries about Barrington, and the vibes continue to be positive about how great these guitars were."

That being said, La Placa is content to maintain his present course in the horn business.

"Guitars and horns are very different when it comes to marketing, which is my forte," he said. "Horns are much like the automobile business, where dealership loyalty is a given. Guitars continue to vacillate widely with music fads and performer tastes. Dealers who focus on the guitar business are always looking for the latest 'hot' or 'new' brand, at the expense of their last 'hot' or 'new' brand."

1989 Barrington bass catalog cover.

SIX

BUNKER

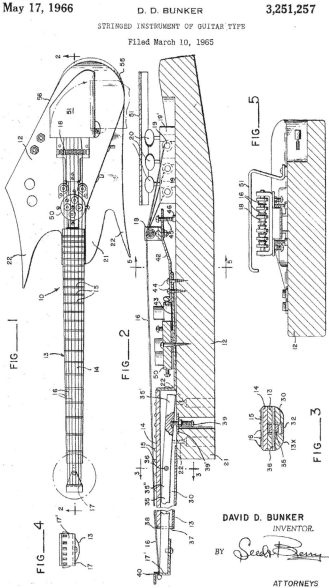

May 17, 1966   D. D. BUNKER   3,251,257

STRINGED INSTRUMENT OF GUITAR TYPE

Filed March 10, 1965

DAVID D. BUNKER
INVENTOR.

BY

ATTORNEYS

Bunker patent line drawing.

Made and marketed before Steinberger headless instruments or the Kramer "Duke" headless series, the early 1970s Bunker "Pro-Bass" bass was radical-looking for its time, but to most observers, such instruments probably weren't as unusual as some of the other creations of musician/inventor Dave Bunker, longtime innovator from the Pacific Northwest.

Bunker is probably best-known among guitar aficionados for his unique doubleneck Touch Guitar and the two-handed tapping system by which such instruments are played. Bunker's invention of a unique instrument and a unique playing style preceded instruments such as the Chapman Stick by many years.

Bunker Pro-Bass, 1970s. *Vintage Guitar Magazine* archive

On the other hand, Bunker's Pro series of guitars and basses were strung and played like standard instruments, but their design and aesthetics were quite unusual.

Bunker first filed for a patent on a headless guitar in March of 1965, and his design was approved in May 1966. The design of the patented instrument generally conformed to the style of what became the ProStar series.

"I had an all-girl band that played Vegas," Bunker recalled, "and I was trying to cut some weight off of the body for the instruments they would use. I wanted the guitars to be petite, and wanted them to be easier for the girls to tune. I thought it would be much easier to hold a guitar with your left hand, and tune it with your right hand if the tuners were on the body."

The ProStar guitars and Pro-Bass had Bunker's patented "floating" neck, which utilized a ⅜-inch steel bar acting as a cantilever for both ends. Bunker recounted that the rod weighed some six to eight ounces more than a standard single truss rod. The neck attached to the body using a screw and dowel assembly, according to company literature.

The vestigial Gumby-shaped headstock was "strictly for show," according to Bunker, and could be removed if desired. The ball end of strings anchored in a large bracket at the end of the neck, and a brass nut (often seen on 1970s instruments, as such an item was designed to help sustain) was standard.

ProStar guitars and the Pro-Bass were also early examples of twenty-four-fret electric instruments. Maple fretboards were standard, and their inlay was somewhat unusual. Black dots with white centers (described by Bunker as "plastic inside of plastic") were found on the first octave. An additional set of smaller, solid black dots were also placed at the twelfth fret, and only the smaller markers were used on the fifteenth, seventeenth, nineteenth, and twenty-first frets. Four small black dots adorned the twenty-fourth fret.

The Pro-Bass on the previous page appears to be an early 1970s example, as its scale is 30½ inches, the original length. During its brief life, however, the series was made up primarily of thirty-two-inch scale basses. The matching guitars had a 25½-inch scale, and one of those is also seen here as a bonus.

Bunker ProStar guitar, 1970s.
Heritage Auctions

As for the body silhouette, the ProStar series was designed with ergonomics and balance in mind. Bunker knew full well that a guitar or bass body with tuners mounted on it was going to look striking to some potential players but weird to others, so small cutaway horns were added in attempt to provide a "traditional" reference.

The instruments were usually seen with all-maple construction, although walnut bodies, as well as laminated bodies made from those two woods, were also offered.

Hardware included a massive Bunker-designed brass bridge (check out the length of travel for each saddle, regarding intonation possibilities!). Like brass nuts, brass bridges were sonically-desirable in the Pro-Bass's time.

Dave Bunker remembers that Grover tuners were used on ProStar instruments in the earlier days of the series, and later, Sperzels. The jack was located on the edge of the body, near the G string's tuner key.

The pickup on the Pro-Bass is a DiMarzio, and the mini-toggle offers coil tone selection from the pickup. The two knobs are for volume and tone. Two-pickup versions of the Pro-Bass were also offered.

The company later marketed the Magnum Bass, an active electronics version of the Pro-Bass. That step-up model had the company's own innovative "Super Magnum pickups" which were another Bunker innovation—the system utilized four small pickups; one for each string.

Dave Bunker's reputation had already been forged in the musical instrument world thanks to the Touch Guitar, and he says the reaction to the ProStar series was initially positive, due to its combination of striking looks and traditional playability. The veteran builder says that many guitarists and bassists proclaimed the cutting-edge instrument headless design to be "twenty-five years ahead of its time."

However, the so-called cutting edge can also be the first thing that hits a brick wall, and not enough players stepped up to the ProStar series, which floundered after several years in the marketplace.

Bunker reported that in recent times, interest in his ProStar series has increased, and as of this writing he was planning on building a re-issue of the bass.

SEVEN

CARVIN

In the pantheon of legendary guitar manufacturers, Carvin has been successful with its "factory direct" approach for decades. The company was founded in southern California by Lowell Kiesel (1915–2009), an accomplished lap steel player, in 1946. Carvin expanded its facilities more than once, ultimately building guitars, basses, amplifiers, and sound reinforcement gear at its 82,000-square-foot facility in San Diego. While the company has several retail stores, the bulk of its business is still done direct via phone, mail, and the internet. Customers who ordered a Carvin stringed instrument had dozens of options regarding finishes, body and headstock shapes, woods, inlays, and electronics.

Things didn't start out that way, however. Kiesel's company began by making pickups and selling them to other builders. Considering the founder's instrument of choice, it wasn't any surprise that Carvin began manufacturing and marketing lap steels in the early 1950s.

Once Carvin opted to participate in the rapidly growing solid body Spanish electric guitar market, their earliest offerings were Höfner guitars and basses imported from Germany (the brand would, of course, later become famous worldwide as the maker of the left-handed violin-shaped bass played by Paul McCartney of the Beatles), and Carvin would subsequently make hybrid instruments that utilized parts made by both companies.

This mid-1960s model 74-BG is a bass with a Höfner-made body and neck, and Carvin-made APB-4 pickups—list price $259, "wholesale" (to retail customers) $125, according to the catalog. The company also offered a one-pickup bass, the 84-BG, which listed for $210 and sold for $105.

There was also a matching guitar in the series . . . mainly because they were the same instrument, each with a 25⅛-inch scale, albeit with different pickups, bridges, nuts, and tailpieces. The sonic capabilities of any bass that has a guitar-like scale is dubious, but Carvin's catalog proclaimed that such construction made an instrument "a natural for any guitar player."

The 74-BG had a maple body and bolt-on neck (which had an adjustable truss rod), and a rosewood fretboard with twenty-two frets. The single-play white pickguard housed a three-way pickup toggle switch and volume and tone controls for each pickup.

A bit of controversy might have been in the offing concerning some of the catalog text, as the text stated that the 74-BG was "100% American-made." One would surmise that Carvin's perspective was that a guitar or bass wasn't "made" until its parts (whether domestic, imported, or a combination) were assembled, and such final assembly for this instrument was indeed done in California. In the ensuing decades, other guitar manufacturers have used similar wordplay when imported parts were put together in the US.

And in an advertising spiel about the bass's standard sunburst finish that, decades later, comes off as bizarre-sounding to guitar and bass aficionados, the 1966 Carvin catalog intoned: "The new sunburst finish is outstanding, with a natural maple center blending to a dark edge, hand-rubbed to a fine piano finish. We realize there are some who like bright colors; however, generally they are considered cheap and inexpensive in appearance. Perhaps someday you may wish to sell your guitar, and the fine sunburst will always have a much better resale than a gaudy color. With a Carvin maple body, you know you are getting a fine piece of wood. However, with a solid color it's just as well you never saw the body before it was painted. That is why we no longer produce guitars in solid color."

In the vintage guitar and bass world, the reverse has turned out to be true—standard sunburst instruments of all brands usually fetch less than, er, "gaudy colors," and Carvin would later change its strategy. By the late twentieth century, the company was offering dozens of custom color options for potential customers.

Carvin 74-BG, mid-1960s. *Bill Ingalls Jr.*

Doubleneck instruments have always been in a unique niche in the guitar market, for good reason. They seem to have an image of superiority or insinuation that they are intended for pro players; i.e., those who could deftly switch from one instrument to another in the middle of a song. Though they look hyper-cool when strapped on, donning them usually reveals that they're heavy and cumbersome.

And while doubleneck instruments are an acquired taste, Carvin nevertheless offered such a configuration from the late 1950s until the early 1990s.

"The first doublenecks debuted in 1959," said Kevin Wright, webmaster for www.carvinmuseum.com, "and you could get a six-string guitar/short-scale four-string bass, or a six-string guitar/eight-string mandolin—pretty revolutionary for the time."

This mid-1960s 4-BS is one of Carvin's earlier doubleneck styles, with Carvin's own pickups and Höfner necks (the same length of which avers the basic-guitar-that-utilizes-bass-parts concept). The minimalist body saves weight (catalog hype said that the instrument weighed approximately nine lbs.), and the 4-BS was only thirteen inches wide. The guitar side has a bridge and vibrato system made by the Bigsby company.

The controls on this primitive two-fer are less complicated than a potential player might think, but the four toggle switches on the center plate are simply off-on switches for each pickup. There's also a master volume control, master tone control, and jack. Simple as that.

In the middle of the guitar boom decade, the 4-BS listed for $457, but sold for a "wholesale price" of $229.90, with a deposit of $80 required when an order was placed. The Bigsby vibrato system added $29.90 to the price, and the purchase of a hardshell, plush-lined case was mandatory ("due to protection and packaging," said the catalog). The case listed for $49, and sold for $29.90 with a requisite $10 deposit.

The LB70, introduced in 1976, was the company's first effort at a thirty-four-inch scale instrument (the "LB" prefix stood for "Long Bass"), and it was also the last of the "Höfner hybrids." The full-scale Fender Precision Bass had become the industry standard since it was introduced a quarter-century earlier, and like many other brands and models, the LB70 had a blatantly Precision-like silhouette. The instrument shown here is a 1977 stereo example.

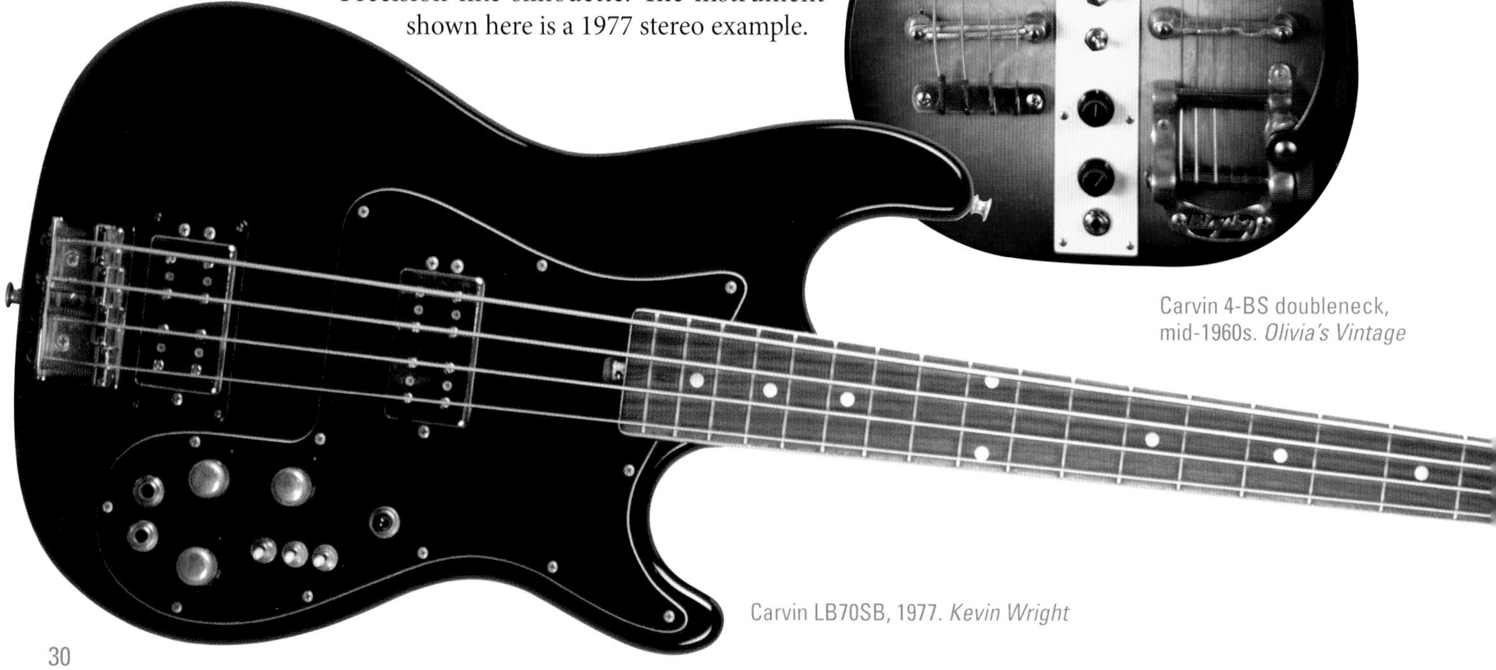

Carvin 4-BS doubleneck, mid-1960s. *Olivia's Vintage*

Carvin LB70SB, 1977. *Kevin Wright*

The LB70 featured a Höfner-made, German hard rock maple neck and a Carvin-made solid maple body. The 1977 Carvin catalog touted its weight at 10½ pounds.

The Fender-like headstock sported Schaller M4SL tuning machines. The neck had twenty frets on a bound rosewood fretboard with mother-of-pearl dot markers, and its truss rod was adjustable at the neck/body juncture.

The neck dimensions measured, according to catalog text, "1⁹⁄₁₆ inches wide at the nut, 2⅜ inches wide at heel, ⅞ inches thick at fifth fret. Guaranteed to play with all strings less than ³⁄₃₂ inch away from the twentieth fret, without any buzzing frets."

The body had a laminated black celluloid pickguard (also Höfner-made), and a "hand-rubbed, durable polyester finish" that came in black only for a standard LB70B, but in two finishes for the stereo version—black (LB70SB) or clear (LB70SC).

The first pickups found on the LB70 were open-coil, APH-4N humbucking pickups, but in 1977, those items acquired chrome pickup covers and became known as APH-8 pickups. That annum would be the only year the LB70 had such pickups, as in 1978, Carvin's new M22B pickups, which sported twenty-two polepieces, were introduced on the only bass in the company's catalog (and it wasn't the LB70).

The LB70's intonatable bridge's plate and saddles were made of brass, to facilitate sustainability. Note the close proximity of the APH-8 treble pickup to the bridge, which was unusual in such times.

The standard LB70B had Gibson-like controls, with a separate volume and tone control for each pickup, and a three-way pickup toggle switch, as well as a phase switch. One electronic option was dual-coil to single-coil switching. The input jack was also on the top of the pickguard.

The controls on this LB70SB stereo version are obviously more complex. The three-way pickup toggle is still there, but has been moved a bit further up the pickguard from its location on a standard LB70B.

This example also has three mini-toggles, consisting of two coil-splitter switches (one of each pickup), and a phase switch. Because of a plethora of knobs and switches on the LB70SB and LB70SC (and a limited amount of space on the pickguard), the models had individual volume controls, but a master tone control. Curiously, this knob incongruity on the stereo model wasn't pointed out in the 1977 catalog.

The presence of two input jacks visually tags this LB70SB as a stereo instrument, but the wiring of the inputs was similar to Rickenbacker's "Ric-O-Sound" configuration— plugging into one jack with a regular cord would still allow both pickups to be utilized in a mono signal if desired.

In the 1977 Carvin catalog, the LB70S listed for $520, with a manufacturer-direct price of $259. The stereo LB70SB and LB70SC listed for $600, with a $299 manufacturer-direct price. One requisite item was the HC17 hardshell case ($86 list, $46 manufacturer-direct); by that time, Carvin instruments were not sold without cases.

The LB70 may have been an admirable, dual-humbucker utility instrument for many players, but the handwriting was (temporarily) on the wall regarding Carvin basses with bolt-on necks. As noted earlier, there was only one bass in the 1978 catalog, the CB100, an un-Fender-like single-cutaway instrument with a bolt-on neck that had a 2+2 headstock (two tuners on each side, à la Gibson basses), and the company's new M22B pickups. Soon afterwards, the company began concentrating on set-neck models, to be followed in the 1980s by neck-through designs.

"The late 1970s were a transitional period for Carvin," says Kevin Wright. "The company began moving away from assembling Höfner-supplied bodies and necks equipped with Carvin electronics to designing and building their own guitars and basses completely in-house."

The LB70 would disappear from Carvin catalogs for several years, but the model number was resurrected in 1988, in a configuration that Wright pronounced as, " . . . the cornerstone of Carvin's new neck-through series basses. It's still a popular model to this day, and has been supplemented with five-string and six-string versions."

♪

Carvin's DN640 was a unique example in the doubleneck genre. Unlike production models from other manufacturers such as Gibson and Rickenbacker, its bass neck was on the bottom instead of the top. Introduced in 1980, the DN640 and a six-string/twelve-string twin neck companion, the DN612, were Carvin's first modern/all-US-made doublenecks. Moreover, this "reverse-neck" layout was only one of several unique facets of the DN640.

As for the model designation, "DN" stands for doubleneck, and "6" and "4" indicate the number of strings on each neck. Simple as that.

The original owner of the DN640K on page 32 had it made with Hawaiian koa wood—thus the additional "K"

in the model number. In more recent times, koa has gained respect as a tone wood, and has accordingly increased in price. The instrument has set-neck construction and ebony fretboards.

The guitar neck has a 24¾-inch scale, à la Gibson, while the bass neck's scale is the standard thirty-four inches. Each neck has a brass nut, which were standard on most domestic Carvin guitars and basses until 1988.

The owner also opted for gold hardware—tuners, bridges, and tailpiece, all by Schaller. The only other option Carvin offered at the time were block-shaped fretboard inlays. Finish choices in the time frame that this doubleneck was available were also limited—white, black, red, or natural.

The pickups are Carvin's own twenty-two-polepiece humbuckers—M22s on the guitar, M22Bs on the bass. The edge-to-edge polepiece design helped prevent signal loss during string bending.

Logic also permeates the layout of the controls. Each neck has a volume control for each pickup, a master tone, and a three-way pickup toggle. Each line of three mini-toggles consists of coil-tap switches for each pickup and a phase switch.

The mini-toggle in the middle of the body (near the pickup selector) is the neck selector.

The two output jacks are wired for separate necks, allowing separate amplification for guitar (lower jack) and bass (upper jack). However, both necks can be run through just the lower jack.

Another potential plus for the DN640 was that its body was somewhat smaller than competing doublenecks, inferring less bulkiness. Perhaps its design had been inspired by the earlier 4-BS and similar models.

Other Carvin doublenecks included two-bass-neck examples (one fretted, one fretless), bass/guitar doublenecks with the bass on top, and two-fers with a Kahler bass vibrato and Floyd Rose guitar vibrato. There was even one left-handed six-string bass/six-string guitar.

And of course, Carvin built other doublenecks that didn't have a bass neck, but the DN640K was a unique and underrated example of twin-neck instruments built by American manufacturers.

Carvin officially discontinued production of doublenecks in 1993.

The 1980s are also remembered as the "angular era" by many guitar enthusiasts, as guitars and basses in all sorts of oddball shapes were marketed. Many "hair bands" used such instruments onstage and in the then-new music video facet of entertainment, competing to be noticed on the fledgling MTV cable channel (which went on the air in 1981).

Carvin entered the unique-body-silhouette fray in 1984, with the introduction of its V220 guitar, which was endorsed by such players as Craig Chaquico (Starship) and Marty Friedman.

The bass companion to the V220 was the V440, which became available in late 1985, but wasn't officially introduced until the 1986 catalog.

"The V440 was introduced in the mid-1980s due to the popularity of our V220 series guitar, and the many requests that we received for a similar style bass," said Carvin vice-president Mark Kiesel. "Several hundred V440 basses were produced over a three-year period."

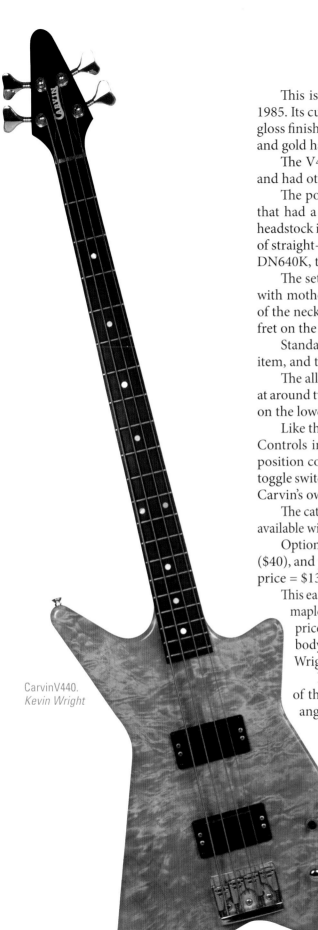

CarvinV440.
Kevin Wright

This is an early example of the V440 that was special-ordered on October 7, 1985. Its custom features include a solid, two-piece figured maple body with a clear gloss finish (standard finishes were white, black, blue, and red), a flame maple neck, and gold hardware.

The V440 featured all maple construction, even in its standard configuration, and had other unique features besides its body silhouette.

The pointed headstock is notable, as this instrument was the first Carvin bass that had a straight-pull lineup for strings. Carvin didn't have a four-in-line bass headstock in its line at the time, and what's more, there's no mention of the advantages of straight-pull strings (on guitars or basses) in Carvin catalogs of that era. Like the DN640K, the nut is brass.

The set-in neck is made of Eastern hardrock maple, and the fretboard is ebony with mother-of-pearl dots, and has twenty nickel-silver jumbo frets. The juncture of the neck and body is at the seventeenth fret on the bass side, and the eighteenth fret on the treble side.

Standard V440 bodies were two-piece Eastern maple, just like this special order item, and the dimensions were fifteen inches wide and 1¾ inches deep.

The all-maple construction of the V440 made it pretty hefty (this one weighs in at around twelve pounds), but its body style, with a lengthy "tail" housing the controls on the lower bout meant that it balanced well.

Like the DN640K, the V440 used two Carvin M22B bass humbucking pickups. Controls included a volume control for each pickup, a master tone control, two-position coil splitter mini-toggle switches for each pickup, and a three-way pickup toggle switch. Chrome hardware was standard, and included the Schaller tuners and Carvin's own TB8 bridge.

The catalog list price for the V440 was $799, but its "Pro Net" price was $399. It was available with a Kahler bass vibrato system (V440T, list price = $1,039, Pro Net = $519).

Options included a premium koa body ($40), black hardware ($20), gold hardware ($40), and pearl finishes ($20). Once again, purchase of an HC20 hardshell case (list price = $139, Pro Net = $79) was mandatory.

This early example, made in 1985, was ordered for $635 plus the case, and the quilted maple body was special-ordered; i.e., it was never an option. Accordingly, the base price of $399, plus the $40 gold hardware option mean that the figured maple body cost around $200 more. Quite an expensive upgrade. What's more, Kevin Wright says this is the only example of a figured maple body V440 he's ever seen.

No player of huge acclaim endorsed the V440, although John McManus of the Irish band Mama's Boys was seen on a catalog page that featured the angular bass.

"As metal bands changed during the late 1980s, so did their taste for guitars and basses so the V440 was slowly phased out," Mark Kiesel recounted. Production of the model ceased in 1988.

A short-lived contribution to the often-lampooned hair band decade, the Carvin V440 was well-made, balanced, and versatile.

The DN440T doubleneck exemplifies the construction changes and innovations—some visible, some hidden—that Carvin had incorporated a mere half-decade after the previously-seen DN640K was made.

The year 1988 was an annum in which Carvin initiated a number of design and construction changes, many of which are found in this bass. The new-for-1988

DN440 used the also-new-for-the-same-year single-neck LB70 as a foundation, and it helps to remember that while the LB70's model name was re-introduced, the newer edition was a neck-through model instead of the bolt-on type as profiled earlier.

Steve McDonald, the founding bassist for the raucous California rock band Redd Kross, ordered this four-over-four bass (one fretless neck, one with twenty-four frets) from Carvin in late 1987, and it was completed early the following year (and the model's designation wasn't official until 1988, as well).

On this instrument, the "T" suffix refers to "tremolo," a perhaps-intentional, shades-of-Fender misnomer for the Kahler vibrato system found on the lower fretted neck (when Fender introduced the Stratocaster guitar in the mid-1950s, it had dubbed the vibrato system to be a tremolo, and what's more, the tremolo circuit on Fender amplifiers was called the Vibrato channel!).

The construction of the DN440T was neck-through, and this example has maple necks and maple body sections. This custom-order example still had a standard sixteen-inch radius on both necks as well as standard ebony fingerboards.

Espousing an 1980s vibe, this twin-neck bass had "pointy" headstocks and black chrome hardware (tuners, straight bridge on the fretless side, and the aforementioned Kahler on the fretted side). A Pearl Purple finish underlines the notion that the DN440T was built in the "Me Decade."

Electronics for this instrument consisted of two Carvin H13B stacked humbuckers, which also debuted in 1988, on each neck. The "13" in the model number refers to the number of edge-to-edge polepieces found on the pickup. This model of pickup was short-lived.

As is the case with almost any doubleneck instrument, switching for each or both necks has the potential to get complicated, but like the DN640K, the layout of this example's controls are logical . . . once their function is learned. Each neck has a master volume and master tone control. The mini-toggles on each neck (from the switch closest to the tone knob to the switch closest to the butt-end of the body) are three-way coil-selection switch for the neck pickup (double coil, single coil, or off), coil-selection switch for the bridge pickup (same three-way switching), and a phase switch. Since each coil switch has an "off" position, no pickup selection toggle switch is necessary.

The extra switch located somewhat above and between the volume and tone knobs for the fretted neck is, as might be expected, a two-way neck selection switch.

It almost goes without saying that the all-maple construction of this instrument would require as wide of a strap as possible when it's being played. It weighs approximately seventeen pounds; by comparison, the DN640K profiled earlier weighs approximately thirteen pounds.

Kevin Wright reports that the four-over-four configuration wasn't a common beast among Carvin's doublenecks.

"I've only seen three others," Wright said of this instrument's design. "One was a NAMM (National Association of Music Merchants) bass that Carvin made; there was at least one four/five-string example, and a white four/four. Carvin made 12/6 guitars, 6/4 guitar/basses, and 4/4 basses, and I've also seen a few oddballs from the same era as the DN440T, like a 6/6 guitar for different tunings. The DN612, six-string guitar/twelve-string guitar, was the most popular doubleneck Carvin made."

While Carvin phased out of making doubleneck instruments, models as this DN440T exemplify the company's orientation towards making custom-order instruments to exacting specifications, then and now.

In early 2015, Carvin's guitar and bass manufacturing operation became a separate operation known as Kiesel Guitars, with the same emphasis on custom-order instruments. The company's unique niche in the American guitar marketplace continues to be successful.

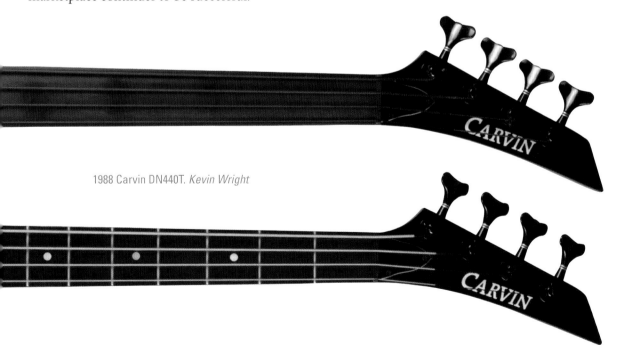

1988 Carvin DN440T. *Kevin Wright*

CHAPTER EIGHT

In their time, the Danelectro company of New Jersey (founded in the late 1940s) epitomized the term "no frills" . . . but many a Baby Boomer cut his/her musical teeth on such inexpensive instruments (which usually sported a Sears Silvertone brand), and may wish he/she still had the guitar or bass on which he/she started his/her respective musical paths.

The construction features of most "classic" Danelectro-made guitars and basses included a Masonite-over-a-wood-frame body with adhesive grained side trim, a neck with a Brazilian rosewood fretboard, a non-adjustable truss rod ("Two steel I-beams," according to a catalog), a primitive but slightly-intonatable bridge/tailpiece unit, an aluminum nut, and "lipstick tube" pickups—Danelectro founder Nate Daniel enclosed the magnets and wiring of his pickups in actual lipstick tubes, having cut a deal with a supplier to the cosmetics industry.

And when an initial bass guitar model was introduced by Danelectro (and Sears) in 1956, said instrument was exactly that—a true bass guitar, with six strings instead of four, but with a short bass scale instead of a guitar-like scale. Tuned down an octave compared to standard guitars, the instrument was a first-of-its-kind model, preceding the similar Gibson EB-6 (first listed in 1959) and Fender's Bass VI (introduced in late 1961).

Danelectro 3412 Short Horn, early 1960s. *Heritage Auctions*

Danelectro's first four-string electric bass was the model 3412 Short Horn, introduced in late 1958. It sported a copper finish and a white "seal" pickguard (check out a horizontal view of the silhouette). The instrument's neck only had fifteen frets (joining the body at the thirteenth fret), and a short scale, which meant that between its light weight, as well as a smaller fretboard and scale, the bass was very easy to play, especially for converted guitarists.

The headstock silhouette is known as the "Coke bottle" shape in vintage guitar vernacular, and the small metallic label on the headstock (just above the nut) proclaims that the instrument is "Totally Shielded" (against interference from fluorescent lights, electric motors, etc.).

The Short Horn 3412 was only available in a bronze finish, but also came in a six-string version (model 3612).

6 String Bass . . .

Combines the best of Spanish guitar and big string bass. Tuning is the same as on a regular guitar, but one octave lower. Bottom four strings are tuned exactly the same as a big bass. The Danelectro bass has six strings, double pickup, extremely soft action, non-warp neck, fully adjustable bridge. It can be used as a 4 string bass by removing the 2 top strings and centering the remaining 4. Choice of three popular colors.

BLACK LACQUER, ivory binding
UB-2 Black $135

BRONZE LACQUER, ivory binding
UB-2 Bronze $135

IVORY LEATHERETTE, black binding
UB-2 Ivory $135

SPARE SET OF 6 POLISHED STRINGS
UB-2S $7.50

Danelectro six-string bass, 1958 (catalog image).

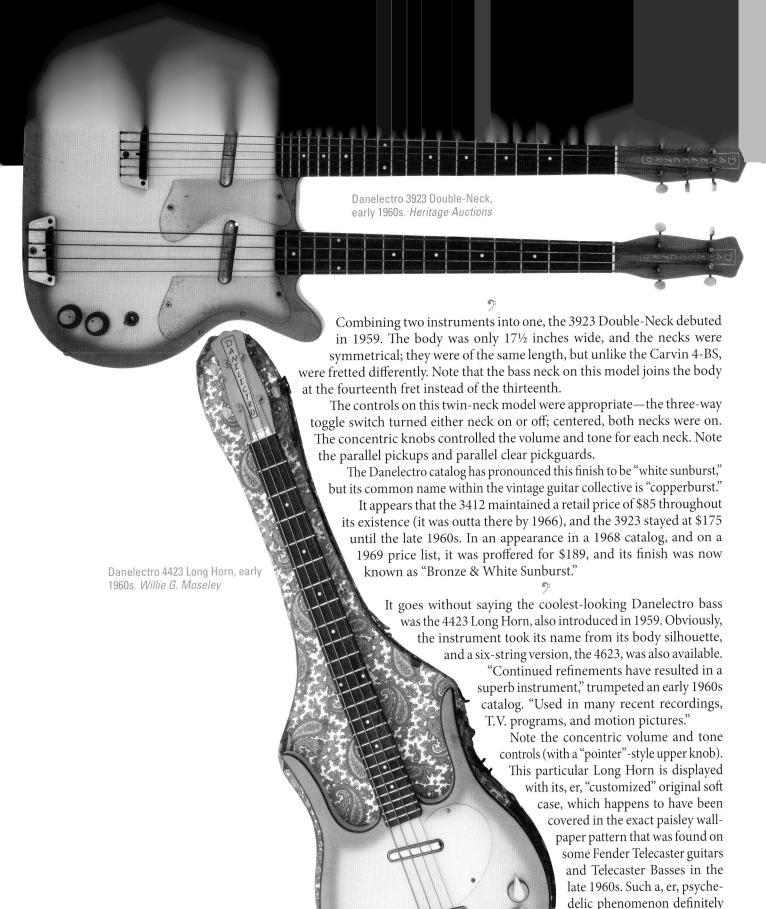

Danelectro 3923 Double-Neck, early 1960s. *Heritage Auctions*

Danelectro 4423 Long Horn, early 1960s. *Willie G. Moseley*

Combining two instruments into one, the 3923 Double-Neck debuted in 1959. The body was only 17½ inches wide, and the necks were symmetrical; they were of the same length, but unlike the Carvin 4-BS, were fretted differently. Note that the bass neck on this model joins the body at the fourteenth fret instead of the thirteenth.

The controls on this twin-neck model were appropriate—the three-way toggle switch turned either neck on or off; centered, both necks were on. The concentric knobs controlled the volume and tone for each neck. Note the parallel pickups and parallel clear pickguards.

The Danelectro catalog has pronounced this finish to be "white sunburst," but its common name within the vintage guitar collective is "copperburst."

It appears that the 3412 maintained a retail price of $85 throughout its existence (it was outta there by 1966), and the 3923 stayed at $175 until the late 1960s. In an appearance in a 1968 catalog, and on a 1969 price list, it was proffered for $189, and its finish was now known as "Bronze & White Sunburst."

It goes without saying the coolest-looking Danelectro bass was the 4423 Long Horn, also introduced in 1959. Obviously, the instrument took its name from its body silhouette, and a six-string version, the 4623, was also available.

"Continued refinements have resulted in a superb instrument," trumpeted an early 1960s catalog. "Used in many recent recordings, T.V. programs, and motion pictures."

Note the concentric volume and tone controls (with a "pointer"-style upper knob). This particular Long Horn is displayed with its, er, "customized" original soft case, which happens to have been covered in the exact paisley wallpaper pattern that was found on some Fender Telecaster guitars and Telecaster Basses in the late 1960s. Such a, er, psyche-delic phenomenon definitely increases the "cool" factor of this particular instrument.

Silvertone 1373L, late 1950s. *Bill Ingalls Jr.*

The marketing relationship between Sears, Roebuck & Company and Danelectro was always one-sided. For the duration of their interdependency, Danelectro made many more budget guitars and amplifiers bearing the Silvertone name (Sears' house brand) than ones that bore the Danelectro brand.

Many Baby Boomers scurried to Sears to purchase an electric guitar after seeing the Beatles on "The Ed Sullivan Show" in 1964, and probably more often than not, said Silvertone guitar was a Danelectro-made instrument with its amplifier built into the carrying case.

"I had one of those; who *didn't*?" recalled noted guitarist Jon Butcher in a mid-1990s interview. "When I got it, I thought it was the coolest thing ever. Open up the case, and there you are, ready to rock! I wish I had it now."

The Danelectro-Sears connection had begun in the late 1940s, when Daniels' company began supplying amplifiers to the giant retailer. When Danelectro began building guitars as well, Sears signed on, displaying such models as the wood-bodied one-pickup 1375L and two-pickup 1377L guitars in a 1954 catalog.

The Sears six-string bass guitar was numbered as the 1376L which it was introduced as in 1956, but was re-numbered as the 1373L the next year. A 1958 Sears catalog touted the six-string bass's sonic capabilities: "Play either bass or guitar. Tunes like a guitar, only one octave lower. Total range of four octaves."

The two-pickup 1373L had a short scale, with twenty-four frets on a rosewood fingerboard that had dot markers. Controls included concentric volume and tone knobs (volume being the smaller and upper portion), and a three-way pickup toggle switch. It was finished in black enamel,

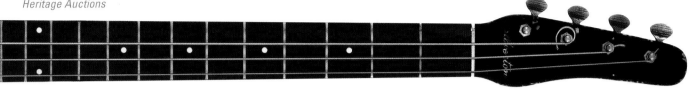

and its textured side trim was an "ivory" color, according to the Sears catalog. A clear pickguard with silver/white trim was flush-mounted on the treble side of the body. Its overall dimensions were 43¼ inches long and 13¼ inches wide. A soft case, cord, pick, and instructions were included for the price of $109.95.

In 1959, Sears went more mainstream regarding electric basses, as the six-string 1373L was replaced by a one-pickup, four-string model known as the 1444L. It had many facets in common with its predecessor, but its headstock had a four-on-a-side "dolphin nose" profile, with somewhat-primitive "skate key" tuners. Curiously, the 1959 Sears catalog illustration shows the 1444L with a white pickguard, but most examples seen in the vintage guitar market have the same clear pickguard as the 1373L.

The 1444L would actually last through about half of the 1960s, when it was supplanted by two wooden Danelectro-made models with offset, Fender Jazzmaster-style bodies, and Fender-style headstocks. Danelectro, by then under the MCA corporate umbrella, was closed in 1968.

However, the Masonite-bodied Danelectros and corresponding Sears basses garnered—and still command—the most interest from players and collectors, for nostalgic as well as sonic reasons. Their unique, quasi-chambered construction, as well as their short scale and lipstick tube pickups all combined to give such basses a unique sound, then and now.

A Danelectro six-string bass was used by Duane Eddy on such songs as "Because They're Young," and the same instrument, when doubled with an upright bass, was responsible for the fabled Nashville "tick-tack" recording technique. In a 2007 interview, legendary producer/guitarist Jerry Kennedy noted that he had owned and played such a six-string bass, and credited producer Harold Bradley as the innovator of that unique sound.

Four-string Silvertone/Danelectros also interest veteran players—the Kentucky Headhunters' lead guitarist, Greg Martin, owned an old Silvertone-by-Danelectro four-string 1444L, and praised its "'She's-About-A-Mover'-by-the-Sir-Douglas-Quintet sound."

"They just honk," Little Feat's Paul Barrére once said of such instruments, and to many bass lovers, such a succinct observation is right on the money.

NINE

DEAN

"At last! A New Standard of Excellence" trumpeted the cover of Dean Guitars' first three-page brochure when upstart Evanston, Illinois luthier Dean Zelinsky debuted three radical-looking solid body electric guitars in 1977. The startling aesthetics of the instruments were obvious from the top down, as they sported oversized, V-shaped headstocks that displayed the winged Dean logo. However, two of the three body silhouettes had been seen for the first time almost two decades earlier—the Dean "Z" owed its shape to the late 1950s Gibson Explorer, and the body of the new company's "V" model looked like a circa 1958 Gibson Flying V (not surprisingly, considering the model name).

However, the body of the third model was a combination of the other two—the ML's lower bout took its look from the "V," while the upper bout was based on the "Z."

Dean Guitars would grow rapidly and would create other unique-looking guitar models, as well as bass versions of their first three items. Ultimately, the ML bass seemed to command a disproportionate amount of attention, since it too had an, er, original-if-derivative silhouette.

ML basses came in two versions, the ML II (two pickups) or the ML I (one pickup). Both models had a maple neck with a twenty-two-fret rosewood fretboard, which joined the body at the eighteenth fret. MLs had mahogany bodies, but the ML II also had a curly maple top. The body and neck were also bound on the ML II, while the ML I was unbound.

Standard colors cited on a 1981 price list (on which the ML was the only bass listed), included Cherry, Black, Brasiliaburst, Cherryburst, Walnut, and Natural. White or a custom color added $100 to the suggested list price. Custom colors were listed separately, and included Baby Blue, Electric Blue, Yellow, Pink, Opaque Red, Purple, Blueburst, Pinkburst, and Silver.

Dean ML. *Willie G. Moseley*

Cream-colored DiMarzio humbucking pickups were usually standard, but custom pickup layouts were available. Both ML bass models had an "active tone circuit," according to the 1981 price list. The controls on the ML II included two volume knobs and a master tone knob, with the three-way pickup toggle switch on the extended treble cutaway (à la an Explorer) and the jack on the top near the end of the lower "wing" (à la a Flying V). The standard bridge was a Leo Quan Badass.

The aforementioned 1981 price list also noted that left-handed versions of any model were $199 extra.

By the time a 1983 four-page brochure was released, Dean had relocated to Chicago, and a November 1984 price list included several basses, including a "Z Standard" model, but the ML was missing.

The Z Standard bass had two pickups in a "P/J" configuration, which means that the ML shown here may have been some sort of transitional item, as it has an ML body with P/J pickups. What's more, it has gold hardware, and an unusual silverburst finish that is similar to the Gibson finish of the same name. While that color did appear as an option on the 1984 price list, veteran bass retailer Bob Hynosky said that the bass is the only example of an early Dean bass model he's seen in that color.

The angular silhouettes of early Dean guitars and basses were a perfect complement to the early 1980s advent of MTV (Music Television), and such instruments showed up in several primeval videos. What's more, advertisements for early Dean instruments often included scantily clad female models, brandishing guitars and basses in provocative (and occasionally controversial) poses.

The Cars were exemplary in their exploitation of uniquely-shaped instruments for videos, and Dean models figured into the Boston-based band's strategy. Lead guitarist Elliot Easton appeared in the company's 1981 catalog, sporting a left-handed ML guitar with block fret markers, while bassist Ben Orr (1947–2000) played a black ML II model in concert, and in the video of "You Might Think."

"We played them for a relatively short period of time, but I guess it was when the Cars had a high visibility, so we got associated with them," Easton reflected.

And as for his own Dean ML guitars, " . . . they've been gone for decades, hanging in Hard Rock Cafes around the world!" said the veteran southpaw guitar slinger.

The Dean brand has been through more than one ownership change in its history.

Some of Zelinsky's more recent guitar and bass silhouettes are also non-traditional, and the way for such aesthetically-wild items was pioneered by instruments such as this ML bass.

CHAPTER TEN

In the early 1970s—long before the "unplugged" concept of popular music became a unique way to purvey acoustic songs (including ones that had been heard in earlier "electric" versions)—California musician/retailer/stringmaker Ernie Ball bought a Mexican guitarron (a large acoustic bass found in mariachi bands), and as an experiment, placed frets on its neck.

Ball liked what he came up with, and tried to interest major guitar companies of the viability of an acoustic fretted bass in the guitar market, to no avail, so he opted to build such instruments himself.

There had been, of course, prior attempts at manufacturing and marketing acoustic bass instruments that played (somewhat) like a guitar. As noted in the initial chapter, Gibson's humungous Style J Mando-bass, which was made from 1912 to circa 1930, had a forty-two-inch scale (the same as an upright bass), and some four decades after the demise of that instrument, Ball's attempt at an acoustic fretted bass turned out to be innovative and eye-catching but short-lived.

Guitar manufacturing legend George Fullerton had departed the Fender company five years after it was acquired by CBS in 1965, and would work with Ball to create the prototype instruments.

Ernie Ball's Earthwood acoustic basses hit the market in 1972. Perhaps their most intriguing facet was the use of wood wherever possible, including parts that would stereotypically have been metal or plastic—on the latter-day 1983 example shown here, the truss rod cover, fret markers, soundhole trim, and body and headstock binding are all wood. Note the flame maple overlay on the headstock. Many Earthwood basses had maple fretboards and/or wood pickguards.

The bodies of Earthwood basses came in two different depths, 6⅝ inches and 8¼ inches—this one has the shallower dimension. The body is 18¾ inches wide at the lower bout. Its top is two-piece spruce, and the sides are made from bookmatched walnut pieces that flare in opposite directions from center vertical strips of wood at the top and bottom of the body. The back is also walnut, and it, too, is bookmatched.

Earthwood Bass, 1983.
Bill Ingalls Jr.

The maple neck is bolted on, and a small panel on the back covers the three neck bolts, as well as a tilt-neck adjustment hole for an Allen wrench. The instrument's serial number (1021) is stamped on the assembly that houses the neck bolts inside the body.

Interestingly, the strings are loaded into this beast through the soundhole, then up through holes in the bridge.

Technically, this example is an electric instrument—there's a Barcus-Berry "Hot Dot" pickup mounted under the bridge, and the cord from the amplifier plugs into the large lower strap button. There are, however, no controls—no volume, tone/equalization, or active circuitry of any kind. The general line of thought of a player whenever one of these was wired up was probably to hope like hell it didn't feed back (which these basses had a tendency to do when amplified).

For most would-be Earthwood bass players, words like "cumbersome" or "ergonomically-challenged" would probably be polite terms used to describe the experience of plunking on one of these, but the guitarron on which it was based wasn't exactly sleek and slim, either.

Nevertheless, these gargantuan instruments can generate a generous and resonant sound once (and if) a player gets used to the bulkiness. They can add a unique and usually-appreciated low-end sonic facet to any pickin' and grinnin' session in nearly any acoustic-oriented genre . . . and they're still a lot smaller than a doghouse bass.

Earthwood acoustic basses and other instruments were made sporadically for slightly more than a decade, with production coming to an end in 1985. The Earthwood brand name lives on as the moniker for Ernie Ball's #2070 phosphor-bronze acoustic bass strings.

The total number of Earthwood basses that were made is nebulous, but they are relatively rare—and big—birds.

CHAPTER ELEVEN

By the advent of the 1960s, European nations that were both winners and losers in World War II had recuperated from post-war reconstruction to the point that their respective industrial bases were once again viable. Many musical instrument manufacturers were crafting traditional products that were popular in their respective countries, but some companies were also monitoring new innovations in the marketplace, such as solid body electric guitars. Accordingly, many European firms began to develop and market their own styles.

The Oliviero Pigini company of Recanati, Italy, had been founded in 1959. While Pigini had focused on accordions, a fairly abrupt decline of interest in that instrument prompted the company's expansion into guitar production in the early 1960s.

The company's earliest Eko brand offerings covered a lot of ground, including acoustic flat-tops and archtops, jazz boxes, solid body electrics, and a few basses.

Early promotional hype about Eko guitars included referencing the country in which the instruments were made—a brochure from an English instrument distributor, Dallas, used phrases such as, " . . . styled the Italian way, which has set the post-war fashion from clothes to cars!" and "Consider the buzz-free fingerboard laminated with woods air-dried under the Italian sun."

Many Eko solid body instruments featured "glitter finishes vacuum-bonded on to (sic) smooth streamlined bodies," according to company literature. Basically, Pigini was taking leftover sparkle and pearloid accordion material and attaching it to wooden guitar bodies.

The very earliest incarnations of such celluloid-covered instruments had featured multiple-push-button pickup controls and roller/thumbwheel-type volume and tone controls on the upper part of the body.

Two Eko basses sporting flamboyant plastic finishes were also proffered in the company's 1962 catalog. The 1100/2 had the same body as the 500 series (13¾ inches wide, seventeen inches long, and 1⅝ inches deep), and the relatively-rare 1150/2 was a violin-shaped instrument (11½ inches wide, eighteen inches long, and 1⅝ inches deep).

While the 1100/2 would be promoted as a matching instrument for the 500 series of guitars, the 1150/2 did not have a guitar counterpart.

The basses had a thirty-inch scale on a bound neck with twenty frets. Note that the pearloid markers were one diameter on the third, fifth, seventh, and ninth frets, switching to a smaller size at the twelfth fret.

The headstocks had different styles, seeming to "coordinate" with the stereotypes of the body silhouettes—the 1100/2 headstock had a bound, Fender-like four-on-a-side style, while the 1150/2 proffered a scrolled look. Truss rods could be accessed for adjustment through the headstock via a small, three-screw plate.

Both basses had two pickups touted as "double-polarity" (indicating they were a humbucking design). The four switches on the top portion of the body were labeled (left to right from the player's viewpoint) "M" (both pickups), "1" (neck

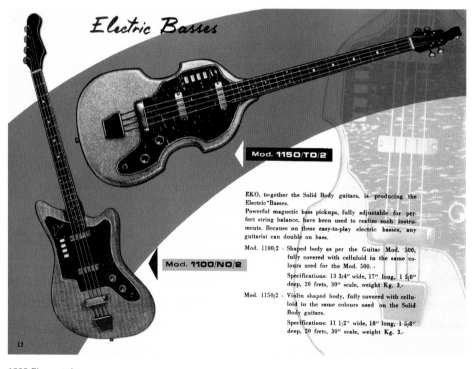

Electric Basses

Mod. 1150/TO/2

Mod. 1100/NO/2

EKO, to-gether the Solid Body guitars, is producing the Electric Basses.
Powerful magnetic bass pickups, fully adjustable for perfect string balance, have been used to realize such instruments. Because on these easy-to-play electric basses, any guitarist can double on bass.

Mod. 1100/2 - Shaped body as per the Guitar Mod. 500, fully covered with celluloid in the same colours used for the Mod. 500. -
Specifications: 13 3/4" wide, 17" long, 1 5/8" deep, 20 frets, 30" scale, weight Kg. 3.-

Mod. 1150/2 - Violin shaped body, fully covered with celluloid in the same colours used on the Solid Body guitars.
Specifications: 11 1/2" wide, 18" long, 1 5/8" deep, 20 frets, 30" scale, weight Kg. 3.-

12

1962 Eko catalog page.

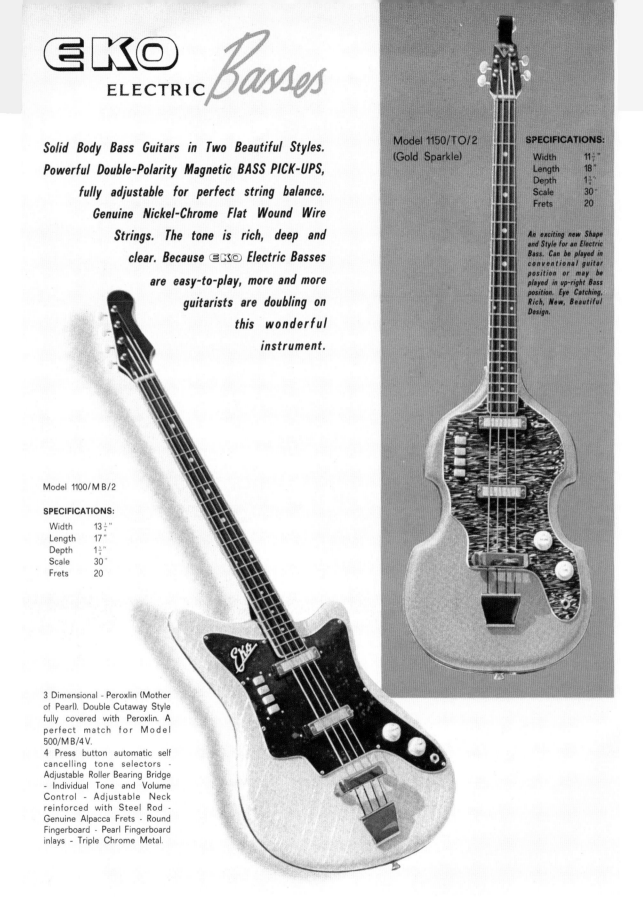

EKO ELECTRIC *Basses*

Solid Body Bass Guitars in Two Beautiful Styles. Powerful Double-Polarity Magnetic BASS PICK-UPS, fully adjustable for perfect string balance. Genuine Nickel-Chrome Flat Wound Wire Strings. The tone is rich, deep and clear. Because EKO Electric Basses are easy-to-play, more and more guitarists are doubling on this wonderful instrument.

Model 1150/TO/2
(Gold Sparkle)

SPECIFICATIONS:

Width	11½"
Length	18"
Depth	1¾"
Scale	30"
Frets	20

An exciting new Shape and Style for an Electric Bass. Can be played in conventional guitar position or may be played in up-right Bass position. Eye Catching, Rich, New, Beautiful Design.

Model 1100/MB/2

SPECIFICATIONS:

Width	13½"
Length	17"
Depth	1⅝"
Scale	30"
Frets	20

3 Dimensional - Peroxlin (Mother of Pearl). Double Cutaway Style fully covered with Peroxlin. A perfect match for Model 500/MB/4V.
4 Press button automatic self cancelling tone selectors - Adjustable Roller Bearing Bridge - Individual Tone and Volume Control - Adjustable Neck reinforced with Steel Rod - Genuine Alpacca Frets - Round Fingerboard - Pearl Fingerboard inlays - Triple Chrome Metal.

1964 Eko catalog page.

EKO

pickup), "2" (bridge pickup), and "0" (off). Electronics were installed through top-mounted pickguards that were usually five-layer, sporting tortoiseshell patterns.

In the 1962 catalog, the following designations of colors were available on Eko's solid body guitars and basses: "NO"—Hazel top, mahogany back, "MB"—White mother-of-pearl top, black back, "TA"—Silver sparkle top, black back, "TB"—Blue sparkle top, black back, "TO"—Gold sparkle top, mother-of-pearl back, "TR"—Red sparkle top, mother-of-pearl back, "RN"—Striped brown top, striped mahogany back (i.e., faux wood).

The edges of the celluloid were covered with a gold strip along the rim of the body.

By the time a 1963 guitar brochure was released, solid body guitar and bass models with traditional finishes had become part of the Eko lineup.

Moreover, the 1963 list of decorative accordion material available on plastic-covered instruments was more nebulous—the text touted "celluloid-covered bodies" (saying nothing about colors of the tops and backs), and the "RN"/Striped finish was discontinued.

Such a lack of specificity regarding tops and backs may have hinted that the celluloid series was available with any combination of colors, but it's doubtful Pigini was alluding to a primeval pick-and-choose/custom shop concept.

Three new basses—two hollow body models and a solid body "all-wood" bass—were shown in the 1963 brochure, and other basses were merely listed, including the 1100/2 and 1150/2 "celluloid" models.

More than one version of Eko's 1964 catalog featured color illustrations, and the two celluloid basses were back on display in those issues. Their page referred to the 1100/2 that was illustrated as "3 Dimensional—Peroxlin (Mother of Pearl). Double Cutaway Style fully covered with Peroxlin." The instruments themselves remained unchanged regarding electronics, dimensions, and hardware, etc.

The 1100/2 shown here is a definitive example of Eko's "celluloid" instruments, sporting a blue sparkle top and a white mother-of-pearl back, separated by the ubiquitous gold strip.

Sparkle/pearloid-bodied Ekos were out of the company's catalog by 1965. It's curious that their wild aesthetics debuted before the Sixties' guitar boom got seriously underway, but the garish models from Italy didn't carry over into that phenomenon.

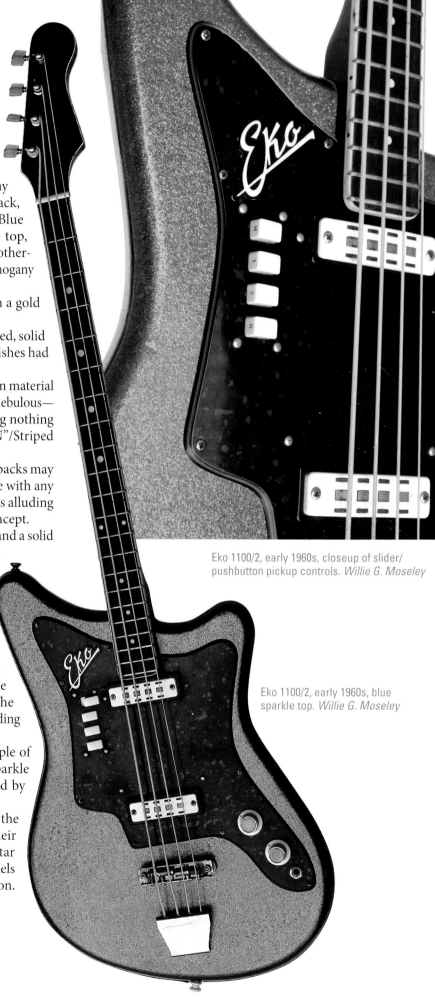

Eko 1100/2, early 1960s, closeup of slider/pushbutton pickup controls. *Willie G. Moseley*

Eko 1100/2, early 1960s, blue sparkle top. *Willie G. Moseley*

While Eko's early 1960s sparkle and pearloid solid body guitars and basses may not have represented anything memorable regarding their fidelity, they're usually at the forefront of a discussion regarding the aesthetics of that decade's kitschy instruments that are now considered retro-cool.

The Beatles' February 1964 appearance on "The Ed Sullivan Show" has been pronounced the most important event in the history of rock music. It inspired thousands, if not millions, of teenagers to play in a band.

And many budding bassists aspired to own an example of Paul McCartney's violin-shaped bass, which was a German-made Höfner. However, budget constraints forced many kids to consider cheaper instruments than McCartney's "Beatle Bass," and the Eko 995 was a commendable alternative.

One of Oliviero Pigini's accordion clients was the Lo Duca Bros. Musical Instruments company of Milwaukee, which joined forces with the Italian manufacturer as a distributor of Eko guitars in the US.

One might also speculate as to what extent the aforementioned 1150/2 affected the design and development of Eko's violin-shaped 995 bass which debuted in the mid-1960s and became one of the company's best-known instruments, but the 995 had a hollow body configuration, and would become Eko's best-selling model in the US.

The 995 was just different enough from Höfner's Beatle Bass to conjure up its own mystique. It, too, was a short-scale, lightweight two-pickup instrument, but like Eko's early sparkle instruments, it had some cheesy appointments that were often associated with Italian-made instruments.

One of the most intriguing aesthetic features is found at the very top—the headstock's unusual square protuberance with a Gothic "E" logo was certainly eye-catching . . . and compared to other headstocks and logos of the time, was probably considered to be downright weird by many observers. Definitely not a standard rock and roll vibe.

The bound fretboard on the example on page 48 has twenty-one frets, and joins the body at the sixteenth fret (Lo Duca Bros. literature proclaimed that the fretboard was ebony). The hyper-slim bolt-on neck has a five-piece laminated construction; it's maple with rosewood stringers. It measures 1⅜ inches wide at the nut, and there's also a zero fret at that juncture. The serial number is embossed on the neck plate.

The Oliviero Pigini company also made Vox guitars and basses in the same era, and the Eko 995 had the same truss rod adjustment system at the butt end of the neck as many Vox instruments. Note the different-sized dot markers on the fretboard, which are also found on some Vox basses.

The body is thirteen inches wide and 2¾ inches deep. It features an arched spruce top and a maple back and sides, and has three-layer binding (white-black-white) on the edges. Its "Dura-Glos" finish is called "Honey Brown."

Electronics include two height-adjustable pickups with staple-type polepieces. Like the earlier Eko catalogs, a Lo Duca Bros. catalog refers to the pickups as having "double polarity."

The four-position pickup toggle switch has a standard three-way operation plus an "off" position. Control knobs are master volume and master tone.

Hardware on the 995 includes cheapo tuners, and a harp-shaped tailpiece.

The pickguard is made from clear plastic that had a gold logo screenprinted on the underside, followed by the application of brown paint. The oversized white fingerrest is also plastic.

The 995's popularity means that numerous variants of the bass exist, including 995s that have a standard three-way pickup toggle switch instead of the four-position rotary switch seen here. Alternate tuners may be encountered, as well as white or black pickguards and black pickups.

Eko also made hollow body violin-shaped guitars, marketing them as the 395 series, which included a six-string with a trapeze tailpiece, a six-string with a vibrato, and a twelve-string model.

Members of the Grassroots play Eko products in a late 1960s magazine ad.

In the late 1960s, the frontline endorsers for Eko's 395 and 995 instruments were the Grassroots ("Temptation Eyes," "Live for Today," etc.), and the band appeared in an ad to promote the models.

In the same era, left-handed bassist Doug Lubahn played a flipped-over 995 (still strung "righty") with his own band, Clear Light, and also used the instrument as the in-studio bassist for the Doors on songs such as "You're Lost Little Girl," "People Are Strange," and "I Can't See Your Face In My Mind," among others.

"The Eko had a beautifully rounded sound if you played it with a pick," Lubahn recalled in a 2010 interview. "If you tried your fingers, though, it didn't sound so hot."

In more recent times, low-end sonic innovator Les Claypool of Primus was seen plunking on a vintage Eko 995.

Eko must have been doing something right with the 995 bass model, considering its popularity in its time. It wasn't the fanciest Beatle Bass wanna-be, but it wasn't the worst of the genre, either. Many Baby Boomer bassists, upon encountering this model, would probably nod their heads knowingly and mutter, "Yeah, I remember those."

Eko 995, late 1960s. *Olivia's Vintage*

TWELVE

EPCOR

One of briefest, therefore rarest, brands to emerge from the somewhat-murky history of Bakersfield, California-area builders in the mid-1960s (see Mosrite, Hallmark, Gruggett, and Standel) was Epcor, a private label line built by Joe Hall's Hallmark company in Arvin.

The brand was the dream of Ed Preager, a successful manufacturer's representative who resided in Beverly Hills. Preager was reportedly a spiffy dresser who also drove a Cadillac and sported a Rolex watch, and he was seeking a guitar line to sell somewhat on the side; i.e., his own brand would not conflict with the lines that had contributed to his success in sales.

Preager approached Hall in September of 1967, wanting to create a budget-priced hollow body line, which was a contradictory goal since hollow body instruments are inherently more expensive to produce than solid body guitars and basses. Nevertheless, Hall and Preager came to an agreement to create the Epcor line, and set a goal of producing 200 instruments per month, including six-string guitars, twelve-string guitars, and basses. The brand name combined Preager's initials with the first three letters of "corporation."

One idea that saved manufacturing time and expense was the importing of pre-finished instrument bodies from Italy, leaving the creation of the necks and pickups to Hallmark.

The laminated body was the same for all instruments, and came in two finishes; red or three-tone sunburst. It featured front- and rear-edge binding (five-layer white/black/white/black/white on top), as well as single-ply bound f-holes.

The headstock had two contoured portions that meant the silhouette was supposed to allude to an "E," and to most guitar enthusiasts, it would seem obvious that this idea was inspired by the "M" headstock of the nearby Mosrite company.

The bolt-on maple neck was two-piece and was unbound, with a rosewood fretboard. The scale was 30½ inches.

Hardware and other parts included bridges made by the Bigsby company, Kluson tuners and tailpieces, and Hallmark strap buttons and knobs. Pickups were Hallmark's own design. Note the angled neck pickup, which was seen on more than one brand of Bakerfield-area instruments.

As it turned out, an estimated thirty Epcor instruments of all styles were made by Hallmark before the deal fell apart for financial reasons, although Hall reportedly assembled a few more instruments, perhaps utilizing other brand names, from leftover parts.

"My guess is that about thirty-five instruments exist today," said Bob Shade, owner of the present-day Hallmark guitar company. "There are no shipping records available, so it is really hard to know how many were made. The necks were very fast, and the pickups were powerful. This is the only Epcor bass I have encountered, and it plays and sounds excellent."

Epcor bass, late 1960s.
Michael G. Stewart

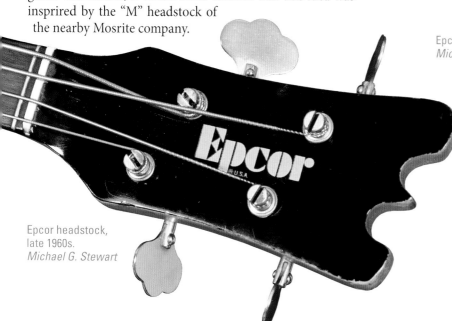

Epcor headstock, late 1960s.
Michael G. Stewart

THIRTEEN

EPIPHONE

The legend of Ted McCarty's leadership of the Gibson guitar company and the innovative instruments that the company produced during his seventeen-year tenure (1948–1965) are well-known to many guitar enthusiasts.

However, one successful "innovation" for which McCarty was praised was a marketing ploy instead of an actual product.

Gibson's parent company, Chicago Music Instrument (CMI) purchased the foundering Epiphone company in 1957. Epiphone's respected line of upright basses had actually been the primary reason the Windy City distributor had sought to acquire the New York-based manufacturer.

Ultimately, production of "doghouse" basses was a boondoggle for CMI, but McCarty realized that owning the Epiphone brand name meant that Gibson could offer Epiphone brand instruments and amplifers to stores that were not Gibson franchise dealerships, but that handled other CMI lines. Such Epiphone guitars and basses were also made to the same quality standards in the Gibson factory in Kalamazoo, Michigan, and oftentimes, Epiphones and their Gibson counterparts had only minor cosmetic differences.

In a 1999 interview, McCarty noted that the semi-hollow, thinline ES-335 was his favorite instrument of the models that were developed and marketed while he was the head of Gibson, and he averred that he personally designed that configuration.

Accordingly, the first Epiphone-by-Gibson electric bass, the EB232 Rivoli, was an amalgam of a unique and relatively new type of instrument, a unique type of construction, and Ted McCarty's unique marketing strategy.

The Rivoli was, indeed, a fraternal twin of Gibson's EB-2 semi-hollow bass when the alternate-brand model was first introduced in 1959. Each had a thinline maple body that was sixteen inches wide, nineteen inches long, and 1¾ inches deep. Both instruments had double rounded cutaways and unbound f-holes. The same center wood block inside the body was found on both models.

The neck was mahogany, and the rosewood fretboard had twenty frets with dot markers on a 30½-inch scale. Like its Gibson counterpart, the headstock on the original configuration of the Epiphone semi-hollow bass originally had rear-projecting, banjo-style tuners, and the plain, one-piece bridge/tailpiece was non-intonatable, but had an angled portion that attempted to facilitate tuning stability.

The original Rivoli also had a massive single-coil pickup mounted near the neck, and simple volume and tone controls. Like the EB-2, it began its existence in natural and sunburst finishes.

Epiphone EB232 Rivoli, mid-1960s (missing handrest). *Heritage Auctions*

Epiphone EB232C Rivoli, 1967. *Bill Ingalls Jr.*

As the EB-2 began to evolve in 1959 and 1960, so did the slightly-newer Rivoli. Each model acquired standard/right-angle tuners, a humbucking pickup, a pushbutton "baritone" switch, and a flip-up string mute (that was controlled by a sliding mechanism that ran under the bridge).

The outright differences in the Rivoli and the EB-2 were cosmetic: The models had different headstock silhouettes with different pearloid inlay in each. The pickguards also had different configurations, and the Epiphone model had a trademark circular "E" on its scratchplate, as well.

Curiously, part of such "evolution" for both models may have been pointed in the direction of "extinction," as they were temporarily discontinued in the early 1960s, only to be reinstated in 1964, when semi-hollow Epiphone and Gibson basses became a boon to many original "British Invasion" bands—and in this portion of their respective chronologies, perhaps it's appropriate to rank the Epiphone Rivoli ahead of the Gibson EB-2, due to more visibility for the Epiphone twin in the hands of notable English bassists. The British Invasion abruptly and permanently altered the American popular music scene, and the Rivoli quickly acquired an image of being a pre-eminent/frontline bass in the mid-1960s English pop/rock phenomenon.

The Epiphone brand was marketed in Great Britain by the Rosetti distributorship, and many English bass players gravitated to the Rivoli's sound, light weight, and playability. Moreover, the quality of American instruments was better than the cheap European guitars and basses that many players had first acquired as beginners' instruments.

Sunburst-finished Rivolis were utilized by bassists in bands such as the Animals (Chas Chandler), the Yardbirds (Paul Samwell-Smith), Gerry & the Pacemakers (Les Chadwick), and the Small Faces (Ronnie Lane).

The Animals, who came out of Newcastle-upon-Tyne in northeast England, purveyed a grittier sound that reflected the band's formative times in the coal-mining metropolis (compared to the upbeat pop being offered by other aggregations), and Chandler reportedly played the classic intro licks to "We've Gotta Get Out Of This Place" and "It's My Life" on his Epiphone Rivoli.

From 1964 to 1966, John Entwistle (1944–2002) counted on a sunburst Rivoli as well as a natural-finished EB-2 as part of his low-end arsenal (it was in late 1964 that Entwistle's band, the High Numbers, changed its name to The Who).

Jimmy Page was seen playing a sunburst Rivoli during his tenure with the Yardbirds, although it may have been the instrument played by Samwell-Smith (who had left the band). Moreover, Yardbirds rhythm guitarist Chris Dreja played what was, again, possibly the same instrument when he switched to the bass slot, as Page became the band's sole guitarist during its final incarnation.

Later in the decade, Free's Andy Fraser utilized a natural-finish Rivoli (historical photos indicate that it was modified).

A Cherry finish (noted by the "C" suffix) became an option in 1966, and is seen on a 1967 example on page 51. It also sports a handrest, which was not seen on all examples (not even on the one in the 1966 Epiphone catalog). The circular "E" logo is no longer on this Rivoli's tortoiseshell pickguard.

The Rivoli was discontinued again in 1969, but made a brief re-appearance in 1970 with two pickups.

Epiphone's experience in the solid body bass field didn't parallel the Gibson chronology, as Gibson entered that facet of the market in 1953, but a solid body Epiphone bass, the EBS Newport, didn't show up until it appeared in a 1960 catalog.

The Newport was a short-scale, all mahogany instrument that was basically the same as Gibson's EB-0, although the EB-0 had a two-cutaway asymmetrical body while the Newport had a plank-like, two-cutaway symmetrical body that measured 12¾ inches wide, 15⅝ long, and 1⅜ inches deep. Its silhouette and body dimensions matched early versions of Epiphone guitar models such as the Crestwood and the Coronet.

The headstock on the original version of the Newport was a variant of the traditional Gibson "mustache" headstock as found on other Epi-by-Gibson instruments. Unlike the Gibson EB-0, which began its existence with rear-projecting, banjo-style tuners (à la the Electric Bass and the EB-2, as well as the Epiphone Rivoli), it appears that the Newport had traditional electric bass tuners from the get-go.

The neck had a rosewood fretboard that joined the body at the eighteenth fret. The body featured a wooden fingerrest as well as a handrest over the strings to facilitate easier playing.

Like the EB-0 of the same era, the Newport's single black humbucking pickup was mounted near the neck, and it had the bridge/tailpiece as the Rivoli and corresponding Gibson models. The catalog description referred to the "Attractive pickguard with white-black-white reveal edges." The instrument's volume and tone knobs installed from the rear of the body.

The 1960 catalog also proffered a two-pickup EBD "Newport Deluxe" bass (with "deluxe trim"), which was not shown.

The 1962 Newport shown here is in nice shape, but its fingerrest (mounted on the pickguard) and its handrest have been removed.

Epiphone EBS Newport, mid-1960s. *Heritage Auctions*

Epiphone EBS Newport, 1962. *Heritage Auctions*

By the time the 1964 catalog was released, the Newport had, like Gibson's EB-0, gone through numerous cosmetic changes (as had Epiphone solid body guitars). Such pronounced differences may have been introduced in an effort to draw even more of a distinction between the Gibson and Epiphone brands.

The second version of the Newport had an asymmetrical body that alluded to an atrophied treble cutaway; i.e., the bass cutaway appeared to be the same as found on the earlier symmetrical-bodied bass, but the treble cutaway appeared to have shrunk.

The EBS Newport now had a chrome pickup, and a four-on-a-side headstock that has what has become known as a "batwing" silhouette in vintage guitar lingo. The catalog noted that the neck joined the body at the eighteenth fret. It also had plainer-looking control knobs (standard for some solid body Epiphone guitars as well), and the controls and jack were now mounted through a longer pickguard.

Unlike the earlier Newport, the later example seen here has its fingerrest and handrest.

Epiphone also marketed a full-scale, two-pickup bass in the mid-1960s called the EBDL Embassy, which was considered by some bass enthusiasts to have been the alternate brand's version of the Gibson Thunderbird bass.

Mid-1960s catalogs also referenced three custom colors that were exclusive to Epiphone; "California Coral," "Sunset Yellow," and "Pacific Blue." Those finishes were available on any Epiphone solid body instrument at extra cost.

In 1970, Gibson opted to abandon the side-by-side manufacturing of Epiphones and Gibsons in Kalamazoo, and the Epiphone brand was switched to Asian production, which is still the case today. Accordingly, some 1960s Epiphone guitars and basses are probably much rarer than their Gibson counterparts from the same era.

Mid-1960s catalog page.

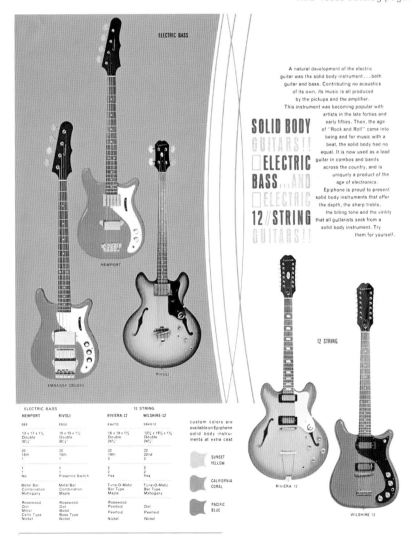

FOURTEEN

FENDER

"The actual, original parts that are left are the tuning pegs, the bridge, and the neck plate," Tim Bogert said of his longtime favorite (four-string) performance bass. "I was always f***ing around with it."

When Vanilla Fudge pioneered the progressive rock movement in the latter half of the 1960s, Bogert acquired more than one Fender Precision Bass, and installed Telecaster Bass necks on them. Introduced in that same era, Telecaster Basses had the same basic configuration of original 1950s Precision Basses, and Bogert preferred the Tele Bass neck's chunkier feel.

"I stripped the finish off of a couple of them," Bogert said of his P-Bass bodies, "because I liked a light color, which showed up better under all of the strobes and black lights."

Bogert would own this particular instrument for around three decades, using it with not only the Fudge, but with Cactus, and Beck, Bogert and Appice as well. And like any musician who is dedicated to his/her craft, he would constantly refine the bass, trying out new parts and replacing worn parts. From the top down, this instrument epitomizes a veritable and perpetually viable "Frankenstein" utility instrument, having gone through numerous configurations in its history.

The maple neck, for example, is the third that has been on this bass. It has an early P-Bass look and feel, as well as a plethora of bird's-eye flecks. Bogert acquired the neck from a guitar parts supplier that allowed him to personally search through their inventory of necks until he found the one that looked and felt right. He also had an original 1950s Fender Precision Bass decal placed on the headstock.

Bogert also installed a brass nut on the instrument, in an effort to get increased sustain.

Tim Bogert's utility Fender bass. *Darlene Ward*

Sharp-eyed Fender bass aficionados will note that there are no holes in the body under the holes in the pickguard on either side of the pickup, where the arched handrest/pickup cover would normally be installed. Nor are there holes in the body on either side of the bridge, where the bridge cover would have been installed.

That's because, perhaps not surprisingly, the body itself is also a replacement item.

"The body is something Fender gave me in the late 1980s," Bogert recounted. "I was an endorser of theirs for a long time, and we had a very friendly relationship; they treated me very well. I had an earlier maple body, but had chewed it up over the years, and I asked them for another one, because I've always liked a maple neck and a maple body. The (current) neck was on the old body for a few years before I got the maple body."

The bridge that is one of the remaining original parts wasn't always on this instrument. When it had an earlier body, Bogert tried out a Leo Quan Badass bridge on the bass for a while.

The two small chrome caps on the pickguard cover the former location of two small switches, which controlled two pickups, when a previous body had a second pickup installed on it.

"One was an on/off, and the other was a pickup select," Bogert remembered.

While the pickup isn't an original late-1960s item, the bassist emphasized that it has always been the instrument's, " . . . most important part, because it came off of a 1957 Fender that I got in 1968 or 1969, when we played the Hollywood Bowl with Jimi Hendrix. I got it put into my main bass by the Sam Ash store on Long Island. It's the best-sounding pickup I've ever heard; a great 'chunky' sound. I put the original pickup on this bass nearer the bridge to make it a two pickup instrument, but when I went with a new body, I went back to one pickup . . . and I wanted that '57 pickup."

An obvious eye-catching item is the fingerrest, which was installed on the body between the pickup and the bridge, instead of a normal location on the pickguard. Bogert explained that the part actually served as a thumbrest to allow his fingers to manipulate the strings in a unique manner.

"I started doing that around 1965 or 1966," he said, "when I started working with the Pigeons, which became the Fudge. We would do these crescendos, but the volume on Fenders would drop off really quick if you tried working the volume control; I think the old potentiometers were rated 250 (ohms), and they'd drop off like a rock. I would brace my thumb on that fingerrest and work the volume of the strings manually to make the crescendos smoother, and I learned to do that very precisely."

The late-1980s acquisition of a new maple body would mark the last major modification for this bass. It was at that time that he reverted to the original bridge and one pickup.

"The idea was kind of like restoring a motorcycle or a car," he said of his decision to return to a simpler layout. Perhaps the "restoration" notion was a bit nostalgic for Bogert as well. By then he had begun playing basses with more than four strings, and this instrument was usually relegated to storage.

"Around the 1980s, I started playing multi-stringed instruments," Bogert recalled, "and now, I play a (six-string) contrabass, for the most part."

In the late 1990s, Bogert finally parted ways with his former utility bass, selling to New York music producer/collector Randolf Pratt, who still owns it as of this writing. Pratt also acquired Vanilla Fudge guitarist Vince Martell's 1963 Gibson ES-335.

While Tim's bass has been through multiple modifications, including a replacement body and more than one replacement neck, it's still an important piece of progressive rock history.

Like any innovative company, Fender would not be satisfied with the success of its Precision Bass, and developed a second model, the two-pickup Jazz Bass, introducing it in 1960.

The original Jazz Bass had the distinction of being the first Fender bass model to appear with a new brand name logo on its headstock. The previous, original-style Fender script name on the headstock is known as the "spaghetti" logo among guitar collectors, and the newer, gold-colored, "more aerodynamic" logo is sometimes called the "transition"/ "transitional" logo. While some guitar buffs might have originally thought the term indicates that the logo change is connected to the purchase of the original Fender company by the gargantuan CBS conglomerate in 1965, that perception is incorrect by a half-decade. In fact, most of the earlier-introduced Fender models had begun the, er, transition from the "spaghetti" logo to the new logo by 1964.

The Jazz Bass was an improvement on the Precision Bass in several ways. While the body still had an arm bevel and "belly cut" contouring (as did all frontline Fenders except the two-pickup Telecaster and single-pickup Esquire guitars), its silhouette was an "offset waist" style, which was first seen on Fender's Jazzmaster guitar in the late 1950s. Such a shape meant that the instrument would be comfortable when played in a standing or sitting position, as the lower waist would be in alignment with a player's thigh when said player was seated.

The neck of the Jazz had a 1½-inch width at the nut (slimmer than the Precision). Its unbound rosewood fretboard had dot markers.

Pickups for Fender's second electric bass were two rectangular-shaped, single-coil units with non-adjustable polepieces. They were hidden under a chrome handrest (covering the pickup closer to the neck juncture), and under a large chrome plate nicknamed "the ashtray" (which covered not only the pickup closer to the bridge, but also the bridge itself). Many times, one or both covers were removed, and the "ashtray" often lived up to its moniker for many musicians.

The earliest Jazz Basses had two concentric volume-and-tone knobs (the smaller/inner knob was the volume control), and such versions of the Jazz Bass have become known as "stack-knob" variants. In 1962, the control configuration switched to a three-knobs-in-a-row layout (two volume controls and one master tone control; the latter had a smaller knob).

String mutes, designed to better emulate the sound of an upright/doghouse bass, were found on original Jazz Basses, but were outta there by 1963.

Like Bill Black's 1960 P-Bass, the stock 1961 and 1966 Jazz Basses seen here each have a classic three-tone Fender sunburst finish, and a reddish/rust-colored tortoiseshell pickguard. Similar instruments were seen in the mid-to-late 1960s in the hands of players such as Jack Casady (Jefferson Airplane), Bruce Barthol (Country Joe & the Fish), and Noel Redding (Jimi Hendrix Experience), among others.

These stock examples still have both pickup covers, and the 1966 Jazz Bass also has "egg"-shaped tuners. Many mid-1960s Jazz Basses also came from the factory with a third strap button attached to the back of the headstock, in case a player wanted to stretch a strap the full length of the instrument in an attempt to acquire better balance, but the 1966 example doesn't have that amenity (and most players would probably proclaim that the Jazz Bass is nicely-balanced, anyway).

But this 1966 Jazz Bass, which was made soon after the acquisition of the original Fender company by CBS, is one of the shorter-lived—if not the shortest—variants of the original standard-production Jazz Bass model, and the application of a "transitional" nickname is potentially redundant, and has nothing to do with headstock logos.

The CBS acquisition resulted in numerous cosmetic and construction changes to numerous Fender instrument models, and the Jazz Bass wasn't immune from such production transitions. Beginning in late 1965, the neck of the Jazz was bound in white, with black dot side markers. About a year later, the fretboard markers changed from dots to blocks.

Accordingly, a "transitional" Jazz Bass with a bound neck and dot markers is a unique Fender item that most guitar enthusiasts will consider one of the more interesting early CBS-era models. Its neck cosmetics exemplify why sometimes other criteria besides "pre-CBS" figure into the mix for players and collectors of Fender basses.

Fender Fine Electric Instruments

NEW FENDER JAZZ BASS—This is Fender's newest addition to the field of electric basses and represents the standards by which others will be compared. The two pickups have two poll pieces for each string giving excellent and true string tone response.* Tandem tone and volume controls for each pickup permit mixing for wide bass tone selection. In addition, it features Fender's new faster-action neck with rosewood finger-board and adjustable truss-rod for perfect neck alignment. For playing ease and comfort, the body is comfort-contoured and shaped with the "offset"* waist design, fitting the instrument to the player's body and placing the player's arm in a natural position over the strings. Individual bridges are adjustable for both accurate string lengths and comfortable string heights. Every bassist will find the new Fender Jazz Bass is truly an artists' instrument, combining all the fine features of the original Fender Bass plus these many developments and improvements which make it the most advanced electric bass on today's market.
*Patent Pending

JAZZ BASS

FENDER PRECISION BASS—One of the most popular of modern instrument developments, the Fender Precision Bass has rapidly become the choice of bassists in every field. Requires only a fraction of playing effort as compared with old style acoustic basses; compact in size and very large in performance. Fast-action neck facilitates playing technique, playing in tune and is extremely comfortable. Adjustable neck truss-rod assures perfect neck alignment. Individual bridges are adjustable for custom string heights and perfect string length between bridges and nut. Split pickups produce true bass tones and require only a fraction of the playing effort that went into playing old style bass. In addition, considerably more volume is obtainable. Its portability permits freedom of movement on stage and the fact that it is easy to carry is readily appreciated by every bass player. Its fine tone quality, playing ease and comfort has made the Fender Precision Bass a stock item in many of the nation's top musical organizations.

PRECISION BASS

FENDER JAZZMASTER—There is no more convincing proof of the fine playing qualities of the Fender Jazzmaster than its rapid acceptance by guitarists throughout the country during the past year. This remarkable guitar incorporates all the well-known Fender developments including the new "off-set" body design, smooth tremolo action plus separate rhythm and lead tone circuits. In addition, it offers a comfort contoured body and truss-rod reinforced fast-action neck with rosewood fingerboard for effortless playing and faster playing technique. Every convenience is provided including the tremolo lock, adjustable master bridge channel with individually adjustable two-way bridges and completely adjustable high fidelity pickups. The Jazzmaster' represents one of the finest additions to the Fender line and far surpasses other instruments in its price class.

FENDER STRATOCASTER GUITAR—Perfection in a solid body comfort-contoured professional guitar providing all of the finest Fender features. Choice hardwood body finished with a golden sunburst shading, white maple neck with rosewood fingerboard, white pickguard, and lustrous chrome metal parts. Three advanced style adjustable pickups, one volume control, two tone controls and a three-position instant tone change switch. The adjustable Fender bridge insures perfect intonation and softest action. The neck has the famous Fender truss rod. The Stratocaster is available with or without the Fender built-in tremolo.

The Jordanaires

Monk Montgomery

FENDER BASSMAN AMP—Specially designed for use with the Fender Jazz Bass and Fender Precision Bass and may be used with other instruments due to its wide tone response and circuit design. Its unparalleled performance is readily recognized by all qualified listeners.
Features four 10" heavy duty Jensen speakers, bass, mid-range, treble and presence tone controls, two volume controls, four inputs, on-off switch, ground switch and standby switch. Heavy duty solid wood cabinet covered with two-ply striped luggage linen. Size. Height, 23"; Width, 22½", Depth, 10½".

STRATOCASTER GUITAR

Unsurpassed in the field of Fine Music

The photo of the Jazz Bass in this page from a 1960 insert in Down Beat magazine showed it in its original, short-lived "stack-knob" configuration.

The 1962 Olympic white custom color Fender Jazz Bass (with matching headstock) on page 58 is obviously a collectible instrument, but there's an extra "people" facet to it, since it's owned by country music star Steve Wariner, c.g.p., and there's a decades-old family connection to his ownership.

Wariner is known as a lightning-fast guitarist, but in his earlier days he played bass behind more than one legendary Nashville singer.

The instrument is missing its handrest, "ashtray"/bridge and tailpiece cover, and mutes, but is otherwise fully original, with one interesting modification. Wariner's enthusiastic recollections about his acquisition and use of this bass are fascinating.

"I guess it was around 1962 or 1963," he recounted. "We lived in Fishers, Indiana; it was a small lazy farm town then, and it is anything but that now. It's pretty much grown into the north side of Indianapolis these days.

"My Uncle Jimmy Wariner was always the coolest guy! He lived in south central Kentucky but visited us often with his recent bride from Chicago, our new Aunt Becky. I always really looked up to him. He was a huge influence on me, as well as my music. He played lead guitar in a cool country band called Jay Hammond and the D.J.s. I thought it was awesome that they actually had 45s out on jukeboxes! They were a four-piece combo and they all wore matching flashy show clothes. Really impressive!

"I remember Jimmy and Becky had been to Chicago once to visit her mom, and they stopped in on their way back to Kentucky. Jimmy had his brand-spankin'-new Fender Jaguar guitar and Fender Jazz Bass with him— both Olympic White—that he got while they were in Chicago; he also

Fender Jazz Bass, 1961. *Olivia's Vintage*

Fender Jazz Bass, 1966. *Bill Ingalls Jr.*

A close-up look at the 1966 Jazz Bass's neck binding and dot inlay. *Bill Ingalls Jr.*

Fender Jazz Bass, 1962, Olympic White, owned by Steve Wariner. *Willie G. Moseley*

bought a new Fender Showman amp! I was amazed when he pulled back those metal legs on that Showman and let it tilt slightly back; I had never seen anything like it in person. Fantastic!

"Later, as a young teen, I joined the D.J.s for one summer, and got to play with Uncle Jimmy. We played on a live TV show out of Bowling Green, airing every Saturday night. Years later I realized other young teens who occasionally performed there were Ricky Skaggs and Keith Whitley. That time playing and traveling with Uncle Jimmy —in the baddest 1966 red Chevelle SS 396 ever—is something I will never forget."

Fast forward to 1973, when Wariner was a senior in high school, and got his stereotypical big break:

"I met Dottie West at the Nashville Country Club in Indianapolis, which was a country music club where I occasionally played while going to high school. She heard me and offered me a road job that night . . . as her bass player! Her current bass guy was leaving, and besides, she had a killer guitar player in Jimmy Johnson. I was a guitar player, but Dottie wanted a bass player who could sing, and I said 'Yeah, I can do that!' I jumped at the chance, and joined her at my semester break of my senior year; my grades were pretty good so I was able to leave early—and I did graduate. My Uncle Jimmy gave me that Fender Jazz Bass for the gig since I didn't even own a bass!"

Wariner would work with West for three years, after which he took a gig with singer Bob Luman.

"He grabbed me backstage at the Opry one night," Wariner said of Luman, "and asked me to go to Texas for the weekend, since his bass player had just left him. They were leaving . . . in just a few hours! I went, and wound up staying with him two years."

The young guitarist-turned-bassist would use the Jazz Bass on recordings with both West and Luman, but it was during his tenure with Luman that Steve had his first traumatic experience with this instrument:

"One night, after playing a funky little club in North Carolina, I sat bolt upright in my bunk on the bus ride home—I had left my bass at the edge of the stage, and we were halfway to Nashville!"

"I called for two weeks every day and finally got the (club) manager. Days later, he called back, said he'd found it, and he was putting it on a Greyhound bus to the Nashville bus station. I went at the designated arrival time, met the bus coming in, and as the driver opened the luggage bay, I asked him if he had an instrument. He looked around and said, 'Is this it?' He pulled out my bass and handed it to me. Close call!"

Wariner also used this bass when he played with Chet Atkins, and considers himself fortunate that the instrument didn't get damaged or demolished by airlines:

"While I was working with Luman, Chet had signed me to a recording contract with RCA. He was also my producer, and we became great friends immediately. When Luman passed away, Chet offered me the bass job with him. I had never had a 'flying only' gig. We flew all over; even Europe several times. That Fender bass was just tossed under the plane over and over, in its original Fender case. Nowadays, I look back and say, 'What was I thinking?'"

"Chet asked me to play on some of his recordings, and of course I used Uncle Jimmy's Jazz. The ones that stick out the most are *Chet Live from Paris and Nashville*, and *Neck and Neck* with Chet and Mark Knopfler."

Steve is one of four guitarists to whom Atkins awarded the honorary designation of "c.g.p." (certified guitar player), and he was a pallbearer at Atkins's funeral.

Steve Wariner onstage with Bob Luman in April 1977, playing his 1962 Fender Jazz Bass.

The only "modification" to the Jazz Bass was done during Wariner's time with West.

"While I worked for Dottie, I had talked to Steve Shafer, a top session bass guy of the day, about a slight hum I had experienced recently," Wariner remembered. "He took my bass and put a drop of epoxy on the pickup poles to eliminate it. It sure worked; looking back, though, I wonder if it had not simply been the studio I was in."

Nevertheless, the epoxy remains in place, and even though he's been ensconced as a top-flight singer and guitarist for decades, Wariner still uses the instrument on occasion.

"I still have the original ashtray, but I'm not sure about the hand rest," he said. "I love this old bass! When I pick it up and put my hands on it, it brings back great memories from my whole life. Sometimes I still use it to record, and occasionally I'll use a pick. It has flatwounds on it that are probably twenty years old!"

Loopy, goofy, and loping, Norman Greenbaum's spring 1970 hit single "Spirit in the Sky" was sort of a "caboose" on the psychedelic era of the late 1960s, the music of which was primarily centered in San Francisco. That's where "Spirit in the Sky" was recorded, and this is the bass that was used on that song. It's a 1963 Jazz Bass that belonged to Doug Killmer (1947–2005).

Parts-wise, the "Spirit" bass seems to be all original, " . . . except for a bridge screw or two," according to Russ DaShiell, Killmer's childhood friend and longtime musical associate, who was lead guitarist on the "Spirit" recording sessions. Cosmetically, however, it's obvious that its body has had its finish stripped, and there's also been a pad added to it.

"It was originally a sunburst," DaShiell recounted. "Around the time of the 'Spirit' sessions, Doug stripped the finish off his bass, and added a deerskin pad above the pickguard. He decided he didn't like the sunburst finish, and then proceeded to scrape it off using the edge of a knife blade. By the end of the day it was down to the wood; he added the deerskin pad later, after the wood itself started to wear down."

Nevertheless, some of the wear still seen on the body was also caused by Killmer's playing technique over the decades . . . and by the way, DaShiell says that Killmer always played with his fingers, not a pick.

After "Spirit in the Sky" became a hit, Norman Greenbaum's musical aggregation ended up opening shows for Chicago, the Moody Blues, Spirit, Iron Butterfly, Grand Funk Railroad, and the Doors. The band also appeared on Dick Clark's "American Bandstand," and Doug Killmer can be seen playing this bass in the photo from that episode. The single would end up as *Cashbox* magazine's Number One song for 1970, outranking such hits as "Bridge Over Troubled Water" by Simon and Garfunkel (#5), and the Beatles' "Let It Be" (#9).

When Killmer was diagnosed with a terminal illness, he consigned the Jazz Bass to DaShiell. Sadly, the twosome's last communications in 2005, were about the disposition of this instrument. The late bassist's survivors included his wife and three children.

Many aging Baby Boomers fondly recall the upbeat tone and unique sounds of "Spirit in the Sky," which was indeed a definitive example of "One-Hit-Wonderdom" for

In this old photo of a television broadcast, bassist Doug Killmer is shown playing this 1963 Jazz Bass with Norman Greenbaum's band on an April 1970 edition of "American Bandstand." Other members, from the left, are drummer Bill Meeker, Greenbaum, and lead guitarist Russ DaShiell.

Norman Greenbaum and his associates, including the now-departed bassist who is heard on the iconic song. One can only wonder to what extent the lyrics of the song might now seem ironic.

𝄢

It would be an understatement to say that REO Speedwagon bassist Bruce Hall and "Butter," his primary utility Jazz Bass, have been through a lot together. Born and raised in the side-by-side college towns of Champaign-Urbana, Illinois, the veteran bassist, who has now been with the platinum-selling rock band for decades, acquired his mainstay Jazz Bass when he was sixteen. Interestingly, the aspiring teenage player purchased the instrument from REO Speedwagon's original bassist, Greg Philbin, whom Hall would replace in 1978.

Applying a feminine connotation to his favorite instrument, Hall recalled: "Greg had bought her new, and had either sanded her down himself, or had it done, which was kind of a fad back then. I don't know what color she was originally, but he'd put a coat of varnish on her; it was a nice job."

In addition to the missing finish, the pickguard had been removed. Otherwise, the bass was stock, and was an example of Fender's second version of the Jazz Bass.

"I played her in the bars for years before I joined REO Speedwagon," Hall recounted. "One night, I happened to leave her in the equipment van; this was during the winter, so the finish cracked. I was upset, but as time went on, I thought it looked cooler. In fact, I later took her to the Fender Custom Shop—I take her down there once or twice a year—and they took pictures of her, because they wanted to see if they could duplicate the look when they were 'relic'-ing instruments."

"The first (REO Speedwagon) record I was on was *You Can Tune a Piano but You Can't Tuna Fish*, and I used 'Butter' on that album," Hall continued. "I started getting into some other basses; (former REO guitarist) Gary Richrath knew some guy who would bring him old Les Pauls, and the same guy started bringing me sunburst Precision Basses from the 1950s. I bought two of those and used them on the *Hi Infidelity* album and tour.

"I'd left 'Butter' at home, because I didn't want anything to happen to her," he noted, "but now those 1950s P-Basses are at home, and 'Butter' is back out with me."

Over the decades, "Butter" has been through what Hall considers to have been appropriate modifications for utility instruments. A reproduction laminated tortoiseshell pickguard has been installed, and the original bridge, which was rusted out, was replaced by a Leo Quan Badass bridge around 1982. A brass nut was added by a Los Angeles guitar shop.

One of the biggest modifications for 'Butter' was the installation of EMG active pickups and circuitry, and the decision caused Hall a moderate amount of angst before he opted to proceed.

"I'd gotten used to active pickups with Spector basses," Hall recounted. "When (guitarist) Dave Amato joined the band, he turned me on to those. They had EMGs in them, and I really liked their sound; you could get more tone out of them. The 'original Fender sound' is very distinct, and is good for certain things, but is not good for everything."

Accordingly, "Butter" eventually underwent a transmogrification to active bass status, and Hall was delighted with the result (but he's kept the original pickups, of course). The control knob arrangement now consists of a master volume knob, a pan pot, and a stacked treble and bass knob.

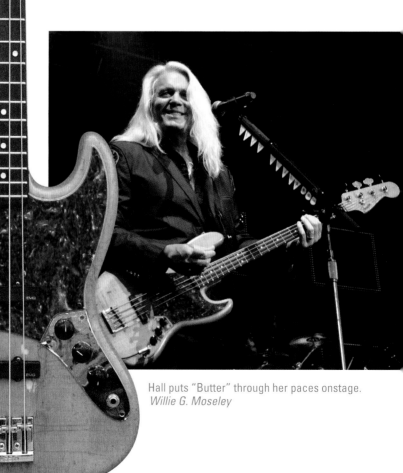

Hall puts "Butter" through her paces onstage.
Willie G. Moseley

Fender Jazz Bass, 1965, owned by Bruce Hall. *Willie G. Moseley*

However, the pan pot doesn't matter all that much to Hall, as he uses the pickup closer to the neck exclusively, and the bassist has mused about an even more radical modification.

"I've been talking to some of the guys down at Fender," he said. "I've been thinking about maybe moving the (bridge/treble) pickup and putting it right next to the other pickup. That ought to sound interesting!"

When advised of Asia/King Crimson bassist John Wetton's analogy that active basses are the sonic equivalent of an automobile that's had a supercharger added to the engine, Hall enthused, "That's exactly right! That's what it feels like, and you can still get a lot of the same sounds that you can get with passive pickups, but with active, it's like having more colors to paint with."

Like any veteran musician, Bruce Hall understands that instruments are tools of the trade, and while he's modified his 1965 Jazz Bass numerous times, such improvements have always enabled him to enhance his music and his career. "Butter" remains his favorite bass, and such will always be the case.

"She and I grew up together," Hall said with a smile.

The legend of the Fender brand's travails in the 1970s and early 1980s is well-known in the vintage/used guitar market. The quality of many of their US-made products was considered abhorrent, as were many of their so-called innovations. And the 1985 purchase of the company from CBS by a number of investors by no means guaranteed the brand's survival—the fabled Fullerton, California, factory was closed, and the company had to count on imported guitars and basses from Japan to fill the gaps in their lineup of standard instruments as Fender struggled to make a comeback.

Many Japanese Fender guitars and basses of that era are immediately recognizable, as they have black headstocks. Being as how it was the 1980s, black hardware was also often seen on such instruments. However, some new-from-Japan models also had new ideas that had merit for working musicians, and such was the case for the Jazz Bass Special, introduced in the latter half of that decade.

Intended as a hybrid lineup that interpolated ideas from both the Precision Bass and the Jazz Bass, the Jazz Bass Special series came in both active and passive models. The addition of "Power" to the model name indicated the active variant, and two small lightning bolts by the model name on the headstock underlined the use of active circuitry, powered by a 9-volt battery installed in the back.

Another distinguishing feature of the headstock of the Power Jazz Bass Special was a textured-looking overlay under a clear coat surrounded by black, offering a type of holographic effect. Standard/passive Jazz Bass Specials usually had a solid black headstock.

The perceived melding of Precision and Jazz features on this series matched up a slim, Jazz-like neck that was 1½ inches wide at the nut with a P-Bass body silhouette (i.e., parallel "waists"). Both the standard and Power models had carbon graphite nuts and were among the first Fender models to offer a pickup configuration that consisted of one offset Precision-style unit and one straight Jazz-style unit. This arrangement has now become known—generically—as a "P/J" layout in bass parlance and is found on countless models by umpteen manufacturers.

Both models had rosewood fingerboards with a 7¼-inch radius. Curiously, the fretted variant of the passive Jazz Bass Special had a twenty-fret neck, while its Power sibling had twenty-two frets.

The treble cutaway on the Power version is more offset compared to the standard model. The Power model's cutaway horns also have beveled contours inside, which also assists in facilitating access way up the fretboard. The top edge of the treble-side bevel joins the neck at the twenty-first fret!

The jack was a side-mounted item on Jazz Bass Specials, whereas original Jazz Basses and Precision Basses had top-mounted jacks.

While the electronic innovations on the Power Jazz Bass Special make sense and aren't particularly complicated, a player would still need to take the time to learn the functions of the knobs and switches.

At first glance, one might think the Power version's two upper knobs are volume controls while the lower knob is a master tone control. Not so. The upper controls consist of a volume control and tone control (and the latter does not have a center detent),

Fender Power Jazz Bass Special, late 1980s. *Bill Ingalls Jr.*

and the lower knob works a "TBX circuit control" that offers "frequency sweep," according to the owner's manual. The TBX knob does have a center detent; moving the knob counter-clockwise filters off high frequencies, and rotating it in a clockwise direction adds presence and brightness.

The larger switch is a simple three-way pickup toggle (and remember, original Jazz Basses didn't have such, even though they were two-pickup instruments), but the three-way mini-toggle (called a "circuit switch" in the owner's manual) is a different matter. Known as the "A.T.E. (Active Tone Enhancement) circuit," this portion of the Power Jazz Bass Special's active electronics offered a "Passive" option (the tone control acted like a normal tone control), a "Low

Frequency Boost," and a "Midrange Boost," depending on the position of the mini-toggle. Fender literature proclaimed that the circuit, " . . . can add low end 'pop' or high end 'brilliance' to the sound of the instrument."

Among noted players, Richard Cousins, bassist for the Robert Cray Band, was seen onstage in the late 1980s with a silver Japanese Fender bass of this configuration circa Cray's *Strong Persuader* album, i.e., when such instruments were new.

The Power Jazz Bass Special and its standard/passive variant lasted into the 1990s, and are relatively inexpensive in today's used instrument market. Like other imported Fenders of their era, they may have been considered (by

Fender Fine Electric Instruments

JAZZ BASS

FENDER JAZZ BASS—This is Fender's newest addition to the field of electric basses and represents the standards by which others will be compared. The two pickups have two poll pieces for each string giving excellent and true string tone response. Tandem tone and volume controls for each pickup permit mixing for wide bass tone selection. In addition, it features Fender's new faster-action neck with rosewood finger-board and adjustable truss-rod for perfect neck alignment. For playing ease and comfort, the body is comfort-contoured and shaped with the "offset"* waist design, fitting the instrument to the player's body and placing the player's arm in a natural position over the strings. Individual bridges are adjustable for both accurate string lengths and comfortable string heights. Every bassist will find the new Fender Jazz Bass is truly an artists' instrument, combining all the fine features of the original Fender Bass plus these many developments and improvements which make it the most advanced electric bass on today's market.
*Patent Pending

NEW FENDER BASS GUITAR—The New six-string Bass Guitar is the finest on today's market. It is tuned one octave below that of the spanish guitar. This instrument incorporates three pickups that can be used together or in any combination, making a total of seven tone changes plus separate tone and volume controls. The Bass Guitar has a 21 fret, extra-slim faster action neck with rosewood fingerboard and adjustable truss-rod for perfect neck alignment. This remarkable new guitar incorporates all the Fender developments including the comfort-contoured "off-set" body design, and smooth tremolo action. Every convenience is provided including the "floating-bridge" with six individual bridges each adjustable for string length and height, and individually adjustable high fidelity pickups. The Bass Guitar is a fine addition to the Fender line and answers the demand for a high-quality six-string bass.

FENDER PRECISION BASS—One of the most popular of modern instrument developments, the Fender Precision Bass has rapidly become the choice of bassists in every field. Requires only a fraction of playing effort as compared with old style acoustic basses; compact in size and very large in performance. Fast-action neck facilitates playing technique, playing in tune and is extremely comfortable. Adjustable neck truss-rod assures perfect neck alignment. Individual bridges are adjustable for custom string heights and perfect string length between bridges and nut. Split pickups produce true bass tones and require only a fraction of the playing effort that went into playing old style bass. In addition, considerably more volume is obtainable. Its portability permits freedom of movement on stage and the fact that it is easy to carry is readily appreciated by every bass player. Its fine tone quality, playing ease and comfort has made the Fender Precision Bass a stock item in many of the nation's top musical organizations.

PRECISION BASS

New!

BASS GUITAR

FENDER JAZZMASTER—There is no more convincing proof of the fine playing qualities of the Fender Jazzmaster than its rapid acceptance by guitarists throughout the world during the past few years. This remarkable guitar incorporates all the well-known Fender developments including the new "off-set" body design, smooth tremolo action plus separate rhythm and lead tone circuits. In addition, it offers a comfort contoured body and truss-rod reinforced fast-action neck with rosewood fingerboard for effortless playing and faster playing technique. Every convenience is provided including the tremolo lock, adjustable master bridge channel with individually adjustable two-way bridges and completely adjustable high fidelity pickups. The Jazzmaster represents one of the finest additions to the Fender line and far surpasses other instruments in its price class.

JAZZMASTER

STRATOCASTER GUITAR

FENDER STRATOCASTER GUITAR—Perfection in a solid body comfort-contoured professional guitar providing all of the finest Fender features. Choice hardwood body finished with a golden sunburst shading, white maple neck with rosewood fingerboard, white pickguard, and lustrous chrome metal parts. Three advanced style adjustable pickups, one volume control, two tone controls and a three-position instant tone change switch. The adjustable Fender bridge insures perfect intonation and softest action. The neck has the famous Fender truss rod. The Stratocaster is available with or without the Fender built-in tremolo.

Unsurpassed in the field of Fine Music

On a page in Fender's 1961 Down Beat insert, the "NEW!" instrument designation had been switched from the Jazz Bass to the "Bass Guitar."

players and/or company employees) to have been "temporary," but several worthwhile innovations that made sense for working musicians went into the design and construction of these basses. Perhaps such basses didn't (or don't) get the respect they may have deserved because of the company's arduous efforts to survive that were ongoing when these instruments were introduced.

Curiously, Fender waited a decade to introduce a true bass guitar, but it was markedly different from the Danelectro and Gibson products that had preceded it.

Fender's bass guitar was initially called exactly that—in a 1961 pull-out brochure found in *Down Beat* magazine, the new instrument was pronounced to be the "Bass Guitar" as it was displayed near Fender's already-popular Precision Bass and one-year-old Jazz Bass.

By the time the next year's pull-out brochure was found in *Down Beat*, the Bass Guitar was known as the "Bass VI."

The Bass VI was Fender's first short-scale bass instrument and owed a lot to the Jazzmaster guitar, which had appeared a few years earlier. The new low-end instrument had a maple neck with twenty-one frets on a rosewood fretboard with dot position markers. The Bass VI had a thirty-inch scale, and the neck joined the body at the seventeenth fret on the bass side and the twenty-first fret on the treble side.

Like a Jazzmaster, the Bass VI body had offset waists, and also sported a Jazzmaster-style "floating" vibrato system. Unlike the Stratocaster's single-unit vibrato system, both the bridge (which had individual intonatable saddles and a snap-on cover) and the vibrato tailpiece were both in motion when the vibrato arm was manipulated. Once again, Fender erroneously switched terminology in its advertising

Fender Bass VI, Olympic White, 1962. *Vintage Guitar Magazine* archive

Fender Bass VI, Candy Apple Red, 1964. *Vintage Guitar Magazine* archive

Fender Bass VI, mid-1960s. *Willie G. Moseley*

hype (as it had done with the Stratocaster and amplifiers) for its description of the Bass VI's "smooth tremolo action" (when the device was actually a vibrato).

The Bass VI offered a plethora of versatility, as its three single-coil pickups had separate off-on switches (found in a plate on the treble cutaway), allowing a total of seven different pickup combinations. Master volume and tone controls were found in a metal plate beside the pickguard.

Within two years after its introduction, the Bass VI had received a foam rubber mute and serrated metal pickup surrounds (à la the Jaguar guitar introduced in 1962). A fourth switch, pronounced in company literature to be a "tone modification switch," was now found next to the three pickup switches.

Like other Fender models, the Bass VI would receive neck binding in the mid-1960s, followed soon afterwards by block markers.

The most notable Fender Bass VI player of the 1960s was Jack Bruce, who utilized that model (in a standard Sunburst finish) while he was still with the Graham Bond Organization. When guitarist John McLaughlin departed from that band he was not replaced, as Bruce held down the low end and tried to venture into "guitar territory" whenever possible.

In a 2002 interview, Bruce recalled that, " . . . when (McLaughlin) left, we got Dick Heckstall-Smith on saxophone. So with no guitar, I was able to play little guitar-like solos."

Fender Bass V, 1966, Candy Apple Red.
Vintage Guitar Magazine archive

Fender Bass V, circa 1968. *Heritage Auctions*

Fender Bass V, circa 1969, Lake Placid Blue.
Willie G. Moseley

Bruce also utilized the same instrument in the early days of Cream. Primeval concerts by the legendary supergroup saw Eric Clapton with an original single-cutaway Les Paul Standard guitar in a sunburst finish, with Bruce on his Bass VI. When Clapton's "'Burst" was stolen, he acquired a 1964 Gibson SG, which would receive a psychedelic paint job from a Dutch art collective known as The Fool (and the same moniker has been applied to Clapton's iconic instrument). Bruce's Bass VI also received the same treatment from the same group, but the experience left him frustrated.

"When it got painted, the neck was so sticky I couldn't play it," Bruce recounted. "I used some borrowed instruments and started looking for something new, and that's when I found the Gibson EB-3, which was very important, because I wanted to develop a style of playing that was very guitar-like, instead of playing root notes. I used La Bella light-gauge strings, which I could bend."

Shown on page 63 are a 1962 Bass VI with three pickup switches, a Candy Apple Red 1964 example with the fourth switch and a matching headstock (missing its vibrato arm and bridge cover), and a standard Sunburst finish mid-1960s example.

The Bass VI lasted until 1975, much longer than other true bass guitars by other manufacturers. It was re-introduced as a Japanese import in 1995, and discontinued again in 1997.

The Bass VI wasn't the first instrument of its type, but it had some unique innovations that could generate unique sounds.

Just as many bassists have probably had discussions with their peers concerning the viability of electric stringed basses vs. keyboard bass instruments, conversations have also transpired comparing five-string electric basses to standard four-string instruments, and the question has been raised as to whether keyboard basses and/or five-string models would ever supplant the original four-string version.

The bottom line in the "four-strings-versus-five" confab should be that the four-string electric bass is alive and well, but the five-string version, with an extra lower string usually tuned to B below the standard E of a four-string model, has made impressive inroads into the musical landscape of contemporary music.

Accordingly, such schmooze sessions about four-string and five-string basses probably never address the original five-string electric bass, the Fender Bass V, which was developed by Leo Fender and associates in the "pre-CBS" era, and was made from 1965 to 1970.

However, the original five-string bass's extra string was a higher-tuned item rather than a lower-tuned string. Its high C string was tuned above the G string of a standard bass, but the extra string was just the beginning of the Bass V's unique (and ultimately unsuccessful) approach.

Examined from the top down, the Bass V has an expected elongated headstock in the classic Fender silhouette that accompanies the extra string and its tuning key, and there's also a string retainer, under which the D, G, and C strings pass.

The length of the fretboard is immediately striking (and/or alienating)—it's only fifteen frets. The commendable notion behind the innovation of a high C string on a bass was that a player could reach higher, guitar-like notes by simply moving over to the C string instead of fretting way up the neck, which, its creators apparently thought, rendered such higher-range frets unnecessary.

The scale of the Bass V was still the industry-standard thirty-four inches, just like the Precision Bass and the Jazz Bass. However, the noticeable distance between the end of the Bass V's fretboard and the bridge on the body may have also looked, like the short neck, awkward to some observers.

Early examples of the Bass V had dot inlay on the rosewood fretboard on a maple neck, but about a year after its introduction, it acquired block inlays and a bound neck, as did other Fender models around the same time.

The body of the Bass V had traditional Fender contouring, as well as a slimmer, "stretched" appearance compared to other Fender basses, perhaps to give it some kind of visual "balance" with the abbreviated neck.

Like all Fender electric guitars and basses, the Bass V came in standard colors and custom colors, and seen here is a rare 1966 Candy Apple Red variant with a matching headstock, as well as later examples (with block fretboard inlay) in standard Sunburst, and Lake Placid Blue.

A multi-laminated pickguard and a fingerrest were also found on the Bass V, as were volume and tone knobs for the solitary pickup, which is another unique item. It's a split-oval design, not unlike the pickups on the Electric XII twelve-string guitar, introduced around the same time as the Bass V. The bass side portion of the Bass V's pickup handles the E and A strings, while the treble side takes care of the D, G, and C strings. Curiously, the split-oval pickups on the Electric XII were installed in a reverse configuration to the Bass V's pickup—when the Electric XII's body is viewed vertically, each half of its two pickups were higher on the bass side than the treble side.

Some early publicity photos of the Bass V show it with a handrest covering the pickup, just like the Precision Bass and Jazz Bass. The bridge cover looks, appropriately, like a cross between the bridge covers found on the Precision and Jazz. While it's shaped more like a P-Bass bridge cover, it still has the "flying F" logo as seen on the large Jazz Bass bridge cover. Like other Fender basses, a foam mute was installed on the underside.

The handrest has been removed on the Bass Vs seen here, and the bridge cover has also been removed from the sunburst Bass V.

The bridge itself has five individual and intonatable string saddles. The Bass V's strings install through the rear of the body, and its holes are reinforced with ferrules that are countersunk.

Towards the end of the decade, Fender began to discontinue the matching-headstock look on its custom color instruments, and the circa-1969 example in Lake Placid Blue validates that shift.

The Bass V has the dubious distinction of being the first Fender bass model that was discontinued, as it disappeared from the music instrument marketplace in 1970 . . . which means that yet another use of the "opposite direction" term could be applicable to its lack of success, compared to its predecessors.

Some surplus Bass V bodies were used to make examples of the Fender Swinger/Musiclander, a relatively rare but uninspiring single-pickup guitar that was a "floor sweep" model that used parts from more than one standard-production instrument.

In the ensuing decades, Fender has re-issued all sorts of classic versions of basses that were originally introduced during the company's fabled "pre-CBS" era, but just as the ultimately-unsuccessful uniqueness of the Bass V led to its demise around a half-decade after its introduction, aging Baby Boomers and other stringed instrument enthusiasts aren't particularly interested in a comeback for the Bass V; i.e., such an oddball status apparently hasn't generated enough nostalgia or enthusiasm to merit a modern-day re-issue of the model.

In more than one way, Fender's short-scale Mustang Bass, introduced in 1966, was more of a transitional instrument than many persons may have realized.

Fender had sought to encourage the student guitar market as early as the mid-1950s, when their no-frills single-pickup Musicmaster and two-pickup Duo-Sonic ¾-size models were introduced. An upgrade student model, the two-pickup, twenty-four-inch scale Mustang, came along in 1964, sporting offset waists on its body, as well as a vibrato. Following the lead of the new model, the Musicmaster and Duo-Sonic would also adapt an offset-waist silhouette around that time.

Fender didn't market a short-scale student bass until after the company had been sold to CBS in 1965. Leo Fender had been developing such an instrument, as well as a twelve-string electric guitar, prior to the CBS sale, and the original Mustang Bass would indeed quickly become a popular instrument for students, female players, and players with small hands.

Comfort was the obvious primary asset and intent of the Mustang Bass, and its short, thirty-inch scale was just the tip of the ergonomic iceberg. Its light weight, offset body waists, and body contouring made it extremely easy to play in both sitting and standing positions.

The Mustang Bass's headstock had a classic Fender four-on-a-side silhouette. The tuning keys initially had a rounded/"egg-shaped" profile and would be supplemented later by Schaller "cloverleaf"-shaped keys.

The bolt-on neck was made of maple and had a rosewood fretboard with nineteen frets and pearloid dot markers.

Another indication that the Mustang Bass was a student/budget instrument was its body silhouette. With its stubby cutaway horns and shallower cutaways, it looked more like its six-string student cousins rather than a downsized Precision Bass or Jazz Bass.

Initially, the Mustang Bass body was made of alder, but in its history, other woods were also used, particularly on natural-finished examples. As for its debut colors, the first-of-its-kind Fender bass started out just like its namesake guitar, in red, light blue, or white. Instruments finished in the first two colors had white pearloid ("mother-of-toilet-seat") pickguards, while white Mustang Basses had reddish-colored tortoiseshell scratchplates.

Fender Mustang Bass, 1966. *Heritage Auctions*

Fender Mustang Bass, 1967.
Vintage Guitar Magazine archives

Like the P-Bass, the Mustang Bass had a single, offset/split-coil pickup, but its housings were oval-shaped. The volume and tone control configuration gave a nod to the Jazz Bass, however, as the knobs were installed on a chrome plate instead of on an extended portion of the pickguard.

Strings loaded through the rear of the body, and the large bridge plate had individual and intonatable string saddles, as well as foam mutes. Most players usually removed the latter items.

A fingerrest was initially found on the treble side of the pickguard. Some players removed that item or relocated it to the bass side to serve as a thumbrest.

The Mustang Bass and the Mustang guitar would each be offered in an unusual variant in 1969. The "Competition" version of the guitar and bass were offered in upgrade colors with a coordinating racing stripe painted on the body. Color combinations included red (white stripe), burgundy (white stripe), dark metallic blue/Lake Placid Blue (light blue stripe), or yellow-orange (red stripe). Some Competition Mustangs had matching headstocks.

As the Mustang Bass continued its sojourn through the music marketplace, subsequent colors in which it would be offered included sunburst, natural, walnut, black, and wine. Black pickguards would also be introduced. Some white examples also had white pickguards. There was even a Mustang Bass offered in the unusual off-white/ghost-like "Antigua" finish in the late 1970s, as was the case with almost all Fender standard electric models.

Despite any (somewhat expected) sonic shortcomings of the Mustang Bass due to its short scale, the instrument had a decent sound, and numerous notable players used the model. One of its most noteworthy appearances was in the hands of Rolling Stones bassist Bill Wyman during the band's (infamous) 1969 tour, as documented by the movie *Gimme Shelter*. Tina Weymouth, who fit the stereotype of one segment of the instrument's target market, used a Mustang Bass in Talking Heads. Other British purveyors of the Mustang Bass included Trevor Bolder of the Spiders from Mars (David Bowie's band during his "Ziggy Stardust" incarnation), and Alan Lancaster, the original bassist for English boogiemeisters Status Quo. Veteran British guitarist Denny Laine reportedly used a Mustang Bass in concert with Paul McCartney & Wings, when the ex-Beatle opted to switch from bass to guitar or piano.

The original Mustang Bass had run its course after about a decade and a half, and was discontinued in 1981. It was re-introduced in more recent times as an import.

For many aspiring bassists who came of age during the 1960s and 1970s, Fender's Mustang Bass was, in their minds at the time, a requisite instrument to own and play. A Leo Fender design, but a Fender/CBS product, it did indeed have a unique place, not only in the Fender instrument lineup, but in the history of the company.

This page from the 1966 Fender catalog shows the "Coronado Bass" in its earliest configuration.

Fender Coronado
Bass I, black, 1967.
Willie G. Moseley

The original "pre-CBS" Fender company may have designed a number of classic instruments, but a thinline hollow body/semi-hollow series wasn't among such innovations—credit for that style belongs to Gibson, which debuted its thinline Byrdland ES-225T and ES125T hollow body guitars in the mid-1950s, followed by the double-cutaway ES-335 guitar and EB-2 bass, among other semi-hollow thinline models in 1958. And as noted earlier, Epiphone siblings soon followed.

Soon after the CBS acquisition of Fender, the powers that be opted for a Fender series that had a similar look to Gibson's semi-hollow series. However, Fender's lineup was fully-hollow, and had, as expected, bolt-on necks as well as a Fender-like headstock profile.

Luthier Roger Rossmeisl, who had migrated from Rickenbacker to Fender in the early 1960s, had designed Fender's acoustic flat-top lineup, and was tapped to work on the new thinline electric series. The reception to the (well-crafted) acoustic line had been unsuccessful, however, because in the eyes of the guitar-buying public, Fender was a company that made solid body guitars. Perhaps that lack of success should have been a warning to the Fender brass about the viability of a thinline hollow body electric series.

Nevertheless, the Rossmeisl-designed Coronado series was introduced in 1966. The one-pickup bass was first, and the two-pickup version came along in 1967.

Fender Coronado II, 1967. *Olivia's Vintage*

Fender Coronado II, 1968. *Steve Evans*

Fender Coronado II, Wildwood, late 1960s.
Olivia's Vintage

The (one-pickup) Coronado Bass displayed in the 1966–1967 Fender catalog was an instrument with a body that was 1¹¹⁄₁₆ inches in depth. It sported a pickguard and a bound neck with a rosewood fretboard and block fret markers starting on the first fret. The f-holes were unbound, and the bridge and staggered-tailpiece assembly (which had individual "tubes" anchoring each string) were earlier items that usually weren't found on production models, so the instrument in the catalog may have been a prototype. The standard finishes proffered were Sunburst and Cherry Red.

The Coronado series had a "softened" lower portion of its headstock silhouette (no "barb," as found on Fender solid

bodies such as the Precision Bass and Jazz Bass), which is a possible validation of Rossmeisl's involvement, as the headstocks on the earlier acoustic guitar lineup also had a softer profile.

By the time the 1968 catalog debuted, the single pickup bass had been dubbed the Coronado Bass I, and the two-pickup Coronado Bass II was available. Both had the bridge and tailpiece seen on these examples. Both standard finishes were still available, but instruments were also offered in "selected custom finishes available by special order."

As for the hardware, note the egg-shaped/paddle tuners associated with some Fender bass models of that era.

Fender Coronado II, Antigua. 1968.

The tailpiece was another indication of Rossmeisl's influence—the traditional Fender "Flying F" was there, and Rossmeisl had designed a somewhat-similar "R" tailpiece during his tenure at Rickenbacker.

What's more, the control knobs (volume and tone for each pickup) looked like they'd be at home on a Ric guitar or bass.

The Coronado Bass I shown on page 68 is a 1967 custom color black example, and the 1967 Coronado IIs are in standard finishes.

The long, thin f-holes (bound on the Coronado Bass II) are situated beside a thumbrest and a fingerrest. Note the differences in the bridge units.

The pickups on the Coronado series were uninspiring and fraught with problems, including a tendency to feed back, according to longtime Fender employee Bill Carson, who recalled in his autobiography, *Bill Carson: My Life and Times with Fender Instruments*, that "the point of no return" had been reached in production commitment to the series before the pickup problem could be resolved. His recollection included pronouncing the Coronado project to have been a "fiasco."

The term "flop" could not only be applicable to the lack of success of the Coronado series in the marketplace, but also to what happened when the hollow body instruments were strapped on. The lack of a center woodblock inside the body meant that donning a Coronado bass (with a longer and heavier neck than a guitar) revealed a strong tendency for its headstock to take an immediate dive towards the ground.

Variants of Coronado thinlines over the years included the Wildwood series (bodies made from beechwood trees that had been injected with dye while growing) as well as basses in the Antigua finish.

No bass player of renown was regularly seen plunking on a Coronado when the series was in production, nor are Coronados highly-sought in the vintage market because of any unique sonic properties.

The failure of the Coronado thinlines as the first series introduced by CBS/Fender was an ominous harbinger of the problems—to include marketing, design, and ultimately, quality—that would plague the company for its two decades of CBS ownership.

Nevertheless, Coronado Basses have their fans among some collectors and players, including Cheap Trick's Tom Petersson, who owns the black Coronado Bass I shown herein. Among his collection are another custom color Coronado Bass I (in Sonic Blue), and two-pickup examples from the Wildwood and Antigua series.

"I think they're all beautiful, and they look good together," said the Cheap Trick bassist. "They sound good; kind of like Guild Starfires, and they're nice and light, too. I've never recorded with them, except at home on demos."

Sitting pretty in south Texas, here's a quintet of late-1960s Fender Telecaster Basses, owned by veteran bassist Ricky Phillips, who has gigged with the Babys, Bad English, and Coverdale-Page during his career. As of this writing, he has occupied the low-end stringed instrument slot in Styx since late 2003.

Most guitar enthusiasts consider original Tele Basses to have been re-issues of the original early-1950s Precision Bass, and the connection is obvious, regarding the slab body, hardware, electronics, and cosmetics (although most Tele Basses had a white pickguard).

The Telecaster Bass was introduced in 1968, and later became available in quasi-psychedelic floral or paisley finishes, as well as a fretless version. Phillips actually cited a guitarist for the Rolling Stones as one of the reasons he was attracted to the earlier incarnation of the model.

"There's a Ron Wood connection," he enthused. "A lot of people aren't aware of how great of a bass player he was in the original Jeff Beck Group, and he used a Telecaster Bass. What he did in that band was phenomenal; he's riffing through entire songs, and playing great stuff. I love that tone, and I always have. I know that when [Jimi] Hendrix played Woodstock, Billy Cox was playing a Tele Bass—probably a brand new one. I got my first '68 when I was in the Babys; I got it at a pawn shop for $100. It had a Strat pickup in it that had an interesting tone, but I replaced it with a proper '68 pickup."

Ricky's fivesome shows varying degrees of wear, and the white bass in the middle has been refinished and has a replacement pickguard as well as a replacement pickup. The handrests have been removed on that Tele Bass and another one as well.

Fender Telecaster
Basses, owned by
Ricky Phillips.
*Dawn Jones-
Garcia*

But Phillips, like many pro musicians, eschews the "is-it-fully-original-including-the-finish" syndrome if a certain utilitarian instrument has a sound he is seeking (other instruments in his collection are refinished as well). For example, he used the modified white Telecaster Bass on "Difference in the World," a song written by Tommy Shaw, on Styx's *Regeneration, Volume I* album. "It sounds amazing," Phillips said of that particular instrument.

Fender Telecaster Bass,
1970s. *Olivia's Vintage*

Fender Telecaster Bass, 1970s.
Olivia's Vintage

Fender Bullet Bass,
1980. *Willie G. Moseley*

Fender Bullet Bass, 1980.
Heritage Auctions

Phillips also respects the bass playing of another erstwhile Jeff Beck bandmate mentioned earlier in this chapter.

"I thought Tim Bogert had a great, raw style with Cactus and Beck, Bogert & Appice," he recalled, "and his tone is very similar to what I get out of those Tele Basses. It's all about the sound."

The Telecaster Bass maintained its retro look until 1972, when it underwent changes in the pickup (which became a humbucking unit with offset polepieces), pickup location (nearer the neck), and the neck/truss rod system, which had been a four-attachment style but became a three-bolt design with a "bullet" truss rod adjustment protuberance on the headstock. Two examples from the second configuration are seen here in standard Blond and Sunburst finishes.

The second generation Tele Bass exemplified an unfortunate propensity of CBS/Fender to take a classic design and modify it—sometimes radically—for reasons that didn't seem to make much sense to many musicians. The model was discontinued in 1979.

At more than one point in its history, the Fender company has tried to manufacture and market lower-priced, relatively plain instruments in an effort to garner a segment of the marketplace that they felt their frontline instruments, such as the Precision Bass and the Jazz Bass, were missing. Such full-scale models had a "budget" vibe (as opposed to a "student model" notion, which implied a short scale), and while the idea was laudable, more than one lower-priced, no-frills bass didn't last too long.

In the early 1980s, Fender (then owned by CBS) was on a downhill slide. Quality problems and the marketing of uninspiring products were contributing factors, and while the introduction of a new, lower-priced "Bullet" series of guitars and basses in 1982 seemed like a good idea at the time, the American-made lineup was discontinued the following year, and production of the series was shifted overseas.

The Bullet Bass was proffered in a thirty-four-inch-long scale (B-34) with a standard full-size body, and a thirty-inch short scale (B-30) with a slightly-downsized body. Both models' bodies had a P-Bass silhouette with parallel "waists" and were made of alder.

This B-34 has the series' Telecaster/original Precision Bass-style headstock on a maple neck with twenty frets. The split-oval pickups resemble Mustang Bass pickups—and that model had been discontinued the year before the Bullet series was introduced. There's a standard P-Bass-style bridge/tailpiece, and Stratocaster-ish volume and tone knobs, and that's about it.

Fender changed ownership for the third time in its history in 1985, and by the end of that decade the company had re-established itself as a formidable factor in the fretted instrument marketplace.

Accordingly, Fender had begun to introduce new stringed instruments, and somewhat unique among the new models was the ultimately-short-lived JP-90 bass. It had some new cosmetic features,

This 1990 Fender catalog image shows the less-rounded body edges of the JP-90, the "pointier" cutaway horns, and the black "pork chop" pickup/pickguard assembly.

Fender JP-90, 1990. *Vintage Guitar Magazine* archive

but also had a "safe" or "standard" electronics configuration for the bass market, and was designed and marketed as a no-frills-but-dependable American-made instrument at an attractive price point.

The JP-90 was one of the earliest collaborations between Fender's US factory in Corona, California, and its then-new *maquilladora* factory located in Ensenada, Baja California, Mexico, on the Pacific coast about seventy-five miles south of Tijuana. Bodies and necks were crafted in Ensenada, then shipped to Corona for assembly, thus validating the JP-90's "Made in the U.S.A." designation.

The JP-90's moniker is self-explanatory to those familiar with guitar jargon: The "JP" intimates at the connection to the Jazz Bass and Precision Bass, and the number references the decade in which it was introduced. Even though the original Jazz Bass was introduced almost a decade after the original Precision Bass, the "J" appeared first in this new model's name, possibly because the JP-90 owed more to the Jazz Bass in its appearance.

From the top down, the JP-90's aesthetics and construction included a slightly smaller traditional Fender headstock, topping a slim maple neck (i.e., a Jazz Bass feel) with a rosewood fretboard, which had twenty frets.

The poplar body had a Jazz Bass-inspired shape, with offset waists, but there were two subtle, modernistic incongruities on the JP-90, as Fender sought to add a bit of a contemporary flair to one of its traditional body silhouettes. The JP-90's cutaway horns were a bit more pointed than those found on Jazz Basses and Precision Basses, and the beveling on its edges wasn't quite as rounded as found on earlier models (and the JP-90 still had a forearm bevel on the front and a "belly cut" bevel on the back). The less-rounded beveling wasn't uncomfortable and did indeed give the instrument a slightly starker look.

Colors for the JP-90's body included Arctic White, Black, and Torino Red.

The JP-90's no-frills concept included its electronics, which consisted of two pickups in the popular "P/J" configuration.

Controls included simple volume and tone controls and a three-way mini-toggle switch for pickup selection. The entire electronics array was set up in a black plastic pickguard which dropped into a routed-out cavity on the front surface of the body.

The JP-90 debuted in the year that is found in its model designation, and the black instrument seen herein is a first-year example. Its introduction was cause for excitement among the Fender sales force as well as authorized dealers, since it was an American-made Fender bass that was being marketed at what was thought to be a viable $499 suggested retail price point.

And not much happened. For better or worse, the JP-90's pickguard silhouette quickly garnered a "pork chop" nickname, for obvious reasons.

Sales of the JP-90 were uninspiring, in spite of its pricing, and it was discontinued by 1994. Apparently, the majority of Fender's bass customers were (and are) traditionalists, favoring Precision Basses and Jazz Basses, including numerous variants (many of which are signature/endorsement instruments) of those two classic Fender bass models.

Ironically, the Bullet Bass and the JP-90 have become, in the used instrument marketplace, what their intent was as new instruments—they're uncomplicated, comfortable, and easy-to-play American-made Fender basses, available at a decent price.

𝄢

By the end of the 1980s, Ricky Phillips's career was successful enough that he could consider ordering a custom-made Fender instrument, with the cosmetic and construction features he wanted, as his primary concert utility bass.

And more than two decades later, the bass created for Phillips by the Fender Custom Shop was still serving him well.

Working closely with then-Custom Shop luthier Larry Brooks, Phillips sought to design an instrument that combined his love of late 1960s Telecaster Basses and other classic instruments with then-cutting-edge sonic innovations, such as a fifth string (low B) and active electronics.

"All of the five-strings that were made back then were basically for jazz guys and looked like a piece of furniture," he recalled. "Different woods, grains, multiple layers. There was not a rock and roll five-string bass out there, because most rock and roll guys didn't play five-strings. I tried to design something that I would be proud to play onstage as a rocker."

In addition to the Tele Bass influence, Phillips interpolated a single f-hole into his design, having garnered such creative inspiration from a Telecaster Thinline guitar that Bad English vocalist John Waite had owned when Waite and Phillips were also together in the Babys (more about the f-hole momentarily). He also requested a matching headstock.

He also specified checkerboard binding, recalling his love of that look on Rickenbacker basses he'd owned. Phillips says that the Custom

Shop ultimately informed him that his bass was the first Custom Shop instrument on which checkerboard binding had been installed.

"Initially, I wanted the checkerboard binding to go all the way around the headstock," he recalled, "but I decided that it would look kind of cheesy, so we just did the neck and the top edge of the body."

The nut is made of bone, per Phillips's request (although he and Brooks also considered various metal and brass nuts), and the bassist tried out more than one bone variant before Brooks carved the appropriate piece.

"I actually like the sound you get with brass nuts and bridge saddles," Phillips said. "It's kind of twangy and cool, but my experience was that I didn't get some of the 'warmth' for the sound I need, so we went with a bone (nut)."

The bass has neck-through construction (not usually associated with Fender instruments) with alder "body wings" on either side. The instrument also sports an ebony fretboard with no surface markers. Phillips allowed Brooks to choose the type of fret wire that worked best with the ebony fretboard.

The single f-hole, bound with plain white binding, runs nearly the full depth of the (solid) body, although that wasn't the original intent, according to the owner.

"I kind of flipped out when I first saw it," Phillips recalled with a laugh. "At the first meeting where I checked the progress on the bass, I saw that (Brooks) had cut a whole chamber out, and I'd just wanted something cosmetic on the top; just for the visual aesthetics. I really got upset, but as it turned out, it was an 'accidental plus' for the sound of the bass."

As for the tuners and bridge, Phillips didn't specify any particular hardware, so what he presumes are stock Fender parts are on the bass, and such hardware has been durable.

Phillips praised Fender's cooperation in acceding to his request for EMG active pickups instead of the active pickups Fender marketed.

"The 'passives'—particularly the ones from the '50s and '60s—are still the instruments that I think sound the best," he detailed, "but when you're playing with an 'arena-type' band, an active bass is able to 'compete' a little bit more; its sound can get through. I had been playing Spectors, and loved the EMG pickups; that's true to this day. Fender couldn't have been cooler in working with me to put Jazz-style EMGs in this bass. All they wanted to do was to get it right and make me happy, and I really respected them for doing that."

Phillips onstage with his trusty Fender Custom Shop five-string bass. *Willie G. Moseley*

There are twice as many control knobs as found on the original 1950s P-Basses and late-1960s Telecaster Basses that inspired this instrument, and Phillips explained the layout.

"The first one is a volume knob," he said. "Next is a pickup pan knob that's notched in the center—when you're singing and playing and making changes, reaching down there becomes sort of second-nature. If you need to change tones, even if it's ever-so-slightly, it's really nice to be able to 'feel' it; you don't have to look. It becomes a natural thing, and it really helps out. The last two knobs are a tone control for the front pickup, and a tone control for the back pickup."

The bassist chose black for the finish and a white mother-of-toilet-seat pickguard, possibly as a subliminal reference to monochrome television, as the vibe that he was trying to create ties in with vintage TV image recollections.

"I can become a kid again," he chuckled, "a twelve-year-old watching the Beatles on Ed Sullivan, or the Doors, or whoever happened to be on my parents' black-and-white TV."

Phillips described the Bad English gig where he first used the new bass as, "…phenomenal. Everyone was really pleased with how it sounded, and it also became my main recording bass from then on. I used it a lot with Coverdale/Page, and it was the bass used on that band's first single, 'Pride and Joy.'"

In the years that Phillips used the bass, it's proven to be an extremely durable instrument, and he's never sent it to Fender for refurbishing or repair, although the pickups have been refurbished by EMG.

"As much as I've beat the crap out of it, you'd think it'd be seriously worn," Phillips reflected, "but there's no place on the finish that has broken through. I'm absolutely amazed at how solid that thing is; it's built like a truck."

Fender Custom Shop bass, early 1990s, owned by Ricky Phillips. *Bill Ingalls Jr.*

FRITZ BROTHERS

Luthier/guitarist Roger Fritz first came to public acclaim in the late 1980s, when he was based in the Mobile, Alabama area, and crafted a guitar line that was co-designed by legendary guitarist Roy Buchanan (1939–1988). The series bore the guitarist's name on the headstock as its brand, and following Buchanan's death about a year after the joint venture commenced, the brand name of such guitars was changed to Fritz Brothers.

Notable guitarists who played instruments that Fritz built in that era included George Harrison, members of the Bangles, and Gary Moore, who proclaimed that his Fritz Brothers guitar had " . . . a Cadillac sort of vibe."

After closing down his own shop on Mobile Bay, Roger ultimately worked in at Gibson in Nashville for a brief time, and backed up singer Shelby Lynne on guitar in concert and on recording sessions. His love of luthiery proved to be an irresistible muse, however, and his brand ultimately re-appeared in the marketplace when he relocated to the other side of the continent and began making electric and acoustic instruments in the bucolic community of Mendocino, California.

While there, Fritz began creating his first "production" (such as it is) bass, a retro-looking model that was obviously inspired by the first Kay electric basses of the 1950s (see the Kay chapter).

The F.B. Bass had its share of (expected) modern updates, such as improved electronics, a larger dovetail at the neck joint, and a two-way adjustable truss rod in its neck, but Roger noted that he was still trying to get his instrument " . . . as close to the original as possible."

Fritz Brothers F.B. Bass, prototype. *Loren Hammer*

As for why he chose the old Kay design to emulate, Roger noted that he had used one in recording sessions, and recalled that, " . . . I just kind of got 'the bug' about it. There were no builders trying to re-create that sound, which is very unique, and there aren't many of those basses left that are in good shape. I decided to make a knock-off in a way that would add some modern features it didn't have but needed, without affecting the tone."

After two years of development, Fritz completed his first prototype, seen here. The instrument's sides and unique arched back are made from solid maple, and the (flat) top is made from laminated figured birch. The top and back edges have triple binding, and Fritz states that the instrument is put together in a manner that resists feedback. Two grades of maple, plain and curly, are offered.

The top has interior struts on its underside that are made from 1x3-inch wood, but the lateral bracing isn't exactly a tone-oriented center-block concept à la the Gibson ES-335 guitar or EB-2 bass. Instead, its main function is to support the pickup and the bridge mounts.

The body is finished in "Vintage Sunburst."

The neck is also maple and has twenty frets on a rosewood fretboard. It's got a twelve-inch fretboard radius, and is a slim 1½-inch wide at the nut, which is made of bone. One improvement that is perhaps not immediately discernable is the thickness of the taper on t he head-stock, which strengthens that area.

Scale on the F.B. Bass is thirty-one inches, the same as found on the Kay original.

The custom "Vibe-O-Sonic" pickup, with just its "blade" portion poking out from inside the body, emulates the original large Kay item, according to Fritz, who says that the pickup is " . . . a big, honkin' magnet. The pickup is made just like the original, and that's one of the key things that makes this bass sound the way it does."

Other electronics include a volume and tone control, and a two-way "deep cut" switch. The latter item contains a .1 and a .01 capacitor stacked on top of each other for two instant tone selections. Fritz is a fan of the retro-tortoiseshell look (the guitar he made for George Harrison had a tortoiseshell pickguard, at Harrison's request), so the pickup surround and the control plate on this neo-retro instrument are in that vintage-style look.

The compensated rosewood bridge is height-adjustable, and the trapeze tailpiece conforms to the look of its 1950s predecessor. The tuners, however, are modern-looking Hipshot Ultralites, which help to give the F.B. Bass a balanced feel that weighs in at around seven pounds.

Roger Fritz. *Loren Hammer*

Roger's new venture received a big boost in June of 2005, when the Rolling Stones acquired two of his new guitars and an F.B. Bass.

Ultimately, Fritz returned to the Mobile Bay area, where he continued his work. He signed on with the Kay company as a consultant regarding imported reissues of classic designs bearing the Kay name. He also makes special versions of such instruments in his own facility. Differences in Fritz's handbuilt Kay version of the F.B. Bass (compared to the original Fritz Bros. variant) usually include a laminated maple top instead of laminated birch and a keystone-shaped headstock.

"This is the Kay custom shop, right here," he said from his shop, located in a rural area in Baldwin County, Alabama. "I can still make a Fritz Bros. F.B. Bass if somebody wants one, but most people prefer the Kay version."

Roger Fritz epitomizes the dedicated, modern-day luthier who painstakingly handcrafts instruments until he gets them done right. That he chose to create an updated version of a unique 1950s bass with a unique sound is a bonus for most vintage guitar and bass enthusiasts.

A quick perusal of the G & L L-1000, the initial single-pickup bass that was produced by Leo Fender's final company, tells an observer that it's more versatile than a standard Fender Precision ever was. This model underlines the legend that Mr. Fender was never satisfied and continued his quest for innovative-and-practical designs until his death in 1991.

Introduced in 1980, L-1000s had a "traditional" silhouette. Their three-bolt neck attachment/truss road system differed from the somewhat-similar but unpopular Fender company three-bolt system, but both styles still had a "bullet" poking out at the headstock end for adjusting the truss rod. The neck on the L-1000 was maple, of course, and body woods were originally ash or mahogany. G & L's premier price list noted that the entire line was available with maple or ebony fretboards, but rosewood was added soon afterwards.

As for a comparison of their respective capabilities, the basic Fender P-Bass had (and has) one pickup with non-adjustable polepieces, one volume control, and one tone control—simple as that. The new G & L bass featured a potent Leo Fender-designed "Magnetic Field Design" (MFD) pickup with eight adjustable pole-pieces and offered more sonic options, yet its controls were laid out logically—the three knobs controlled volume, treble, and bass, and the three-way mini-toggle switch allowed a user to choose between a humbucking pickup setting, single-coil, or single-coil with bass boost—and the L-1000 was a passive instrument.

The bridge on a P-Bass was fairly generic, but the L-1000's "Locktight" bridge was a massive item that helped to increase sustain, and it's still in use on G & L basses more than thirty-five years after the L-1000 debuted.

This mahogany-bodied L-1000 from 1981, has an unusual *déjà vu* vibe going for it. Its Sunburst finish was the only other color besides Natural cited on the company's initial price list, and it has a maple fretboard with black dots, as well as chrome hardware (which was the introductory configuration). Serial numbers were embossed on the bridge until 1983, when a transition to embossing serial numbers on the neck plate began. This one is #B003861.

The bass also gives away the fact that it's an early example due to the very-short-lived slotted polepieces on the pickup (which were replaced by Allen-wrench-adjustable polepieces), as well as the walnut truss rod stripe on the back of the neck (which was eliminated after a couple of years).

Nevertheless, the main thing this mahogany-bodied L-1000 has going for it doesn't have anything to do with production rarity and/or construction features (it's a standard configuration in a standard finish). Instead, it happens to be exemplary of the mystique surrounding "N.O.S." ("New Old Stock") instruments.

"N.O.S." refers to instruments that, for various and sundry (or sometimes unknown) reasons, were never sold when they were originally received from a manufacturer or distributor. Instead, such an item

G & L L-1000, 1981. *Bill Ingalls Jr.*

G & L L-1000, 1981, butt-end view of laminated body grain.
Willie G. Moseley

supposedly stayed on a retailer's premises (usually in storage) for a number of years before finally being exposed for the consideration of stringed instrument players.

The story on #B003861 is that the retailer in question couldn't get a Fender franchise due to another store in the same town being a longtime Fender dealer. Figuring his store could try out Leo Fender's new line as an alternative, the guitar consultant ordered several G & L instruments soon after Leo Fender's new company acquired a rep for that area of the country.

The mahogany bass was placed on layaway by a customer in 1981, but the G & L line proved ultimately unsuccessful for the retailer (which, like many independent music stores, had a core of high school marching bands as its primary clientele). The line was dropped by the retailer, and the L-1000 was apparently forgotten by both customer and store personnel. It stayed stored away in a dark and out-of-the-way portion of the store for sixteen years, and was finally discovered and brought back out for retail sometime in 1997. A week after it was hung back out on a display rack, a guitar enthusiast pounced on it, for obvious reasons.

Corroborating this bass's N.O.S. status is the warranty card, which has never been filled out, as well as other original items found inside the case pocket.

Another fascinating facet is the fact that the instrument appears to be in almost mint condition. Pivot its body in the light, and maybe—just maybe— an observer might be able to see some very, very light skritches on the surface due to shop wear, but those could probably be buffed out.

Like other facets of guitar collecting, encounters with "New Old Stock" instruments are usually unexpected and usually intriguing, causing a guitar

G & L L-1000, 1981, factory mis-matched hardware. *Bill Ingalls Jr.*

G & L L-1000 body, 1983.
Willie G. Moseley

G & L L-2000, 1981.
Willie G. Moseley

buff to wonder why it stayed out of public view for so long. And anytime an N.O.S. instrument is this clean, that's an additional and unexpected bonus that will only increase its desirability.

The ash-bodied 1981 L-1000 on page 79 has some unique cosmetic features. It, too, has an MFD pickup with eight slotted polepieces, which validates that it's also an early example.

As noted earlier, the earliest G & L basses had chrome bridges and control plates, but this bridge has a smooth black finish, while the control plate is still chrome. The factory mis-matched hardware demonstrates that in its earliest days, G & L was pretty much unconcerned about using whatever parts were available.

Then there's the three-piece ash body. While figured wood patterns on ash usually aren't as interesting as maple and other tone woods, this bass was assembled in a manner that displays the grain nearly equidistant and parallel all the way across the entire front, giving an almost multi-laminated look. No wonder it has a natural finish—it would have been a shame to hide such an interesting pattern under a solid color.

And here's a two-pickup L-2000 from that same year, and it, too, has a mismatched bridge and control plate. The L-2000 was initially available in active and passive models—this one's active, and its controls are a bit more complicated. The passive version of the L-2000 was discontinued fairly quickly, but as of this writing, the active L-2000 has been in production ever since it was introduced, thus it is G & L's longest-running bass.

The body of yet another mahogany body/maple neck L-1000 (this one dates from 1983), shows the Allen wrench-type polepieces on the pickup, as well as the black crinkled/textured bridge and control plate that became standard after the smooth black hardware was dropped. However, the inability to see embossed serial numbers very well on the black textured bridge resulted in the serial number being transferred to the neck bolt plate on the back of the body. The neck plate was also crinkled, but the serial number was easier to see.

And by the time this example was made, G & L had also stopped installing truss rods using the method that required the walnut insert strip on the back; i.e. the back of the neck on this bass is solid maple. The L-1000 was discontinued in the early 1990s, soon after Leo Fender's death.

In his time with Fender (and during a short affiliation with Music Man before he co-founded G & L), Leo placed a low priority on developing budget-oriented guitars and basses (other than some student models). He was more concerned with creating serious—if not particularly fancy—products for professional musicians.

G & L's first effort at producing budget guitars came about in the summer of 1982, with the introduction of the SC and HG models. It wasn't until later that year that the first "economy" basses by a true Leo Fender company were marketed, and they happened to be full-scale.

Seeking to offer some of Leo's more recent innovations at a more accessible price, SB-1 and SB-2 basses were no-frills, but while some might surmise that the "S" in the model number stood for "student," these were professional-grade instruments. Their necks were maple, and the headstock silhouette was slightly narrower than that of the L-1000/L-2000. Their maple bodies had a traditional double-cutaway silhouette, and while SB bodies had the same dimensions as G & L's frontline basses, they were more slab-like (no forearm bevel on the front or "belly cut" in the back). Nevertheless, the rounded sides of the body meant that the instruments were relatively comfortable, and they balanced nicely when strapped on.

The beefy bridge was the same as on other G&L basses, and the bridges and control plates on original SBs had the black crinkled/textured finish.

Electronics consisted of one or two of Leo's smaller variants of his Magnetic Field Design pickups. There was no difference in the location of the single pickup on the SB-1 and the pickup closer to the neck on the SB-2.

The SB-1 has a simple volume/tone control layout, while the SB-2 has a Telecaster-like configuration with a three-way toggle switch. In his review of a G & L SC-2 guitar in the February 1997 issue of *Vintage Guitar*, "Gigmeister" columnist Riley Wilson likened the cheap-looking knobs to those " . . . purchased at Radio Shack at 7:30 on a Saturday night, just before the gig," and a better analogy probably doesn't exist.

Early G & L instruments were all over the spectrum in regard to colors, and a list of standard finishes didn't develop until the mid 1980s. While SCs and SBs were reportedly available in (variations of) red, white, and blue, the SB-2 seen here doesn't appear to be a white instrument that has become discolored over the years – its off-white/ivory/bone color is original (i.e., it looks the same under the control plate).

SB basses of this style were around for less than two years. The models later acquired a slightly different body silhouette, pickguards, body beveling, different pickup styles and configurations, and a variety of finishes, thus becoming more traditional-looking. The SB-2 also got a new control system.

However, the original plain, full-scale SB basses were historically intriguing. They were not only good instruments, they represented Leo Fender's first legitimate attempt at creating and marketing a full-scale economy bass marketed by a company in which he had a fiscal interest.

And the SB series basses and their companion SC series guitars represent as good of an opportunity as any to cite the decades-long, uh, "concept"/"mojo" of matching instruments.

During the guitar (and self-contained-band) boom of the 1960s, one method of getting your aggregation noticed was to get equipped with matching instruments (and usually, matching outfits as well). Matching amplifiers were also a plus in some cases.

Many instrumental surf bands followed such a notion. Boulder, Colorado's Astronauts, for example, were notable not only for playing surf music in a land-locked state, but for their use of white Fender instruments and matching suits.

Likewise, the Ventures, who preceded surf music, were seen onstage or in publicity photos with three matching electric stringed instruments, including sunburst Fenders and white Mosrites.

Even bands that were "regional" instead of "national" were noted for their sartorial displays in performance. Some aging Baby Boomers may recall a "circuit band" from Atlanta, the Bushmen, who sported a red Gibson ES-335-type thinline guitar, a red Gibson EB-2D bass, red sparkle Kustom tuck-and-roll amplifiers, a red sparkle drum kit, and matching outfits.

Accordingly, matching guitars and basses seem to have always had a bit of an extra "cool" factor going for them, but the early-1980s G & L SB-1 basses and SC guitars seen here have several other interesting facets besides the similarities in their looks.

Like the original SB basses, SC guitars had maple bodies and maple necks. The six-string instruments had full scales of 25½ inches (with twenty-two frets).

The three-pickup SC-3 shown here and its companion SB-1 were blue, of course, and have yellowed slightly, giving them a slight teal color. To some uninitiated observers, their (dis)coloration could possibly be considered as "original," as their present hue is still quite attractive, but an examination of the finish under these instruments' respective control plates avers that they originally had a more sky-blue color.

And this SC-3 has several additional unique aspects, in spite of being a stock-for-the-times instrument. Its body silhouette (also non-beveled but comfortable) is somewhat of a cross between a traditional single-cutaway Fender Telecaster shape and a double-cutaway body such as a Fender Stratocaster. Moreover, it may appear to be slightly downsized to some observers—or maybe the headstock appears to be too big—but it's still a very balanced instrument.

Electronics include three pickups laid out in a traditional Stratocaster configuration, and they're controlled by a five-way toggle switch and master volume and tone knobs. This example has hyper-rare white pickup covers (most were black). Accounts vary as to how many early "Leo era" G & L instruments had white pickups, but author Paul Bechtoldt has averred that he has a hand-written note from G & L co-founder and early Fender salesman Dale Hyatt (1925–2013) that only a few dozen guitars or basses had such covers.

Another curiosity is the guitar's serial number. According to Bechtoldt's 1994 book, *G & L: Leo's Legacy*, the first example of the SC series was completed on August 31, 1982, but a serial number list in the same book indicates the serial number embossed on the vibrato bridge plate is a 1981 number. Thus, it seems that the early G & L company's use

G & L SC-3, 1983. *Bill Ingalls Jr.*

G & L SB-1, 1983. *Bill Ingalls Jr.*

G & L SB-1, 1984. *Willie G. Moseley*

G & L SC-2, 1984. *Willie G. Moseley*

of embossed serial number bridges wasn't sequential, and was somewhat haphazard, as was also the case for the early Fender company in the 1950s.

One "addition" to this SC-3 is the signature of longtime Leo Fender associate and G & L co-founder George Fullerton on its headstock. Fullerton signed this instrument at a mid-1990s southern California guitar show.

Also shown are an SC-2 and an SB-1 in black, a finish that G & L added later. The configuration of the SC-2 evolved into the ASAT, which had a Telecaster-shaped body. This one dates from 1984. The SC-3, SB-1, and SB-2 would continue in the line longer, undergoing numerous changes to their cosmetics and electronics.

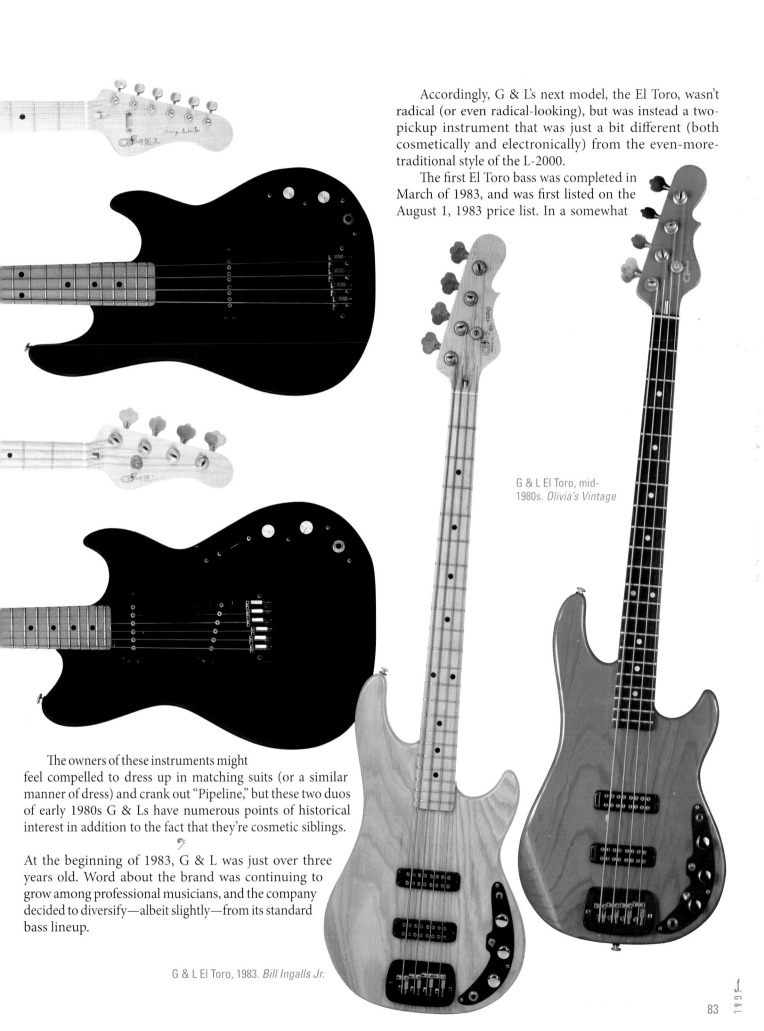

Accordingly, G & L's next model, the El Toro, wasn't radical (or even radical-looking), but was instead a two-pickup instrument that was just a bit different (both cosmetically and electronically) from the even-more-traditional style of the L-2000.

The first El Toro bass was completed in March of 1983, and was first listed on the August 1, 1983 price list. In a somewhat

G & L El Toro, mid-1980s. *Olivia's Vintage*

The owners of these instruments might feel compelled to dress up in matching suits (or a similar manner of dress) and crank out "Pipeline," but these two duos of early 1980s G & Ls have numerous points of historical interest in addition to the fact that they're cosmetic siblings.

𝄢

At the beginning of 1983, G & L was just over three years old. Word about the brand was continuing to grow among professional musicians, and the company decided to diversify—albeit slightly—from its standard bass lineup.

G & L El Toro, 1983. *Bill Ingalls Jr.*

similar scenario to the original marketing idea for the L-2000 (which, as noted earlier, had been offered in active and passive versions when it was introduced in 1980), the El Toro was touted as a passive instrument with an optional pre-amp for $100 more.

However, like the passive version of the L-2000 (which quickly flopped), the passive El Toro ultimately also didn't pass its test in the marketplace, and was discontinued within six months, in favor of a standard active version. The natural-finished example seen is indeed one of the short-lived passive versions of the El Toro, while the red bass is an active model (note the extra mini-toggle switch) from later in the decade.

In 1983 the company began modifying its headstock silhouette, with a "barb" on the lower edge, which these instruments have.

Bodies were made of mahogany, ash, or maple. The very earliest examples of El Toros had a "slab"-type body, à la the original SB series (no belly cut or forearm bevel), but these have the same type of contouring as the frontline L-1000 and L-2000.

Like the natural-finished L-1000 seen earlier, the ash body of the passive El Toro has some striking grain patterns.

At first glance, the El Toro body looks cosmetically similar to L-1000s and L-2000s, but on some examples, there were some slight yet noteworthy aberrations—in a side-by-side comparison to an L-1000, the El Toro's body was slightly smaller, and its forearm bevel on the front and belly cut in the back are more pronounced than the similar contouring found on the L-1000.

The control plate, bridge, and neck mounting plate are in the black crinkled finish.

Then there were the electronics. The El Toro was the first of only two bass models to have the smaller bass humbucking MFD pickups. Those items would later be found on the even rarer Interceptor Bass. The baby 'buckers had four adjustable polepieces for each string, whereas the pickups on the L-1000 and L-2000 had two adjustable polepieces per string. And like other M.F.D. pickups, these lil' humbuckers have a potent sound.

The controls on the passive El Toro include a volume control, treble control, and bass control. In front of the volume control is a black-capped three-way pickup mini-toggle switch, and there's a red two-position splitter-type mini-toggle as well. In one setting of the two-way's position, the pickup switch is operable, but in the other position, the pickup toggle switch is bypassed, and both pickups are boosted for a flat-out, balls-to-the-wall sound—an unusual but perhaps appropriate configuration for a passive instrument.

The active El Toro's system was like the L-2000, with the extra switch offering different electronic pickup settings.

Finish-wise, El Toros, like many other early G & Ls, were all over the map. Another natural-finish example has been seen that looks exactly like this one, except for an original black headstock, which was sometimes an in-house designation that the instrument was to have been displayed at a National Association of Music Merchandisers (NAMM) trade show.

As happened to numerous other G & L models, the El Toro was dropped from the company's June 1991 price list, but it appears that the model actually wasn't built after 1988, when G & L began marketing—and concentrating on—models that had a reproduction of Leo Fender's signature on the upper bout.

Overall, fewer than 1,200 G & L El Toros (active and passive) were estimated to have been made in a five-year period. They're interesting and rarer alternatives to L-1000s and L-2000s, as well as other brands and models of the same era.

𝄢

Five-string basses with a low 'B' string have now been a viable option in contemporary music for several decades. They actually began to be created in the mid-1970s, with builders such as Alembic among those cited as the early innovators.

G & L climbed onto the five-string bandwagon in the late 1980s. Almost two decades after his Bass V flopped, Leo Fender was reportedly prodded by G & L co-founder Dale Hyatt to develop a five-string "low B" instrument. Hyatt, who had been a longtime and successful sales representative for the Fender Sales company during Fender's "pre-CBS" era, constantly paid close attention to the musical instrument marketplace, and to which items had potential for G & L.

As validated by this 1990 example, some earlier G & L L-5000s had what might have been considered a contradictory overall silhouette, as they had a "4+1"

G & L L-5000, 1990. *Vintage Guitar Magazine* archive

modernistic, sickle-shaped headstock (the design was also found on the Interceptor guitar and bass, as well as some early Comanche guitars), mated to a traditional-looking, double-cutaway body. Later, the five-string headstock would affect the more-often-seen traditional G & L style with the sculptured point on the underside (still as a 4+1).

The neck was made from hard rock maple and offered a 7½-inch radius (which was also pretty much the standard on four-string G & L basses) on a maple or rosewood fingerboard, which had twenty-one frets. The width of the nut on this example is 1¾ inches, but some other neck widths may be encountered on other L-5000s.

Bodies were made of maple, ash, or poplar, and were contoured for comfort.

The solitary pickup was a noticeably offset MFD unit with adjustable polepieces. History buffs would probably take note of the fact that the L-5000's split pickup is offset in an opposite configuration under the five strings (three left, two right) from the earlier Fender Bass V (two left, three right).

The pickguard-mounted controls consisted of volume and tone knobs, with the jack also located on the top.

The bridge was a five-string variant of G & L's massive and highly-regarded unit, with individual and intonatable string saddles. The bridge on this instrument has the black "crinkled" finish.

Other than having a low 'B' string with corresponding parts, the L-5000 bass was a simple and uncomplicated instrument. It didn't have as many innovations as many of the other instruments that had been previously associated with Leo Fender, and the fact that it wasn't "the first of its kind" may have contributed to apparent disinterest among musicians.

However, another factor may have been a lack of active electronics. As a passive, single-pickup bass, the L-5000 may have come across to some potential players as simply a Precision Bass-like instrument with an extra string. Therefore, in the eyes of many bassists who were upgrading from a four-string to a five-string, it might not have had enough pickups and/or enough features (of which onboard active electronics would have been an important selling point).

After BBE purchased G & L in December of 1991 (following Leo's death in March of the same year), interest in the L-5000 apparently waned, although some latter-day examples received "premium finishes" (a post-Leo marketing innovation).

The L-5000, the first 'low B' five-string bass associated with Leo Fender, was discontinued by mid-1993. The quantity of L-5000s created remains unknown, although "500" is a figure that has been bounced around.

The L-5000 is a relatively rare bird, is a "Leo era" G & L instrument, and is the first instrument of its kind to be historically-associated with Leo Fender . . . even if Mr. Fender's involvement with the creation of this model wasn't as "cutting edge" as some of his earlier innovations.

At the very least, this time Leo's company went in the right sonic direction regarding the design and manufacturing of five-string basses.

As it turned out, the first new G & L bass models introduced by the BBE ownership were based on a combination of marketing pragmatism and a nod to the aesthetics of classic and successful models of basses associated with Leo Fender.

Introduced in 1993, the Climax Bass and the LB-100 were quite different from each other, just as their respective forebears were. The active Climax Bass, with its solitary MFD pickup located near the bridge, bore a distinct resemblance to the Music Man Sting Ray, while the LB-100 bass was, to most observers, a near-clone of the Fender Precision Bass. Let's examine the similarities of the two models before diverging:

Both basses had a 7½-inch neck radius on a maple or rosewood fretboard. One intriguing similarity involves the headstock silhouette—while it had the by-then-standard G & L "barb" opposite the posts for the D and G strings, the "hook" near the company logo was new (and obviously, more Fender-like); the same portion of the headstock on earlier G & L bass models was rounded.

While the basses seen here have different fretboard woods, they do have pearl dot inlay (it's black pearl on the LB-100 and the Climax in the see-through green finish). The fretboards each have twenty-one frets, and each body joins the neck at the sixteenth fret on the bass side, and in the middle of the twentieth fret on the treble side.

One marketing difference between the two instruments concerns the moniker of the LB-100, which had originally been named the Legacy Bass. Following the discovery

G & L Climax, 1994.
Bill Ingalls Jr.

G & L Climax, Clear Forest Green,
1994. *Willie G. Moseley*

The Climax Bass came in "standard" and "premier" finishes. The example with the rosewood fretboard is in an attractive metalflake color called "Emerald Blue," a standard finish, and the "Clear Forest Green" finish on the other Climax Bass is a premier finish that shows off the grain on the body.

Standard and premier finishes were also found on the LB-100. This one is in a very cool "Bel Air Green" (standard) color, which would, of course, evoke comparisons to Fender custom colors.

Ultimately, both models were relatively short-lived for G & L. The Climax Bass was discontinued circa 1996, but was succeeded by a next-generation model known as the L-1500. The LB-100 hung around until 2000.

For most knowledgeable guitar enthusiasts, however, there probably wouldn't be much debate that G & L's Climax Bass and the LB-100 were each seeking to emulate Leo Fender's earlier successful models (with other companies) when they were introduced in a time of transition for what had been his last company. These two bass models may not have stayed around too long, but it seemed like their designs were offering an appropriate (if not-so-subliminal), historical tip-of-the-hat to the memory of a guitar manufacturing legend.

of an infringement on a patented name, the Legacy Bass quickly became the LB-100. The name change also occurred in 1993; accordingly, the G & L Legacy Bass is a rare bird.

From the top down, differences begin with the width of the neck at the nut: On the Climax Bass it's 1½ inches, and on the LB-100 it's 1¾ inches.

While the bodies—usually poplar, alder, or ash—are the same width at 12¾ inches, the more-modernistic Climax Bass has, as might be expected, less-rounded edges (à la the Fender JP-90), while the LB-100 body maintains a traditional profile (including its edges).

One highly unusual feature that was found on the back of the Climax Bass body was a rounded and recessed "scoop" around the neck bolt area that was approximately ¼-inch deep.

The pickup on the Climax Bass was an eight-pole MFD, and its 9-volt-powered active circuitry was controlled by two two-way mini-toggles. The three knobs controlled volume, treble, and bass.

The passive LB-100 has an offset, "split-coil vintage" pickup, according to company literature, and standard volume and tone controls.

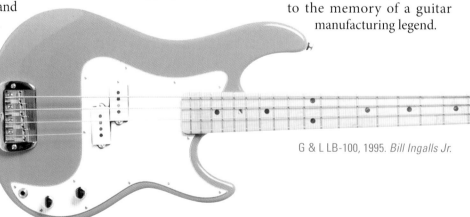

G & L LB-100, 1995. *Bill Ingalls Jr.*

This rear view of a Climax
Bass body shows its unique
"scooped-out" portion and
"sharper" body edges.
Willie G. Moseley

SEVEN

GIBSON

Many stringed instrument enthusiasts cite the 1948–1966 tenure of Gibson president Ted McCarty (1910–2001) as the "golden era" for that company, and the same time frame also saw the introduction and development of the electric bass as an innovation that would permanently alter the contemporary musical landscape.

When it was introduced in the early 1950s, the Gibson Electric Bass (a model number for this instrument wasn't specified) may have come off to some observers as a second example of the staid Kalamazoo, Michigan, manufacturer playing catch-up with the then-upstart Fender company. Gibson had responded to Fender's Telecaster solid body electric guitar with its Les Paul model, but even before the Gibson solid body was introduced, Fender had also marketed the Precision Bass. Noting the immediate and immense popularity of the "Fender Bass," Gibson had no choice but to respond to that innovation as well.

As was the case with the Les Paul guitar, the Kalamazoo company tried for a classy and more traditional look with its solid body bass, which hit the market in 1953. Borrowing from upright bass influences, the Gibson Electric Bass had a violin-shaped, solid mahogany body, finished in brown, that was eleven inches wide and had an arched top. The body also had a small, faux f-hole as well as front-and-back purfling that was painted on (not all Electric Basses had the pseudo-f-hole, however).

The headstock on the Electric Bass featured rear-projecting, banjo-type tuners made by Kluson. The one-piece mahogany neck had an unbound rosewood fretboard with twenty frets (joining the body at the sixteenth fret).

Other differences between the Fender Precision Bass and this instrument included neck attachment (The Electric Bass had a standard Gibson glued-in neck juncture; the P-Bass had a bolt-on neck), and scale length (thirty-four inches for the Precision, 30½ inches for the Electric Bass).

While the Electric Bass could easily be strapped on and played like a guitar, Gibson also offered a telescoping end pin that could be threaded onto the bottom of the body, in an attempt to offer a somewhat downsized look and feel of an upright bass.

The large pickup on the Electric Bass, placed next to the neck juncture, offered a huge, dark sound. Its polepieces were on the side of the top that faced the bridge, and its cover was made of brown Bakelite. Other appointments included a one-piece combination bridge and tailpiece that featured an angled portion for strings in an attempt to evoke primeval intonation and volume and tone controls.

In its time, a Gibson Electric Bass was seen in the hands of Olsie Robinson, who was the bassist for the Upsetters, Little Richard (Penniman)'s crackerjack backing band.

As it turned out, the Gibson Electric Bass wasn't exactly competitive with the Fender during the Eisenhower era. Fewer than 550 were shipped from 1953 to 1958, when the instrument was discontinued in favor of the semi-hollow EB-2. Both basses appeared in the 1958 catalog, in which the Electric Bass was now known as the EB-1.

The example shown here is from the collection of Doug Fieger (1952–2010), lead singer and guitarist for the Knack ("My Sharona," "Good Girls Don't," etc.).

A so-called "re-issue" of the EB-1 was made from 1970–72, but like many Gibson products of that era, there were major differences between the original and the so-called re-issue. The latter item had a different pickup configuration and standard tuners, among other updates.

Felix Pappalardi (1939–1983), bassist for Mountain, was probably the most famous player to utilize an Electric Bass (and he also had EB-1 "re-issues," according to Mountain bandmate Leslie West). Pappalardi had earlier produced Cream's classic *Disraeli Gears*, *Wheels of Fire*, and *Goodbye* albums, and when Cream reunited at the Royal Albert Hall in May of 2005, Jack Bruce utilized one of the violin-shaped basses formerly owned by Cream's late producer.

Gibson Electric Bass, 1950s, owned by Doug Fieger. *Heritage Auctions*

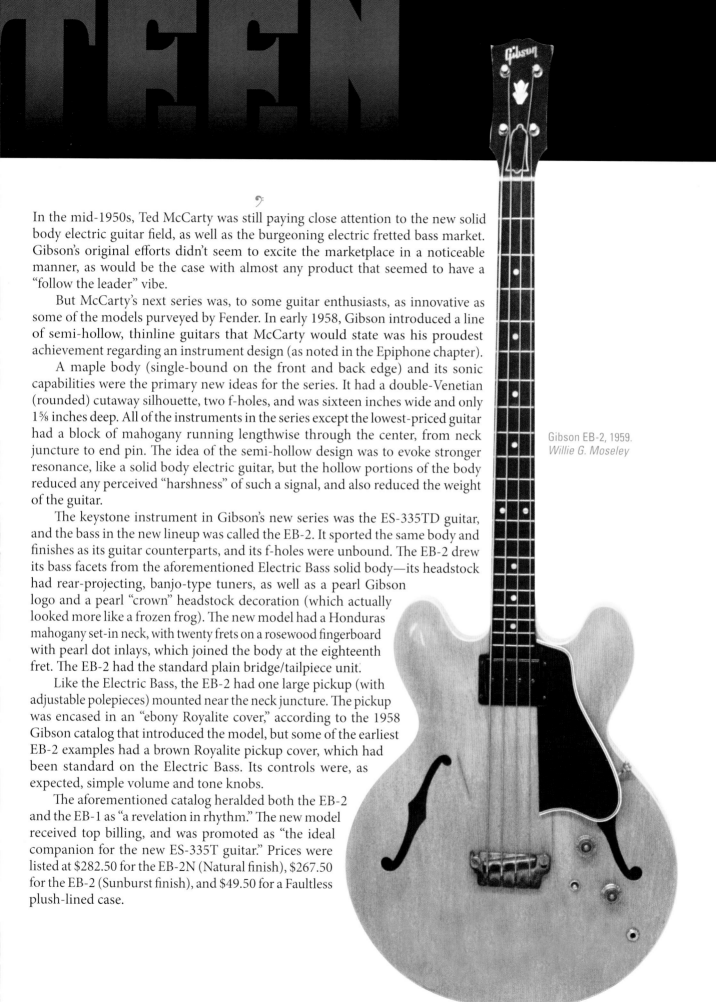

In the mid-1950s, Ted McCarty was still paying close attention to the new solid body electric guitar field, as well as the burgeoning electric fretted bass market. Gibson's original efforts didn't seem to excite the marketplace in a noticeable manner, as would be the case with almost any product that seemed to have a "follow the leader" vibe.

But McCarty's next series was, to some guitar enthusiasts, as innovative as some of the models purveyed by Fender. In early 1958, Gibson introduced a line of semi-hollow, thinline guitars that McCarty would state was his proudest achievement regarding an instrument design (as noted in the Epiphone chapter).

A maple body (single-bound on the front and back edge) and its sonic capabilities were the primary new ideas for the series. It had a double-Venetian (rounded) cutaway silhouette, two f-holes, and was sixteen inches wide and only 1⅝ inches deep. All of the instruments in the series except the lowest-priced guitar had a block of mahogany running lengthwise through the center, from neck juncture to end pin. The idea of the semi-hollow design was to evoke stronger resonance, like a solid body electric guitar, but the hollow portions of the body reduced any perceived "harshness" of such a signal, and also reduced the weight of the guitar.

The keystone instrument in Gibson's new series was the ES-335TD guitar, and the bass in the new lineup was called the EB-2. It sported the same body and finishes as its guitar counterparts, and its f-holes were unbound. The EB-2 drew its bass facets from the aforementioned Electric Bass solid body—its headstock had rear-projecting, banjo-type tuners, as well as a pearl Gibson logo and a pearl "crown" headstock decoration (which actually looked more like a frozen frog). The new model had a Honduras mahogany set-in neck, with twenty frets on a rosewood fingerboard with pearl dot inlays, which joined the body at the eighteenth fret. The EB-2 had the standard plain bridge/tailpiece unit.

Like the Electric Bass, the EB-2 had one large pickup (with adjustable polepieces) mounted near the neck juncture. The pickup was encased in an "ebony Royalite cover," according to the 1958 Gibson catalog that introduced the model, but some of the earliest EB-2 examples had a brown Royalite pickup cover, which had been standard on the Electric Bass. Its controls were, as expected, simple volume and tone knobs.

The aforementioned catalog heralded both the EB-2 and the EB-1 as "a revelation in rhythm." The new model received top billing, and was promoted as "the ideal companion for the new ES-335T guitar." Prices were listed at $282.50 for the EB-2N (Natural finish), $267.50 for the EB-2 (Sunburst finish), and $49.50 for a Faultless plush-lined case.

Gibson EB-2, 1959.
Willie G. Moseley

Changes were already in the offing for the EB-2 the very next year, as the model received a pushbutton tone switch.

"The EB-2 offers great facility and handling ease for all string bass effects," a Gibson catalog trumpeted. "Tremendous sustain and tremolo, fast plucking and slap bass. It even adds a baritone voice with its new Vari-tone switch, which operates easily and quickly to provide two entirely different tonal characteristics."

The natural-finish instrument shown herein does indeed date from 1959, making it a first-year example of that variant of the EB-2.

In spite of its innovative design, Gibson's semi-hollow bass still didn't set the woods on fire sales-wise, and following changes such as right-angle/standard Kluson tuners being introduced in late 1960, the model was discontinued in 1961.

However, the EB-2 was resurrected in 1964, and its ease of playability and light weight would make it popular among many combos as the fabled 1960s guitar boom exploded.

When reintroduced, the EB-2 sported a chrome pickup cover and was available in sunburst finish only; the natural finish was no longer advertised, but in late 1965, Cherry became a second standard finish for the model.

1966 saw the introduction of the two-pickup EB-2D, which had the original large pickup plus a smaller unit near the bridge, like the EB-3 solid body bass of the same era. Unlike the EB-3, the EB-2D's controls were similar to most two-pickup guitars (including thinline guitars in the same series as the EB-2D)—a volume and tone knob for each pickup, and a three-way pickup toggle switch. The baritone switch was also a standard feature on the EB-2D, as seen on this 1967 sunburst example.

Both semi-hollow bass models would become available in Walnut or Sparkling Burgundy finishes in the late 1960s, and like other Gibsons, would be fitted with three-piece mahogany necks. In the latter years of their existence, EB-2s and EB-2Ds would be fitted with a better-grade bridge/tailpiece that offered individualized intonation for each string.

The advent of the 1970s heralded the beginning of Gibson's legendary downward spiral regarding the quality of its instruments, as well as uninspiring new models that were introduced. The EB-2 and EB-2D were discontinued in 1972, and perhaps it's fortunate that those models escaped most of those times. Moreover, they are arguably the most innovative (successful) basses ever introduced by Gibson.

As noted in an earlier chapter, the pioneering company that mass-marketed a "bass guitar" was the Danelectro company of New Jersey, which introduced the innovation in the mid-1950s. Such instruments might have been hard to play exactly like a guitar, but they were intriguing items regarding their sonic capabilities, and other companies soon picked up on the idea.

Gibson's take on a six-string bass, the EB-6, was first listed in 1959, and began to be shipped in quantity in 1960 (when it was first introduced in a Gibson catalog). It was the oddest production model in the Kalamazoo manufacturer's thinline semi-solid series.

Factory ledgers indicate that earlier EB-6s were not registered; a May 13, 1960 entry notes serial numbers A33444 through A33447, which means that the example seen here, sporting serial number A33385, is probably an early example.

Gibson EB-2D, 1967.
Heritage Auctions

The EB-6 shared the same double-cutaway body as the ES-335, EB-2, and other associated instruments, and also shared the same one-piece mahogany neck and 30½-inch scale with the EB-2. The tuners on the headstock of the sibling EB-2 bass were still rear-projecting, banjo-type when the EB-6 was introduced, but the six-string bass guitar had Kluson Deluxe "keystone" tuners from its introduction. The EB-6 also had a pearl Gibson logo and a pearl "crown" headstock decoration.

Hardware on the EB-6 was nickel-plated. A standard guitar humbucking pickup was placed near the neck joint, which meant that string spacing on the EB-6 was the same as on a standard Gibson electric guitar. The one-piece bridge/tailpiece still had an angled portion as a nod to attempted automatic intonation, albeit for six strings.

Controls consisted of volume and tone knobs, plus a pushbutton "baritone switch."

Interestingly, the EB-6 wasn't even seen in the 1960 catalog. The page for "Electric Basses" shows the company's two four-string models, the aforementioned EB-2 and the solid body EB-0, both with rear-projecting tuners. A small box by the picture of the EB-2 describes the EB-6 as an "Electric Six-String Bass," and promotes the instrument as follows: "Like the EB-2, but with six strings, giving a full octave lower guitar tuning on a regular bass scale length. Neck joins the body at the eighteenth fret, providing easy access to all frets on all six strings."

It appears that the EB-6 was only marketed in a standard Gibson Sunburst finish, whereas the EB-2 had been available in Sunburst or Natural when introduced.

List price for the EB-6 in the 1960 catalog was $325.00, and a #538 Faultless plush-lined case ran $57.50.

One might wonder to what extent the lack of a catalog illustration of the EB-6 hurt its potential sales. According to company records, only thirty-four instruments were shipped in 1960, and thirty-three units were shipped in 1961. Those seventy-seven EB-6s are all thought to have been thinline-style instruments.

The EB-6 was changed to a solid body, SG guitar-shaped style in 1962.

Gibson's second solid body entry in the electric bass market looked a bit more modern than the stodgy Electric Bass, but it had the confusing model number of EB-0. The initial version of the new model was only produced from 1959 to early 1961.

Gibson EB-0, 1959. *Olivia's Vintage*

Gibson EB-0, 1960. *Bill Ingalls Jr.*

Unlike the aforementioned Epiphone Newport, the original EB-0 had an asymmetrical double-cutaway solid mahogany body, the silhouette of which was inspired by second-generation Les Paul Jr., Special, and TV models (also introduced in the late 1950s). While those guitar models had necks that allowed full clear-of-the-body access to all frets, the EB-0's one-piece mahogany neck joined the body at the seventeenth fret (out of twenty frets total). The neck was topped with a rosewood fingerboard.

Instruments had a Cherry finish, a black plastic-covered humbucking pickup located near neck joint, a single-ply black plastic pickguard, and the standard bridge/tailpiece unit.

The original version also had rear-projecting, banjo-style tuners, but in 1960, right-angle/standard tuners began to be used shortly before the EB-0's switch to a double pointed-cutaway body

Gibson EB-6, 1960. *Vintage Guitar Magazine* archive

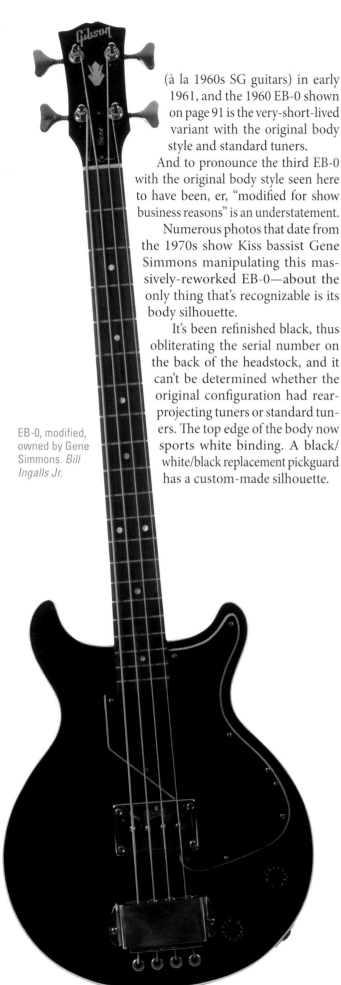

EB-0, modified, owned by Gene Simmons. *Bill Ingalls Jr.*

(à la 1960s SG guitars) in early 1961, and the 1960 EB-0 shown on page 91 is the very-short-lived variant with the original body style and standard tuners.

And to pronounce the third EB-0 with the original body style seen here to have been, er, "modified for show business reasons" is an understatement.

Numerous photos that date from the 1970s show Kiss bassist Gene Simmons manipulating this massively-reworked EB-0—about the only thing that's recognizable is its body silhouette.

It's been refinished black, thus obliterating the serial number on the back of the headstock, and it can't be determined whether the original configuration had rear-projecting tuners or standard tuners. The top edge of the body now sports white binding. A black/white/black replacement pickguard has a custom-made silhouette.

The bass has a circa-1970 replacement Gibson humbucking pickup with a chrome cover, which has been relocated closer to the bridge.

The bridge/tailpiece area has also been considerably modified. Underneath the handrest is a Leo Quan "Badass" bass bridge, and strings now load from the rear of the body, through holes that were drilled into the body; said holes have metal ferrules on each side.

And it's that handrest cover over the bridge that nails this instrument's association with Simmons. There's a noticeable, triangular-shaped patch of wear on the cover, and not only do photos of Simmons show him thonking this bass with his hand resting where the wear is on this item, there is at least one other photo of Simmons with this bass where his hand is not resting on the cover, and the wear thereon is clearly visible.

Curiously, this bass was apparently prepared for further modifications that never happened. There's a diagonal "slice" in the custom-made pickguard, and a couple of extra screws appear to have been installed. Removing the smaller section of the pickguard reveals that a portion of the body has been routed out underneath. There's room to install some active electronic circuitry and (most likely) a 9-volt battery, but the condition of the hollowed-out portion indicates that a conversion of this bass to active status didn't occur.

What's more, earlier photos of Simmons with this instrument don't show the slice in the pickguard.

A couple of fine-tuning points about this instrument need to be addressed about its history as well as its collectability. First, if it was indeed modified and later used by Simmons perhaps more for its visual attributes, such a notion would be understandable, since, to many observers, Kiss has always placed as much—if not more—emphasis on "what it looks like" compared to "what it sounds like." The black-and-white modifications to this bass offer an obvious visual contrast, even in black-and-white photos. However, considering its short scale and not-too-large body, this bass may have looked rather dinky in the hands of some tall dude wearing a bat suit.

Moreover, this EB-0 is, due to its extensive modifications, an obvious example of an instrument that would be more collectible (and more expensive) because of its celebrity association rather than its historical importance as an innovative instrument or classic sound/tone. And celebrity or not, any owner of any instrument is free to modify their instruments to the extent he/she wishes. Might not seem fair, but it goes with the territory (of guitar and bass collecting).

As noted earlier, Gibson switched body shapes for the EB-0 in early 1961, and along with its two-pickup sibling, the EB-3, would be the standard bearer for that brand's basses during the guitar boom of the 1960s. One of the more interesting models during that decade was the EB-0F, which had a built-in distortion device.

Gibson EB-0F, circa 1962. *Heritage Auctions*

Gibson EB-0F, circa 1964. *Vintage Guitar Magazine* archives

And Gibson actually began marketing the FZ-1 in 1962, which was also the first year the EB-0F was marketed.

The SG-shaped version of the EB-0 started out with a black plastic-covered humbucking pickup with centered polepieces, which was mounted near the neck joint. The pickup cover was changed to a metal variant later in 1962.

The regular pickguard for the EB-0 was wing-shaped, and had a five-layer black/white/black/white/black configuration, with a crescent-shaped wood fingerrest mounted on it. Controls were simple volume and tone knobs.

A handrest was usually found on the body. The bridge/tailpiece was the same piece of hardware that had been around since Gibson first introduced the Electric Bass in the early 1950s.

The EB-0F's fuzztone was installed under one section of a longer, two-piece pickguard. Still a black, five-layer style, the pickguard had a seam near the handrest. The upper portion still had a wood fingerrest, while the lower (and extended) portion, which terminated near the volume knob, could be detached for servicing the fuzz unit.

Controls for the fuzztone included "Attack" and "Volume" knobs, as found on the FZ-1 stomp box, and an "In" and "Out" (on/off) switch. The word "FUZZTONE" was etched into the pickguard just below the on/off switch.

The EB-0F was not a big seller for Gibson. Shipping totals for the model in the years it was offered were as follows: 1962, 35; 1963, 74; 1964, 64; 1965, 92. Note the chronologically-appropriate pickups for the two examples seen here, as EB-0Fs switched to chrome pickup covers not long after the model was introduced.

It seems ironic that the EB-0F was discontinued in the same year that the Stones' "Satisfaction" brought the fuzztone into prominence, jumpstarting the sales of those original guitar stomp boxes big-time. The cheesy, intentionally-raunchy sound of such devices—Maestro brand or otherwise—was all over numerous 1960s singles, from the Count Five's "Psychotic Reaction" to the Electric Prunes' "I Had Too Much To Dream (Last Night)" and others.

The Gibson EB-0F was a more-or-less-ahead-of-its-time rarity that could conjure up what's now considered a raucous and retro sound, with no footwork required.

The term "fuzztone" conjures up memories of the buzzing, snarling, barely-musical sound from the 1960s that inspired hundreds of thousands—if not millions—of aspiring rock guitarists.

And "fuzztone" is actually a brand name that became generic in such times, as Gibson's Maestro FZ-1 Fuzz-Tone, a wedge-shaped gizmo with germanium transistors, was the stomp box that seemed to interest most budding players—Keith Richards' use of an FZ-1 on the Rolling Stones' "(I Can't Get No) Satisfaction" in 1965, is often cited as a primary reason for the explosion of popularity for that device in the mid-1960s.

However, the use of a distorted guitar sound as a gimmicky studio effect had already been going on for years prior to the British Invasion; in fact, certain English guitarists may have picked up on the viability of distortion from earlier American performances—Link Wray's "Rumble," for example, was released in 1958, and is often cited as a pioneering example of distorted power chords. Moreover, the Ventures' "The 2000 Pound Bee," recorded in 1962, was proclaimed by founding guitarist Don Wilson to have been one of the first songs to utilize a fuzztone.

One of the more popular/desirable basses seen and heard during the 1960s was the two-pickup big brother of the EB-0, known as the EB-3. Among the notable bassists who manipulated the (usually Cherry-finished) model were Cream's Jack Bruce and San Francisco acid rock musicians such as Big Brother & the Holding Company's Peter Albin. Late in the decade, Free's Andy Fraser was another player who garnered acclaim thanks to his use of an EB-3.

Gibson EB-3, 1962, white custom color.
Vintage Guitar Magazine archives

Gibson EB-3, 1967.
Heritage Auctions

Gibson EB-3, 1968.
Heritage Auctions

Gibson EB-3, 1971.
Heritage Auctions

Gibson EB-3, 1970s.
Heritage Auctions

Technically, the EB-3 was Gibson's first two-pickup bass, but to what extent it should be considered Gibson's "response" to the Fender Jazz Bass is probably debatable, although Gibson's new model was introduced in 1961, the year after the Jazz Bass debuted. The EB-3 was rightfully perceived as a double-pickup version of the EB-0, but it was also more than just a two-pickup model of an originally-one-pickup bass.

Nevertheless, similarities to the EB-0 were obvious. The EB-3 had the same mahogany body and neck, as well as the same short scale as all previous Gibson basses. The headstock featured a "crown" inlay, and the rosewood fingerboard joined the body at the seventeenth fret.

The standard finish for EB-3s (as well as EB-0s) was Cherry, and both solid body basses had dot inlays.

Earliest examples of EB-3s had the standard-for-the-times large black plastic humbucking pickup near the neck, plus a small metal-covered humbucker near the bridge. By 1962, both pickups were encased in metal.

The controls for the EB-3's electronics were versatile. In addition to a volume and tone control knob for each pickup, an unusual four-way rotary switch offered the following pickup options in the following settings:

1. Neck pickup only
2. Both pickups
3. Bridge pickup only
4. Neck pickup with "choke"

The #4 position resulted in a brighter sound that one source has called a "baritone voicing"; i.e., its circuitry was similar to the pushbutton "baritone" switch found on EB-2 basses.

As noted earlier, Jack Bruce would probably be considered by most classic rock guitar lovers as the primary proponent of the EB-3 during the 1960s, as he began playing an EB-3 with Cream.

Bruce also recalled the appeal of his four-string Gibson model in the previously-cited 2002 interview, noting "I wanted to play bass like a guitar, and you can't do that on a regular Fender; you can't bend the strings. And since I was the lead vocalist, I needed some kind of compact instrument that I could more or less forget about while I was singing. But probably the most important reason was that I didn't want it to sound like a Fender; I wanted it to sound very personal. So the EB-3 fit the bill in all of those ways; I was able to get some great distortion, and it didn't sound like a Fender at all!"

Cream's legendary live extended jams, of which Bruce's improvisations and explorations were a vital part, validated his use of the EB-3 in an unforgettable manner.

Obviously, the 1962 EB-3 example seen here doesn't have the standard finish or fretboard inlay from its particular time frame. It has a factory-original white finish and large-block inlay (starting on the first fret) that match the top-of-the-line, three-pickup Les Paul Custom guitar of the same era (the name change of that model to SG Custom came about in 1963). According to Gibson records, it was a special order that was entered as "EB-3 – white" on September 12, 1962. It was reportedly made to match a Les Paul Custom guitar for members of the same band.

EB-3s, like EB-0s, went through several configuration changes in their history, including slotted headstocks for a brief time, as well as the addition of long-scale variants to the series (noted with an "L" suffix after the model number). Company records also indicate that white became available as a finish from 1976–79, but 1979 was also the year the EB-3 was discontinued.

The parade of EB-3s here shows the changes that Gibson's frontline bass went through in the approximately eighteen years of its initial existence—the 1967 model is in the standard Cherry finish, while a 1968 model is in another standard finish, Walnut, which was added later in the decade.

The 1971 EB-3 has the short-lived slotted headstock, which had standard tuners installed on the outside edges, facing backwards.

The mid-1970s EB-3 exemplifies some of the problems Gibson would experience in that decade until the company was sold in the mid-1980s. The headstock was now elongated, with a gold decal logo instead of pearl inlay, and no "crown" inlay. And for whatever reasons, the larger/bass pickup had now been moved to the center of the body (ditto for the solitary pickup on the EB-0). The necks on EB-0s and EB-3s of this era were chunky and uninspiring.

Like most short-scale basses, the EB-3 may have a sonic drawback regarding string resonance, but it's a very comfortable instrument to play, as is usually the case for short-scale basses. What's more, in the hands of legendary players, the model has provided many a memorable low-end riff.

Gibson 1963 catalog page with solid body EB-6.

EB-6
A new and exciting treat for bass players. A six-string electric bass which gives a full octave lower guitar tuning on a regular bass scale length.
FEATURES: New extra thin, custom contoured, double cutaway body design. Slim, fast, low-action neck joins body at the 17th fret. One-piece mahogany neck, adjustable truss rod. Rosewood fingerboard, pearl dot inlays. Combination bridge and tailpiece adjustable horizontally and vertically. Two powerful humbucking pickups. New nickel-plated string damper. Hand brace mounted on pickguard. Heavy-duty machine heads with metal buttons. 12¾″ wide, 16″ long, 1⁹⁄₁₆″ thin, 30½″ scale, 20 frets.

EB-6 Cherry finish
E58 Faultless plush-lined case

EB-3
Here is the ultimate in an all new, ultra thin, hand contoured solid body Gibson Electric Bass. The delicately balanced design automatically adjusts into a natural, comfortable playing position with or without a strap.
FEATURES: New extra thin, custom contoured, double cutaway body design. Nickel-plated metal parts. New, extra slim, fast, low-action neck joins body at 17th fret. One-piece mahogany neck, adjustable truss rod. Rosewood fingerboard, pearl dot inlays. Two powerful humbucking pickups for greater tonal range. New four position switch for versatile tonal response. New nickel-plated string damper. Hand brace mounted on pickguard. Heavy duty individual machine heads with metal buttons. 12¾″ wide, 16″ long, 1⁹⁄₁₆″ thin, 30½″ scale, 20 frets.

EB-3 Cherry finish
540 Faultless plush-lined case
329 Archcraft plush-lined case

EB-0
A new, economy-priced bass by Gibson—it offers clear sustaining bass response, easy and fast playing action, modern cherry-red finish.
FEATURES: Thin, custom contoured, double cutaway body design. Slim, fast, low-action neck joins body beyond 17th fret. One-piece mahogany neck, adjustable truss rod. Rosewood fingerboard, pearl dot inlays. Combination bridge and tailpiece, adjustable horizontally and vertically. Hand brace mounted on pickguard. Powerful humbucking pickup with separate tone and volume controls. 12¾″ wide, 16″ long, 1⁹⁄₁₆″ thin, 30½″ scale, 20 frets.

EB-0 Cherry finish
EB-0F Cherry finish
with built-in Fuzztone
540 Faultless plush-lined case
329 Archcraft plush-lined case

To say things had changed for the EB-6 bass in 1962 is a bit of an understatement. The model was transformed from its one-pickup, thinline configuration into a two-pickup instrument with an SG-style body, and subsequent catalog hype would tout the new version as "A new and exciting treat for bass players."

The EB-6 was displayed in the 1963 catalog beside the EB-3. Both instruments shared the same body dimensions (12¾ inches wide, sixteen inches long, 1⁵⁄₁₆ inches deep) and scale (30½ inches), as well as similar construction features (mahogany body and one-piece mahogany neck, rosewood fretboard with twenty frets) and cosmetic items such as the "crown" logo on the headstock. The necks joined the body at the seventeenth fret on both basses. The only catalogued finish option was cherry.

As for hardware, the headstock of the solid body EB-6 had six large cloverleaf-shaped Kluson tuners (vs. four for the EB-3). Both basses sported handrests and slide-up mutes beneath the one-piece bridge/tailpiece.

But the solid body EB-6's electronics layout underlined why it could be rightfully referred to as a "bass guitar." The instrument had two Gibson humbucking guitar pickups, separate volume and tone controls for each pickup, and a three-way pickup toggle switch, just like Gibson's two-pickup SG electric guitars. While the EB-3 also had separate volume and tone controls, its pickups were, as noted previously, controlled by a four-way rotary switch. Note the slight difference in the array of the controls on both instruments, as displayed on the catalog page.

Gibson EB-6, early 1960s, highly modified, owned by Benjamin Orr. *Willie G. Moseley*

Benjamin Orr with his EB-6 in an outtake image from the photo sessions for the Cars' *Panorama* album. *Paul McAlpine*

The EB-6 was discontinued in 1966. Like the original thinline EB-6, solid body versions of the model are also rare, but the two examples shown here have some additional unique attributes.

An obvious showpiece, the refinished, highly-customized white bass has probably been seen by millions of music fans around the globe. It was owned by bassist Benjamin Orr (1947–2000), and he was brandishing it in a photograph seen in the Cars' 1980 platinum-selling album *Panorama*.

At the time, the bass had already been refinished and already had its mirrored pickguard installed. Moreover, a black pickup toggle surround, absent from the 1963 catalog photo of the EB-6, had been installed on the instrument. A rosewood fingerrest—also not seen in

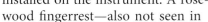

the 1963 catalog illustration—was installed on the new pickguard. The bass's headstock still had the original large tuners.

Veteran photographer Paul McAlpine remembered the sessions that depicted all five members of the Cars, including keyboard player Greg Hawkes and drummer David Robinson, holding cool-looking electric guitars.

"All the guitars used for the cover shoot were favorites of each member of the Cars," McAlpine recounted. "We shot Greg and David with popular-at-the-time electronic mini-keyboard and drum, but went with guitar images in the end selection. The background wall was built especially for this shooting in their rehearsal room, and Greg supplied background programmed music each day; David was the art director for the project."

Orr continued to modify EB-6 after *Panorama* was released. Later additions to the instrument included gold Grover Imperial tuners, gold pickup covers, and gold knobs. Apparently Orr had the bridge tailpiece plated gold, as well (and if it ever had a mute, that item is now missing).

An inspection of the case for this instrument found the EB-6's original tuners, original knobs, original nickel pickup covers, and a Cars guitar pick therein.

The other solid body EB-6 has a 1964 serial number, 157214. It resembles the instrument shown in the 1963 catalog and appears to have all of its original hardware. Its potentiometers date from mid-1965, and all of the internal wiring is original.

However, the "Custom" embossing on the truss rod cover invites a thorough perusal regarding interesting cosmetics and probable alterations.

First of all, there's the unique (for Gibson solid bodies of that era) dark-brown-to-brown sunburst finish, as well as block fret markers and gold knobs.

Like the Orr EB-6, it's missing a mute—if in fact it ever had one—but perhaps its most curious facet is the relocation of the jack from the top of the instrument, reportedly due to a crack at the original location. A pearloid plug is now found near the controls, while the input is now on the rear control plate cover.

How much of the dark sunburst EB-6 is factory original vs. what's been modified, refurbished, or refinished (factory or elsewhere) can make for interesting speculation, but whatever was done when and where, it was a professional undertaking.

Gibson's EB-6 was an interesting if unsuccessful model. Both versions of the instruments were well-crafted in their respective times, and encountering celebrity-associated examples such as the Ben Orr bass or other non-standard instruments is always intriguing.

Following the introduction of the Fender Precision Bass, it took Gibson more than a decade to market a full-scale bass, but the series that premiered in 1963 had a lot more going for it other than just a Fender-like distance from the nut to the bridge.

The redoubtable Thunderbird bass debuted, along with the Firebird guitar series, in 1963. Both lineups featured neck-through construction with body sides glued onto the center portion. Early examples had a two-piece full-length neck, but by the end of the first year, a nine-layer laminated neck was utilized for increased strength.

Gibson Thunderbird IV, 1965,
Cardinal Red. *Steve Evans*

Gibson Thunderbird II,
1964. *Heritage Auctions*

Thunderbird II, 1964, Polaris
White. *Heritage Auctions*

Five years before Firebirds and Thunderbirds were marketed, Gibson had committed an aesthetic marketing blunder with its too-futuristic-for-their-time Flying V and Explorer guitars (and at least one Explorer bass was built). The Firebird/Thunderbird body profile was a softened silhouette of the Explorer, and, to some extent, also seemed to borrow from a flipped-over Fender. Accordingly, they would ultimately acquire a "reverse" appellation to describe their looks.

The Firebird I, III, V, and VII guitars had cosmetic and electronic differences (neck inlay, tailpieces, number of pickups, etc.), but the Thunderbird II and Thunderbird IV were simply one- and two-pickup models with dot fretboard inlays. They featured new humbucking pickups without exposed polepieces and new bridges and stop tailpieces. The single-pickup II had a volume and tone control, and the double-pickup IV featured two volume knobs and a master tone control (and no pickup toggle switch). Original Firebird guitars had banjo-like (and early Gibson electric bass-like) rear-projecting tuners, but Thunderbirds had standard tuners, located exactly where they would be on a Fender instrument.

The standard finish on early T-Birds was a brown Sunburst, but one of the more important marketing innovations for this series was the introduction of Gibson's custom color program (again, après-Fender). Ten colors were available, including Cardinal Red, seen on this 1965 Thunderbird IV. Other colors on the Gibson chart were Heather Poly, Pelham Blue Poly, Golden Mist Poly, Kerry Green, Silver Mist Poly, Inverness Green Poly, Ember Red, Frost Blue, and Polaris White. Some black instruments were also manufactured, but that color wasn't catalogued.

Thunderbirds produce a unique and resonant sound due to their full scale and neck-through design, but they weren't without shortcomings. The term "neck-heavy" is often associated with these instruments, and they've garnered more than their share of broken headstocks.

Also displayed here are a Thunderbird II in a Polaris White custom color and a Thunderbird II in a standard Sunburst finish from the same year.

Over the decades, notable players who thumped original "reverse" Thunderbird basses have included Overend Watts of Mott the Hoople, Wishbone Ash's Martin Turner, and Allen Woody of the Allman Brothers Band and Gov't Mule.

For all of the innovations found on Gibson's original Thunderbird bass series, Fender basses continued to clobber the Kalamazoo company's models throughout the guitar boom of the 1960s. At the very least, the reverse T-Birds exemplified how Gibson was trying to come up with viable alternatives to Fender's Precision Bass and Jazz Bass.

The sales of original F-Birds and T-Birds weren't exactly a runaway success, perhaps because the looks of those instruments may have been a bit too unique for the times.

Accordingly, in mid-1965, Gibson implemented what were perhaps the most dramatic revisions to an existing series in company history (and the manufacturer was reportedly concerned about saving production costs as well). The neck-through style was outta there, as was the "reverse" body shape.

Gibson began making new Firebird and Thunderbird bodies that were a more conventional solid body shape, and the headstocks of Firebirds acquired standard tuners instead of the rear-projecting, banjo-style tuners the original series had. It shouldn't come as any surprise that the new lineup would ultimately be nicknamed "non-reverse" Firebirds and Thunderbirds by guitar buffs.

While the bodies and necks on both series were Honduras mahogany, the primary construction difference in "reverse" and "non-reverse" Firebirds and Thunderbirds was that the newer series had traditional (for Gibson) glued-in necks instead of the original series' neck-through construction.

Gibson
Thunderbird
IV, 1966.
*Heritage
Auctions*

Gibson
Thunderbird
II, 1965.
*Heritage
Auctions*

Gibson
Thunderbird II,
1965, Cherry.
*Heritage
Auctions*

Gibson Firebird III,
1965, Cherry.
*Heritage
Auctions*

While the Thunderbird series of basses also received the set-neck and "non-reverse" silhouette revisions, their electronics, hardware, and layout remained the same as "reverse" examples. There was a slight difference in the layout of the Thunderbird IV's controls—its three knobs had been evenly spaced when laid out on a "reverse" model, but there was a slight gap separating the two volume controls from the master tone control on the "non-reverse" variant.

Many players would probably opine that the ergonomics of "non-reverse" Firebirds and Thunderbirds actually make them more balanced and comfortable than their predecessors (in spite of the ho-hum aesthetics of the "non-reverse" series). The weight of the larger body quadrant where the controls are located on a "non-reverse" instrument tends to place the neck at a more upright angle when it is strapped on.

And non-reverse F-Birds and T-Birds had (and have) their fans. In the heyday of Roxy Music in the 1970s, guitarist Phil Manzanera gigged with "reverse" Firebirds as well as a "non-reverse" model that appeared to have been modified

with full-size humbucking pickups. Lynyrd Skynyrd bassist Leon Wilkeson (1952–2001) was often seen onstage with a non-reverse Thunderbird.

Shown here are a 1966 "non-reverse" Thunderbird IV in standard Sunburst, as well as a standard Thunderbird II from the transition annum of 1965.

However, Cherry-finished Thunderbirds and Firebirds are apparently very rare. While Firebirds and Thunderbirds continued to be offered in Custom Colors, a see-through Cherry finish—standard on other 1960s instruments such as SG-series guitars and solid body EB-series basses—wasn't one of the Custom Color choices.

For many collectors, author Tom Wheeler's comparison of original/"reverse" Gibson Firebirds and Thunderbirds to Errol Flynn and pronouncing the "non-reverse" series to be the fretted instrument equivalent of Elmer Fudd is still valid (and still funny). For others, however, the "non-reverse" instruments may represent a comfortable and easy-to-play collectible.

In 1976, Gibson would reintroduce the "reverse" Thunderbird IV as the Thunderbird 76 (as well as a "reverse" Firebird 76 guitar) as limited edition contributions to America's Bicentennial. The Firebird or Thunderbird logos on white pickguards were etched in coordinating patriotic red and blue. Finishes included Natural Mahogany, White, and Black (Sunburst was also listed for the Firebird).

Bottom line up front: This Melody Maker Bass is a cosmetically different version of Gibson's mainline bass of the same era, the EB-0, but perhaps unexpectedly, it's rarer, too.

Gibson's Melody Maker student series of solid body guitars was introduced in 1959, and went through four different body styles until being discontinued circa 1970. All series of Melody Maker guitars were marketed with headstocks that were narrower than standard Gibson headstocks (although some Melody Makers with wider headstocks were reportedly made shortly before the demise of the series). The line had small, oval-shaped pickups, but still had set-in necks like frontline Gibson models and shared similar hardware and control knobs.

And the frontline EB-0 and Gibson's pursuit of student/beginning players met in the creation and marketing of this instrument.

The SG body style was the fourth and final configuration of Melody Maker guitars, and it wasn't until then that a Melody Maker Bass and a Melody Maker twelve-string guitar were offered to stereotypically fledgling players.

The all-mahogany construction, hardware (including a handrest), large humbucking pickup (and its location at the neck juncture), dot fretboard markers, and scale length seen on this Melody Maker Bass all match what was found on a Cherry-stained Gibson EB-0 in the same era.

The differences? Let's take 'em from the headstock down—there's a cheaper gold-colored Gibson logo on the Melody Maker, vs. a pearl inlay logo on an EB-0, which also usually had the "crown" logo on its headstock; the Melody Maker Bass had a plain headstock.

The profile of the headstock itself is different as well: The sides of the EB-0's headstock curved slightly inwards, whereas the Melody Maker's headstock sides were straight. This was apparently a nod to the narrower headstocks of Melody Maker guitars, which also had straight sides, but the MM Bass headstock was still full-width.

The body of this example is finished in a Sparkling Burgundy color, and the 1968 Gibson price list notes that it was also available in Pelham Blue. The back of the neck of this Melody Maker Bass is finished in a plain natural mahogany; whereas EB-0s sported a Cherry stain over the entire instrument.

Curiously, this Melody Maker bass also has a cosmetic connection to another brand of instruments Gibson was also marketing during the 1960s. The even-less-expensive Kalamazoo line was also aimed at beginners and

Gibson Melody Maker Bass, late 1960s. *Bill Ingalls Jr.*

Gibson Thunderbird, 1977, Bicentennial edition. *Heritage Auctions*

GIBSON

consisted of one- and two-pickup guitars as well as a single-pickup bass. And the white pickguard has exactly the same silhouette as the white pickguard that appeared on Kalamazoo guitars and basses. What's more, the pickup, control knobs, and compass-like markings on the pickguard seen on the MM Bass were also seen on the Kalamazoo KB (see Kalamazoo).

It's an obvious paradox that a budget/student instrument proffered by a major guitar manufacturer is actually rarer than the mainline counterpart of such an instrument, but such is the case with Melody Maker basses vs. the EB-0 bass. Obviously, the even-less-expensive Kalamazoo bass figured into the mix concerning Gibson-manufactured instruments that were intended for beginners, and the bolt-on cheapo guitars and basses named after the city in which Gibsons were made undoubtedly encroached into the potential sales of Melody Maker instruments.

So even if the Melody Maker Bass snitched the pickguard and control knobs from a Kalamazoo bass of the same era, it still ended up as a somewhat-caught-in-the-middle rarity that was only around for about three years, squeezed in between Gibson's lowest-priced and mainline bass products that were marketed in the waning years of the fabled 1960s guitar boom.

In the late 1960s, the Gibson guitar company began re-issuing single-cutaway Les Paul model guitars, as the sonic validity of the original series (which had been supplanted by the SG models) had been promulgated by British blues guitarists such as Peter Green, Eric Clapton, and others. Moreover, the company introduced new Les Paul guitars and basses that attempted to exploit a "best of both worlds" notion, presenting modern technology in a classic guitar body style.

Among the first of these models was the Les Paul Bass, introduced in 1969. The body, made of British Honduras mahogany and finished in walnut, was built in a laminated configuration that the 1970 catalog referred to as "center crossband body construction" (which has become known as a "sandwich body" to guitar enthusiasts). It measured 18¼ inches long, fourteen inches wide, and two inches deep. Like other Gibson bass models, the Les Paul Bass had a "crown" decoration on its headstock, and the neck was three-piece British Honduras mahogany. It had a short scale with a Brazilian rosewood fretboard that had twenty-four frets and dot fret markers.

Electronics consisted of two large, oval-shaped, low-impedance humbucking pickups with chrome surrounds, a pickup toggle switch on the upper bout (like other Les Paul models), three control knobs (Volume, Bass, and Treble), and a small oblong control plate containing a phase switch and a three-position tone selector, for even more instant sonic options. Position-wise on the switch, 1 was "High," 2 was "Norm," and 3 was "Deep Bass." The jack plate was on the side of the body, as was also the case with other Les Pauls.

Hardware included "Schaller design" machine heads, and an intonatable bridge with a flip-up mute hidden under a handrest/cover.

Being a low-impedance instrument only, the Les Paul Bass carried an inference that it was ideal for a studio environment, and its weight was another factor that seemed to discourage its use onstage. The model had to use a low-impedance amplifier, such as Gibson's LP12 (which was introduced in conjunction with the bass), or special adapter cables for a standard amplifier. However, the marketplace quickly rejected such requirements, and the Les Paul Bass was outta there by 1971.

Almost immediately, the Les Paul Triumph Bass replaced the Les Paul Bass, and while it looked similar at initial glance, there were some important cosmetic and electronic differences.

The body and neck construction were the same, but the body was now slightly smaller—17⅞ inches long, 13½ inches wide, and 1¾ inches deep at the rim. Catalog specifications for the Les Paul Triumph also touted the neck width, 1½ inches at the nut, and two inches at the twelfth fret. The standard finish was now natural mahogany instead of walnut.

The Les Paul Triumph's hardware was also the same as seen on the Les Paul Bass, but the flip-up mute was gone from the bridge assembly.

Upgraded cosmetic features were found on the headstock, which was now bound, and sported a split-diamond inlay like a Les Paul Custom guitar. The fretboard now had small block inlay markers instead of dots.

The Les Paul Recording Guitar and the Les Paul Triumph Bass received their own separate brochure in 1971 and 1973. The 1971 photo of the Les Paul Triumph showed a plain truss rod cover and block fret markers beginning on the third fret. This example still has a "Les Paul Bass" truss rod cover and a block marker on the first fret; the extra fret marker showed up on the Les Paul Triumph in the 1973 brochure.

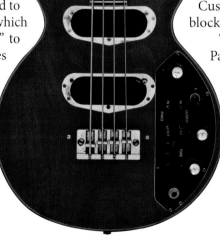

Gibson Les Paul Triumph,
1971. *Heritage Auctions*

The Les Paul Triumph still had oval-shaped low-impedance pickups, and while its electronic features seemed to be a lot more complicated, it was mostly a matter of all of the instrument's controls being installed in a semi-circular, top-mounted control plate. The pickup toggle switch had been relocated from the upper bout of the body and was now found between the Volume knob and the Treble knob. Likewise, the jack was moved from the edge of the body to the rear of the control plate.

The three-position tone switch was still onboard, as was the phase switch, which means that there was actually only one new addition to the controls, but it was an important one—the Les Paul Triumph had a Hi-Lo impedance switch, meaning it could be played through any amplifier; i.e. it could be used onstage like any other instrument instead of having to have a special amplifier or cord.

The model was later offered in a white finish (as were corresponding guitars) and it was displayed in that color (which contrasted nicely with the black pickups and control panel) in Gibson's 1975 and 1978 catalogs. Revised body dimensions were also touted in those publications—17¼ inches long, 12¾ inches wide, and a return to two inches deep, and the scale was now listed as 30⅜ inches.

The Les Paul Triumph was discontinued in 1979, as factory records indicate that forty-four were shipped in that annum. While appearing complicated to some observers, the Triumph was an extremely versatile instrument, at the very least.

By the advent of the 1970s, Gibson had more or less established itself in the new fretted electric bass market with frontline instruments such as the solid body EB-0/EB-3 and Thunderbird series, as well as one- and two-pickup variants of the semi-hollow EB-2 series.

But right or wrong, the "antennae" of many guitar collectors and enthusiasts will probably pop up whenever they encounter a Gibson-made instrument bearing a six-digit serial number with "Made In USA" embossed on the back of its headstock. Such a serial number system was in effect from 1970 through a portion of 1975, which was part of the rough era when the company was owned by the Norlin conglomerate, the tenure of which was considered to have been the company's worst days concerning manufacturing quality. Uninspiring innovations and uninspiring new models were also introduced. Accordingly, guitar collectors will probably examine an instrument from the Norlin era more closely, and for good reason.

True, some unique instruments were introduced by Gibson in the first half of the 1970s, and while some of their bass innovations may have had a bit of merit for players back then, such ideas haven't necessarily meant future collectability (and the same could be said for certain other Gibson instruments in ensuing years and decades).

However, as the 1960s ended, the company was still endeavoring to win its share of the budget market.

Gibson's next effort in the budget bass segment consisted of two basses that were indeed "no frills," but some of their features were also new for the company.

Introduced in 1971, SB-300 and SB-400 differed from each other only in scale length—the SB-300 had Gibson's standard 30½-inch short scale, while the SB-400 had a 34½-inch scale, which had also been adapted to new variants of EB-0s and EB-3s (which had an "L" suffix in the model name to indicate "long" scale).

The bodies of the new early-1970s SB basses retained the classic Gibson double-pointed cutaway SG/EB-0-style silhouette, but were somewhat "chunkier" than earlier frontline basses. Gibson would also adapt the same beefier body (among other changes) to some of its early-1970s standard model basses.

The SB-300 and SB-400 were introduced as being available in a "Highly polished Walnut finish," according to company promotional literature, but it appears that a unique bright cherry finish was also available on the basses from the get-go.

However, both finishes didn't appear to be as "luxurious" as standard Gibson finishes, and over time, some red examples of SB-300s and SB-400s have faded to, for lack of a better description, a hot-pink color.

SG-200—SOLID BODY

If your bag is Rock, Country, Blues, or a combination of each, the exciting new SG-100 and SG-200 offer the finest in quality workmanship and materials at a very popular price. Featuring a new concept in tonal response and body design, each model is equipped with the "bite" and appearance you would normally expect from higher priced Gibson instruments!

FEATURES: Solid Maple neck / Rosewood fingerboard with dotted inlays / Neck width at nut—1-9/16" / 22 frets—nickel silver / Highly polished Walnut finish / Two adjustable pickups / Volume control / Tone control / Two "on-off" slide switches / New flexible bridge / Standby switch / White plastic button machineheads / Engraved "Gibson" hand rest / Chrome-plated parts.

Body dimensions: 13-5/32" x 16¾" x 1⅝"
116—Durabilt case
316—Archcraft case

SG-100 SOLID BODY (not illustrated)—similar to the SG-200, only with single pickup

SB-400—SOLID BODY

This exciting new addition to the Gibson line of quality basses offers the sounds of today! Designed to meet the demands of todays music, the SB-300 with 30½" scale or SB-400 with a long 34½" scale truly offers the "punch" required to support a group! Deep, rich bass tonalities! Clean, clear highs! Available at the touch of a finger!

FEATURES: Solid Maple neck / Rosewood fingerboard with dotted inlays / Neck width at nut—1-11/16" / 20 frets—nickel silver / Metal winged buttons with Schaller machine heads / Newly designed Bridge / Two pickups set in brass mounting rings / Individual slide switches / Volume control / Tone control / Highly polished Walnut finish / Scale length—34½" / Chrome-plated parts.

Body dimensions: 13-5/32" x 17" x 1⅝"
343—Archcraft case
543—Hard Shell Plush case

SB-300 SOLID BODY (not illustrated)—same as the SB-400, except 30½" scale

GIBSON, INC., 7373 NORTH CICERO AVE., LINCOLNWOOD, ILLINOIS 60646

803829   Printed in U.S.A.

1971 Gibson Gazette page.

Both models usually had matching headstocks, a first for Gibson budget electric instruments; however, some examples have been seen sporting a traditional black headstock. The logo was a gold transfer, validating that these were budget instruments (i.e., no pearl inlay). Tuners were by Schaller.

The set-in maple neck had a rosewood fretboard with dot inlays on twenty frets (either scale), and a $1^{11}/_{16}$-inch width at the nut. Curiously, the body wood is not cited in the instruments' listing of specifications.

The bridge offered intonation of individual strings, and its cover sported an embossed Gibson logo.

And most observers could immediately tell that the electronics on Gibson's two new budget basses were definitely different.

The two single-coil pickups were small oval-shaped items, à la Melody Maker guitar pickups, and like the bridge cover, the black plastic covers displayed a Gibson logo. The pickups were surrounded by oval mounting rings made of brass.

While top-mounted controls had appeared on earlier budget Gibson (and Kalamazoo) models, the earlier examples' knobs and switches had been part of the pickguard assembly. However, the SB-300 and SB-400 had a compact assembly that included off-on slider switches for each pickup, master volume and tone knobs, and a jack, all in one oval-shaped chrome plate, which, perhaps not surprisingly, has earned a nickname of "tongue depressor" among some vintage guitar buffs.

Companion guitars to the SB series basses were also introduced at the same time, including the SG-100 (one pickup), SG-200 (two pickups), SG-250 (two pickups, cherry sunburst finish), and the ES-320, a thinline model. There was also a "Sam Ash SG-100," which was a limited edition of approximately 250 one-pickup guitars in cherry sunburst made for the longtime music retailer. All of the new guitars had the same Melody Maker-style pickups and oval-shaped control plates.

However, oblong plates on a sleek SG-shaped body looked aesthetically awkward. Accordingly, 1972 saw the introduction of two models that would ultimately replace the SB-300 and SB-400.

The short-scale SB-350 and long-scale SB-450 sported better-grade walnut and cherry finishes, as well as back-to-standard-color black headstocks. However, said headstocks had a new, elongated silhouette, which was also found on frontline Gibson basses of the same era.

Gibson SB-400,
1971. *Luke Hobbs*

Gibson SB-400, 1971. *Luke Hobbs*

Gibson SB-450, 1972. *Heritage Auctions*

A natural-finish version of the two new basses was also available; it had a matching natural-finish headstock with a black logo. Again, however, some black headstocks may be encountered.

One interesting point of comparison between these two bass series is their respective neck junctures—the earlier series joined the body at the eighteenth fret, while the later series joined the body at the sixteenth fret.

A concise chronology of Gibson's early 1970s budget basses indicates that the SB-300 and SB-400 were produced from 1971–1973, while the SB-350 and SB-450 were made from 1972–1974, with some examples of the SB-450 reportedly being shipped as late as 1978 or 1979.

Perhaps a "budget-is-as-budget-does" attitude is appropriate regarding Gibson's early 1970s lower-end basses and their status in the vintage guitar marketplace. They were functional-if-not-inspirational in their time, and they usually sell for less than frontline Gibson instruments of the same era.

At first glance, the Gibson EB-4L, introduced in 1972, could have been mistaken for an EB-0L, which was a long-scale version of Gibson's frontline single-pickup production bass.

Therefore, an initial reaction to the introduction of the EB-4L might have been something along the lines of "What's the big deal?," as it looked quite similar to other Gibson basses.

The EB-4L's all-mahogany construction was similar to EB-0s and EB-3s, and like its similarly-shaped progenitors, the EB-4L came in Cherry and Walnut finishes. Unfortunately, it sported the "chunkier" SG-shaped body of the early 1970s, and its neck felt pretty beefy (and uninspiring) as well, exemplifying the dearth of quality in instruments from that time period.

Like the mid-1970s EB-3 seen earlier, the EB-4L had no decorative headstock inlay, and what's more, the Gibson script logo isn't pearl either. Its cheaper gold logo on an elongated headstock seemed to add to the EB-4L's lack of aesthetic inspiration.

The neck joined the body at the seventeenth fret (note the rounded end of the fretboard), and the rosewood fingerboard with dot markers was unbound.

The silhouette of the multi-layered pickguard was, for some reason, truncated with a rounded notch (that it apparently didn't need).

What Gibson was apparently trying to accomplish with the EB-4L—thus apparently validating the different model number—was the incorporation of more professional sonic options into a familiar-looking instrument. Take a close look at the pickup: While it seems to be the same

Curiously, the SB-350 had twenty-one frets, while the SB-450 had twenty frets.

The pickups on the new models were mini-humbuckers encased in black plastic. Instead of a "tongue depressor," the top-mounted controls (which had the same basic setup as their predecessors) were found on a black plastic, half-moon shaped plate. Originally, a Gibson two-point intonatable bridge was found on the SB-350 and SB-450 (as seen on the SB-450 shown here, as the bridge cover has been removed; the SB-350 has a replacement bridge), but later examples had Gibson's new three-point bridge, which was found on later 1970s frontline basses as well.

Gibson EB-4L, mid-1970s. *Vintage Guitar Magazine* archives

Gibson L-9S Ripper, mid-1970s. *Heritage Auctions*

Ⓐ **FOUR POSITION TRANSFER SWITCH.**
Position 1. Activates both pickups in a series in phase configuration. (Series wiring achieves a bit more "bite" than might otherwise be obtained.)
Position 2. Activates back pickup only for maximum treble response.
Position 3. Activates both pickups in an in phase, parallel wiring configuration. ("Parallel" resulting in more bottom end response.)
Position 4. Activates both pickups in series, out of phase for a very funky, dirty type tonality.

Ⓑ **VOLUME CONTROL**

Ⓒ **MIDRANGE CONTROL.** *Position* 0 gives the minimum midrange response. 10 delivers maximum midrange.

Ⓓ **TONE CONTROL.** At 0, it delivers maximum bass, at 10, maximum treble.

Ⓔ **INPUT JACK**

L-9S

L-9S Ripper spec sheet.

size as original large Gibson bass humbuckers, it has an offset, "2+2" polepiece configuration, and was designed by the redoubtable Bill Lawrence.

There's also a three-position toggle switch that works coil-tap configurations, which can evoke various tones from the pickup. It's mounted in a tiny oval-shaped plate made from the same material as the pickguard.

The bridge (under a chrome cover) featured individual saddles for intonation, and some bridges on other EB-4Ls offered a mute.

Any full-scale version of an instrument that is also available as a short-scale model should resonate better and should have better sustain, particularly if said full-scale variant has a set-in neck. Such would have been the idea behind Gibson's EB-0Ls, EB-3Ls, and EB-4Ls, with some extra sonic capabilities added to the last model. A simple strategy, but not successful, and Gibson would go on to other ultimately uninspiring and unsuccessful bass debacles later in the 1970s.

The EB-4L was on Gibson's price lists from 1972 to 1975. The last examples were reportedly shipped in 1979.

An EB-4L might make an excellent utility instrument for someone who wants to gig with a full-scale, SG-shaped instrument, but be forewarned that it won't have the slim, sleek profile and feel of a 1960s EB-0 or EB-3. It may actually sound better, due to a long scale, but it will most likely feel a lot beefier. It's a definitive example of something that didn't work for Gibson when it was new and calls into question any hype about collectability of certain guitars or basses, just because they might be rare and/or were short-lived, and were made by a major manufacturer.

The EB-4L has the distinction of being the first Gibson SG-shaped bass introduced as a full-scale instrument . . . for whatever that's worth.

During the dark days of the 1970s, Gibson did indeed introduce new basses with new construction styles and new sonic innovations. The initial market push was made for a trio of basses with a new body silhouette.

The most versatile among the trio was the L-9S Ripper, which was the only model with a set-in neck. Debuting in 1973, it was offered in a sunburst finish with an ebony fretboard, or a natural finish with a maple fretboard (and the pearl position markers on the latter configuration were hard to see).

The L-9S Ripper had two Super Humbucking pickups and an electronics configuration that was dubbed the "Q System," which interpolated master volume, tone, and mid-range roll-off controls with a four-position rotary pickup selector offered the following options in the control's respective positions:

1. both pickups in a "series in phase configuration"
2. bridge pickup only
3. both pickups in "phase, parallel wiring
4. both pickups in "series, out of phase"

Ripper ad with short pickguard.

Rick Danko onstage in 1979 with an L-9S Ripper. *Wikimedia Commons*

It sounds like Peter Cetera's playing a lot of basses.
But, he's just playing a lot of bass. A Gibson.

Since *Only The Beginning*, Chicago has played just about every style of music, and pleased just about every type of music critic. In a group that well rounded, a lesser bassist would be spread too thin. So would a lesser bass. But, Peter Cetera plays it all. All on one bass — Gibson.

If the Gibson Ripper that Peter plays had just one sound, it would be an excellent bass. But, the Ripper is loaded with excellent sounds. The Q System tunes and fine tunes the electronics from funky fundamental tones to rich, raunchy sounds — right on your cue. Just turn the four position transfer switch and tune the midrange and treble roll-off controls. The Super Humbuckers sound especially superb, because we matched their sensitive electronics with the Q System's special electronics.

The Ripper's uniquely contoured, extra solid body gives every sound a uniquely powerful presence. You can mount the strings on the adjustable bridge for the traditional sound and feel. Or, mount them right through the body to get more of the body resonating for more sound. The new string tension gives you a great new feel too. And you know those strings feel good just listening to the smooth, fast, effortless way Peter Cetera's fingers move across the fretboard.

The Ripper is just one amazing bass from Gibson. There's the Grabber with its versatile sliding pickup. The G-3 with its three special design, single coil pickups. Les Pauls with built-in mini-mixing consoles. The traditional EB-3. And more. So, if you've been hearing too much of the same old bass line — 'colour your world.' With a Gibson.

Gibson
Another quality product from Norlin

7373 N. Cicero Avenue, Lincolnwood, Illinois 60646
51 Nantucket Boulevard, Scarborough, Ontario, Canada

For the new Gibson catalog, send $1.75 for postage and handling to: Norlin Music – Advertising, 7373 N. Cicero Ave., Lincolnwood, Illinois 60646

Ripper ad with Peter Cetera, 1979.

The standard model had undergone changes by 1975. The body wood switched to alder, and the sunburst finish was discontinued in favor of black. A fretless version was introduced that year, and in addition to being available in black and natural finishes, the fretless variant was also offered in sunburst.

Interestingly, one earlier ad for the Ripper showed a shorter pickguard with the treble/bridge pickup installed directly on the body, and no bridge cover.

The Ripper did gain several frontline users/endorsers, including Greg Lake (1947–2016) of Emerson, Lake & Palmer, Mel Schacher (Grand Funk Railroad), Suzi Quatro, Louis Johnson (1955–2015), and Chicago's Peter Cetera, who posed with one for an ad in 1979.

Rick Danko (1943–1999), bassist for The Band, regularly played a Ripper, as seen in Martin Scorsese's *The Last Waltz*, the renowned documentary chronicling the final concert of that iconic quintet. Danko used the model in subsequent musical ventures as well.

In late 1974, Gibson introduced the Grabber, which used the same maple body. However, the new model had a bolt-on neck and a tapered, semi-pointed headstock silhouette that was reminiscent of a Gibson Flying V guitar.

The Grabber was distinguished by a sliding pickup that could evoke different tones simply by moving it. Controls were simple volume and tone knobs.

Grabber ad w/ tortoise pickguard.

Kiss album cover.

Gibson Grabber,
mid-1970s.
*Heritage
Auctions*

Gibson G-3.
Heritage Auctions

It began its run in wine-red or black finishes. It, too, acquired an alder body in 1975, and a natural finish was proffered in 1976. It was only available with a maple fretboard.

The highest profile user of a Grabber was Gene Simmons of Kiss. Simmons was seen brandishing a custom-painted example on the cover of the 1975 album *Kiss Alive*.

The final member of Gibson's new threesome was the G-3, which debuted in 1975, with an alder body, bolt-on maple neck, and a semi-pointed headstock.

Its three single-coil pickups were wired to function as sort of a triple-coil humbucker. Soon after its introduction, the G-3's see-through pickup covers were replaced by black pickup covers.

Controls included volume and tone knobs and a three-way toggle switch that offered neck-and-middle, all three, or middle-and-bridge pickup settings.

Several notable bassists relied on the the G-3, including Kelly Groucutt (1945–2009) of the Electric Light Orchestra, and while The Who's John Entwistle and jazz giant Stanley Clarke posed with G-3s, they didn't make heavy use of the model (if at all).

The Ripper, Grabber, and G-3 were all discontinued in 1982, as Gibson's tailspin began to pick up speed. The models seemed relegated to obscurity until they appeared in the hands of 1990s rockers like Krist Novoselic of Nirvana and Mike Dirnt of Green Day.

However, even such a resurrection from oblivion isn't necessarily enough to state that such basses were truly "classic" models.

𝄢

Possibly the most maligned series of electric instruments in Gibson's history, RD solid body guitars and basses were introduced in 1977. Some guitar buffs would probably have opined that the body silhouette of this instrument looks like a melted "reverse" Thunderbird, and the cynicism would most likely have increased once the instrument was strapped on and played.

"RD" stands for "Research and Development"—no surprise there—and the active versions in the series had circuitry that was designed by Robert Moog, who was an innovator in the early days of keyboard synthesizers.

The RD Artist Bass had all-maple construction, which made it pretty hefty (this Sunburst example weighs in at almost thirteen pounds). It's cumbersome when played in a standing position—although the contoured body is relatively comfortable, the neck seems to extend too far to the left. Players accustomed to plunking their left hand down by reflex/"feel" on the first fret of the E string on a full-scale bass (i.e., an F note) would most likely land somewhere around the A-flat fret on this item.

The RD Artist's scale was Gibson's then-standard 34½ inches, and the neck had three-piece laminated construction with an oft-maligned volute on the back of the neck/headstock joint. The strings loaded through the body. The bridge was Gibson's new three-point style, which would also appear on "re-issues" of the "reverse"-style Thunderbird.

The pearl inlay on the headstock is an image of an f-hole and a lightning bolt, which was supposed to signify Gibson's long-time musical instrument manufacturing history with modern electronic innovations,

Gibson RD Artist Bass, late 1970s. *Bill Ingalls Jr.*

but within the Gibson factory, the logo became known as "the flying shrimp" ... although some observers/cynics may think it's a seahorse with wings.

Original standard finishes included Antique Sunburst, Ebony, Fireburst, and Natural. The instrument usually had an ebony fretboard, although a maple fretboard (with hard-to-see pearl markers) was seen on the Natural-finished instruments.

The pickups are Gibson Series V humbuckers, and to say that the controls would have been confusing to an average player is an understatement. It has separate volume knobs for each pickup, but the master treble and bass knobs have a different type of numerical calibration on their sides. Instead of the normal 1-10 range, they're marked "5-0-5." Centering either control on 0 makes that control passive, clockwise rotation creates boost, and counterclockwise rotation creates a cut in the tone signal.

There's a three-way pickup toggle switch, but the second toggle switch only adds to the potential confusion—it was non-functional when centered, but pushing it in one direction activated a bright circuit that was applicable to both pickups, while switching it in the other direction activated a compression/sustain circuit for the neck pickup only, but an expansion/attack circuit for the bridge pickup only was also activated at the same time.

Gibson RD Artist Bass, late 1970s. *Olivia's Vintage*

Circuitry on RD Artists could be accessed through a plastic panel that covered almost half of the back of the body. A smaller panel on the back housed a 9-volt battery, and there was even a small rubber cap that covered a slot through which a screwdriver could be inserted to adjust compression or expansion.

A passive version of the bass was known as the RD Standard; it came with different pickups, simpler controls, and fewer finishes.

Subsequent variants of RD Artists included (theoretically-less-confusing) circuit controls that were split up into three mini-toggle switches, as well as "CMT" versions with bound, figured maple tops. Regardless of the configuration, RD guitars and basses epitomized Gibson's 1970s problems, which carried over into the first half of the 1980s (all RD models were discontinued by 1982).

Gibson RD Standard, 1978. *Olivia's Vintage*

As far as any association with notable players, an RD Artist Bass was seen in the hands of Frank Maudsley, bassist for A Flock of Seagulls during the early days of MTV, and Nirvana's Krist Novoselic bashed RDs in the 1990s as well.

Any desirability for RDs may ultimately derive from an it's-so-ugly-it's-collectible line of thinking, à la the Ford Edsel. Some studio musicians like RDs in a recording environment because of the instruments' versatility, so such basses do have their fans . . . as do Edsels, as well as A Flock of Seagulls, for that matter.

For a (perceived) last-gasp instrument series by the then-in-a-tailspin Norlin/Gibson guitar company, their "Victory" guitars and basses from the early 1980s actually had a lot going for them . . . including weight.

In the eyes of many observers, the long-revered stringed instrument brand was in serious trouble, as the quality of its instruments had severely deteriorated, and most of its new models that had been introduced during the 1970s had "bombed." The perhaps-ironically-named Victory guitars and basses, introduced in 1981, represented the last attempt by Norlin/Gibson to market a completely new series that would be viable in the perpetually evolving electric stringed instrument business.

Victory guitars and basses had asymmetrical bodies made of maple. In an aesthetic nod to the times, their cutaways had severely offset, horns that ended in a point. The body profile meant that the balance of those instruments was extremely comfortable. The headstocks had a semi-Firebird/Thunderbird silhouette (and even factory literature, including the owner's manual, noted the connection).

It seemed apparent, however, that the Victory Bass series wanted to be an alternative to Fender basses *real* bad, as the early 1980s models were—stylistically—the closest instruments to Fenders that Gibson had ever produced up to that time. Such subtle allusions included a bolt-on maple neck with four-on-a-side tuners, and the aforementioned offset cutaway horns. However, the cutaway horns on Victory Basses were much more offset than those on a Fender Precision Bass or Jazz Bass, and the inside edges of the horns, closest to the neck joint, were sculpted as well.

While the extremely offset silhouette on Victory Bass bodies made them very balanced, the solid maple bodies meant that such instruments were also quite heavy. One would have thought that Gibson had learned a lesson

Gibson Victory Custom, 1982. *Bill Ingalls Jr.*

concerning maple bass bodies when their RD series basses, which had been introduced less than a half-decade earlier, had gone nowhere fast.

Accordingly, a wide guitar strap, to distribute the weight strain better, was/is as requisite for a Victory Bass as it was/is for an RD series bass.

The Victory Bass series consisted of three instruments, two of which, the passive single-pickup Standard and the active two-pickup Artist, were manufactured in large quantities. The two-pickup passive Custom, an example of which is seen here, was limited to no more than 250 instruments and was listed from 1982–1984.

Victory Bass models had a fairly wide rosewood fretboard, which had an offset style itself, consisting of twenty-two "complete" frets but an angled butt-end configuration that had a partial twenty-third fret allowing access to all strings except the lowest, and a partial twenty-fourth fret that allowed the D and G strings to be played in a double-octave manner (and the sculpted-and-offset treble cutaway horn helped to facilitate such). Fretboards also had offset dot markers but no neck binding.

Another nod to the times—albeit sonic rather than visual—was the brass nut.

Pickups were humbuckers, and a mini-toggle switch was available for coil-tapping if desired. The solitary, also-severely-angled pickup on the Standard was installed in a more central position on the body, compared to the closer-to-the-neck-joint location of the same item on the Artist and Custom models. The second pickup on the Artist and Custom was installed at a right angle to the strings in the "bridge" postion instead of an extreme angle.

Pickguard silhouettes were different for the single-pickup model and two-pickup variants, but were a standard five-layer black-white-black-white-black. Standard body colors included Candy Apple Red, Silver, and Antique Fireburst.

The three-position pickup switch for Artist and Custom models was also a mini-toggle. Controls included volume knobs for each pickup and a tone knob. An intonatable Schaller bridge/tailpiece embossed with "Gibson" was also standard.

Gibson apparently made a concerted effort to promote their new series. Magazine advertising in the early 1980s included a "Thrill of Victory" ad showing a player awash in spotlights and footlights, brandishing a silver Victory Artist. An endorsement ad was headed by Dave Kiswiney, then of the Ted Nugent Band, along with Dave Pegg (Jethro Tull) and Ralphe Armstrong (Jean Luc-Ponty), and others. Performance video of Nugent's band documents that Kiswiney did indeed use a silver, two-pickup Victory Bass in concert.

What's more, when the supergroup Asia broke out in the same time period that the Victory series was introduced, bassist John Wetton counted on a Victory Artist to craft his sound.

For all of its merits, the Victory series suffered the same ignominious fate as the other new Gibson models and series of the 1970s and early 1980s. Records indicate that the Victory Standard Bass was discontinued in 1986, the Victory Artist was outta there by 1985, and the Victory Custom was last made in 1987 . . . which indicates that the last of the 250 or so Victory Customs were simply made to use up parts.

Moreover, leftover Victory guitar and bass bodies, as well as other parts, apparently figured into the creation of the mid-to-late 1980s basses such as the Q-80 and other models. Those instruments were marketed after a change in ownership, and again, may have simply been created as "floor sweep" instruments to use up excess bodies, necks, etc.

It's interesting to speculate about to what extent the fate of the Victory series was already sealed when it was introduced in 1981, considering the fortunes of the Gibson company in the previous decade. Be that as it may, Victory Basses can be good utility instruments that balance nicely and have a more-"Fenderish" feel than the Gibson basses that preceded them.

But if played standing up in a concert environment, the addition of hernia insurance might be advisable.

Last but not least, here is a fascinating bass that epitomizes what Gibson's legendary Custom Shop has been doing for decades regarding one-of-a-kind instruments.

It's a twelve-string bass (two sets of strings tuned in guitar range, one bass-range set) that was inspired by Cheap Trick bassist Tom Petersson's efforts to evoke a twelve-string guitar sound and bass sound from a single instrument (see the Hamer chapter for a detailed history).

However, the curious facet of this instrument's own chronology is that Petersson didn't know about its existence until a number of years after it was built.

The bass dates from around 1991, and was built by veteran luthier Phil Jones, who designed and built fascinating prototypes and re-issue guitars and basses for Gibson from July 16, 1984, to July 16, 1999 ("Fifteen years to the day," he recalled with a chuckle.).

Jones averred that the bass was a prototype instrument that was not special-ordered by a rock star or affluent customer.

"I finally convinced Gibson's bean counters to let us design Les Paul-type basses and other shapes with a full thirty-four-inch scale instead of a short scale, that weren't copies of Fenders," Jones recounted, "and I began making bass prototypes with body shapes in addition to the single-cutaway Les Paul silhouette. There was even a V-shaped bass with eight strings and a thirty-two-inch scale, so obviously, the 'Wow, I could've had a V-8' line was heard about that one!"

Gibson Custom Shop twelve-string bass, circa 1991, owned by Tom Petersson. *Willie G. Moseley*

Jones described the twelve-string as being " . . . based on a double-cutaway (Les Paul) Junior with an extended horn for balance."

Woods included a mahogany body, a maple neck, and a twenty-four-fret rosewood fingerboard. Phil noted that the scooped-out portion of the body on the treble side of the neck juncture allows for access to high register notes.

"I designed it as a 'picking bass,'" he said, "and that scoop is also a bit of an homage to Paul Reed Smith's designs."

In spite of the tension of twelve strings, the bass has a standard single-truss rod system on a neck that has a thin elliptical profile, and it has not experienced any problems with bowing.

The pickups are Gibson Thunderbird-type units, and the controls are laid out in a standard two-volume, two-tone configuration. The bridge/tailpiece is a specially-made Leo Quan Badass.

The finish is the same gold color that Gibson uses on its "Goldtop" Les Paul guitars and other instruments.

"I've always loved that original finish on '52 and '53 Les Pauls," Jones said. "It looks really good on that unbound body."

Jones went to work at Nashville's Gruhn Guitars after he left Gibson, and it was at that location where Petersson snagged the instrument.

"I was visiting Gruhn Guitars in Nashville, and Phil was working for them then," Petersson recalled. "This was a number of years after he'd left Gibson. He pulled out this bass and showed it to me; I'd never known it existed until then! He told me he'd been interested in what I'd done with the earlier Hamer instruments and wanted to make his own version of that kind of instrument."

"Well, of course I had to have it," the Cheap Trick bassist chuckled. "Gruhn's was getting ready to put it out for sale, and I would have been pissed if anyone else had gotten it!"

Now well into its second century, Gibson may not be the industry leader regarding electric basses, but that hasn't discouraged the company's Custom Shop from creating exquisite and innovive instruments.

EIGHTEEN

GRETSCH

Let's tell it like it was: In spite of the Gretsch company's high-end image among guitar enthusiasts, the brand was never a serious entry in the electric bass marketplace.

One shouldn't have expected too much when Gretsch's first "bass"—using that term in a liberal manner—was the Bikini, an instrument that was part of a bizarre two-neck design on a collapsible body that debuted in 1961. The Bikini's bass neck was simply a guitar neck with bass hardware, and like most designs of that ilk, sounded terrible due to the lack of resonance.

Gretsch's first serious attempt at marketing an electric bass was the double-cutaway 6070, which was introduced ca. 1963. At first glance, observers might have thought the new Gretsch item was similar to Gibson's innovative EB-2 bass but the differences were numerous: The EB-2 was a short-scale, semi-hollow bass with f-holes, while the 6070 was full-scale, fully hollow, and had painted f-holes on its "Electromatic" body, which was seventeen inches wide and two inches deep. Another feature on such bodies was a circular snap-on pad on the back.

Compared to Gretsch guitars, the 6070 had a unique (and large) assymetrical headstock, with a nameplate instead of an inlaid logo. The tuners were in a 2+2 configuration. The rosewood fretboard is shown in a 1965 catalog as having twenty frets, but twenty-one-fret examples have also been seen.

The body was available only in sunburst, and gold hardware was standard. Both a thumbrest and fingerrest were installed at opposing angles, and the bridge was Gretsch's (non-intonatable) Space Control model.

Electronics consisted of a single Gretsch pickup mounted somewhat close to the bridge, a three-position tone switch on the upper bass bout, and a volume control on the upper treble bout. The lower bout contained a standby switch and a control for a flip-up mute.

The 6070 had an end pin to be fitted onto the bottom of the body, so the instrument could be played upright; in fact, the primary hype in the 1965 catalog noted that it could be played in three positions— "standing," "lap-type," and "cello."

The 6070 would last around ten years, which means the company was owned by Baldwin when it was discontinued.

A short-scale, fully-hollow bass called the 6071 debuted in 1968. Differences also included a single-cutaway body that was sixteen inches wide and finished in "red mahogany" (and the body still had painted f-holes and a pad on the back), as well as a four-on-a-side headstock. Controls were the same as the 6070.

The 6070 had a two-pickup variant (6072), and the 6073 was a two-pickup version of the 6071.

Gretsch tried other bass models during the 1960s, but none were successful, and the most famous, er, "player" seen

Gretsch 6071, late 1960s.
Willie G. Moseley

Gretsch 6070, mid-1960s.
Kevin Borden

Gretsch 7629 Committee Bass (back). *Willie G. Moseley*

Gretsch 7629 Committee Bass, circa 1978. *Bill Ingalls Jr.*

Gretsch 7627 TK 300 Bass, late 1970s. *Heritage Auctions*

with a Gretsch bass was Peter Tork of the Monkees. Somehow, the brand name didn't seem to resonate with potential bass customers, and all four of the aforementioned models were discontinued by the early 1970s.

But some of the instruments introduced during Gretsch's "Baldwin ownership era" are considered to be the lowliest examples to ever bear the Gretsch name.

The solid body 7629 Committee Bass, introduced in 1977, actually had commendable construction and cosmetic attributes. It was a natural-finished, single-pickup instrument, with neck-through construction (three-piece maple/walnut/maple) and two walnut "wings" glued onto either side. The body wings also sported a German carve, so the aesthetics for the Committee looked kinda cool. Overall, the body was thirteen inches wide and 1½ inches deep.

The rosewood fretboard had twenty-two frets, joining the body at the sixteenth. The neck and headstock were bound.

A single Super 'Tron bass pickup had a simple volume and tone control, and the "Terminator bridge tailpiece with individual string adjustment" (to quote the 1978 Gretsch catalog) had a chrome cover. The bridge on this example appears to be a replacement.

The 1978 catalog showed the 7629 with a flush-mounted, clear plastic pickguard, but many, if not most, examples had a tinted/smoked plastic pickguard, as seen here. The control plate on the back of the guitar also matched the pickguard, as the rear view of this example demonstrates (and this view also shows off the neck-through construction).

The TK 300 series, also introduced around the same time as the Committee series, was quite possibly the nadir for the Gretsch brand, and that lineup included a bass. Guitar lovers used to the company's elegant hollow body styles probably didn't know what to make of the homely, angular TK 300 guitar and bass, and such models were probably considered heretical to the Gretsch legacy.

Like its guitar counterpart, the 7627 TK 300 Bass had an elongated headstock with the Gretsch name in large, individual black letters. It featured all maple construction, and the bolt-on neck joined the body at the sixteenth fret. The body was thirteen inches wide and 1⅝ inches deep, and such a slightly-downsized body silhouette coupled with the oversized headstock gave the instrument a lopsided look. While most examples of this model were seen in a natural finish, it was also available in an "Autumn Red Stain" finish (model #7626).

The TK 300 Bass had the same electronics and hardware that the Committee Bass had.

The body's oddball silhouette was amplified by the herky-jerky looking pickguard, which looks like an amateurish design to most Gretsch purists.

To its (perhaps-backhanded) credit, the TK 300 Bass had a belly contour on the back of the body and was relatively comfortable to play. However, it's doubtful that any ergonomics-oriented luthiers got much inspiration from this dubious Gretsch series.

The Gretsch brand name is legendary in the world of guitar collecting, and nice examples of classic Gretsch guitar models can fetch thousands of dollars. However, older Gretsch basses seem to be consigned to the dubious niche of historical curiosity items.

Gretsch White Falcon twelve-string bass prototype, 1959 appointments. *FMIC*

Tom Petersson plays his original Gretsch 12-string bass prototype at an outdoor NHL hockey match. *Carla Dragotti*

𝄢

Gretsch would go through numerous ownership changes over the decades, and 2002 saw the Fender Musical Instrument Company (FMIC) acquiring the rights from the Gretsch family to build and distribute Gretsch instruments.

Accordingly, Gretsch instruments now have their own Custom Shop inside the Fender facility in Corona, California, and three of their most unique creations were the prototypes of a twelve-string bass, commissioned by Tom Petersson, who worked with the Gretsch folks to craft a bass with such a string configuration but sporting a classic Gretsch look.

"I love the look of classic 1950s and 1960s instruments, and Gretsches are a longtime favorite," he said.

Not surprisingly, he chose the top-of-the-line White Falcon as its "platform," keying in the double-cutaway version for a very specific reason.

"George Harrison used a Gretsch Country Gentleman," Petersson said succinctly. "There have been quite a few different White Falcons, but I like the double-cut Country Gent look."

Once he began collaborating with the luthiers in California, concepts and construction came quickly, thanks to his experience with the instrument.

The first prototype was developed by Chris Fleming, who has been with the Fender/Gretsch company since the turn of the century. Based on a 1959 instrument, the bass was given the brand's horizontal headstock logo and thumbnail inlays.

"I started with those cosmetics," Fleming recounted, "then Tom and I decided that a sixteen-inch lower bout, thin profile, and a short-scale neck would be a winning combination." He then turned to builders in the Fender R & D Model Shop, Gretsch Custom Shop, and Jackson Custom Shop.

"It was a matter of creating something that could hold up to the huge pressure that twelve strings exert on an instrument," he said. "We've created many prototypes over the years, but none as unique as this."

The prototype was given a spruce center block, three-piece quarter-sawn maple neck with a mortis-and-tenon joint, and other refinements.

"We had to adjust a couple of things, including pinning the bridge with long studs and adjusting the pickups to suit Tom's needs," Fleming added. Those items were placed in a neck-and-middle layout on the top.

Obviously, a stretched-out headstock had to be designed to accommodate two sets of Gotoh guitar tuners and one set of Gotoh bass tuners.

Hardware was gold-plated and included tuners, pickup covers, a specially-designed bridge, and a "Cadillac" tailpiece.

Second White Falcon prototype, 1955 appointments. *Willie G. Moseley*

Back of third prototype shows the darker green in the two-tone finish. *FMIC*

Petersson and his daughter Lilah on the set of the Today Show with the third White Falcon prototype in Smoke Green finish. *Allison Petersson*

"The bridge I designed for the prototype was 3-D printed—quite expensive—and turned out to be incredibly strong," Fleming added.

After several design revisions by the R & D staff, Petersson acquired the first prototype in time to play it at a National Hockey League outdoor game in the month of February at the TCF Bank Stadium at Minneapolis. The temperature was twenty degrees during the performance.

"They need to be able to take the cold and the heat," Petersson said of such instruments. "Plus, it makes for great-looking finish checking."

The other two basses were created in the Gretsch Custom Shop under the direction of Stephen Stern. Based on a 1955 White Falcon configuration, they, too, have pickups in a neck-and-middle configuration, and similar hardware. Differences include a vertical logo, smaller f-holes, a "comfort pad" on the back, and an armrest on the second prototype.

"We couldn't slip the electronics through (the smaller f-holes)," Stern said. "We also didn't want to route channels or drill through the center block to pass the pots and switch through, so we had to route two access holes in the back."

The finish on the second prototype is off-white with relic'ed touches, while the third instrument is a two-tone Smoke Green finish.

"(It's) like Brian Jones' Gretsch Double Anniversary," Petersson enthused. "I always loved that color with the darker sides and back."

All three instruments have maple laminate bodies and ebony fretboards. Petersson used the Smoke Green bass in television appearances on CMT's "Crossroads" and on the "Today Show" in early 2016, when the band was in New York for the ceremony to mark their induction into the Rock and Roll Hall of Fame.

Stern noted that Petersson came up with changes for the second and third prototypes, emphasizing, "He thought it would spruce up the look, and I agree."

Petersson and the luthiers at Gretsch are all understandably proud of their collaboration.

"Tom is great, and I had a feeling this would be a fun project," Fleming said.

Stern shared that enthusiasm and added, "It's fair to say Tom's basses are the most contradictory instruments we've ever made in the Gretsch Custom Shop."

And as for innovations in retro looks and contemporary sound, it doesn't get much cooler than this trio.

NINETEEN

GRUGGETT

One of the more unusual series of instruments that were created in the Bakersfield area during the 1960s guitar boom was the Stradette lineup, crafted by Bill Gruggett, who also had affiliations with Mosrite and Hallmark.

Gruggett set out on his own in 1967, and designed the Stradette line to look like . . . well, nothing else of its time. And he succeeded—at least, as far as the instruments' aesthetics were concerned. He began building the instruments that bore his surname in his garage, then moved his operation to downtown Bakersfield and hired four employees.

Bill had originally wanted to make basses only, as he was a bass player himself. However, the Stradette line ultimately consisted of not only one-pickup and two-pickup basses, but also a six-string guitar, a twelve-string guitar, and a doubleneck instrument.

THE ALL-NEW *Stradette* Model-Guitar

By

THE **g Gruggett** MFG. CO.

For

The Mod Generation

Gruggett Stradette.
Michael G. Stewart

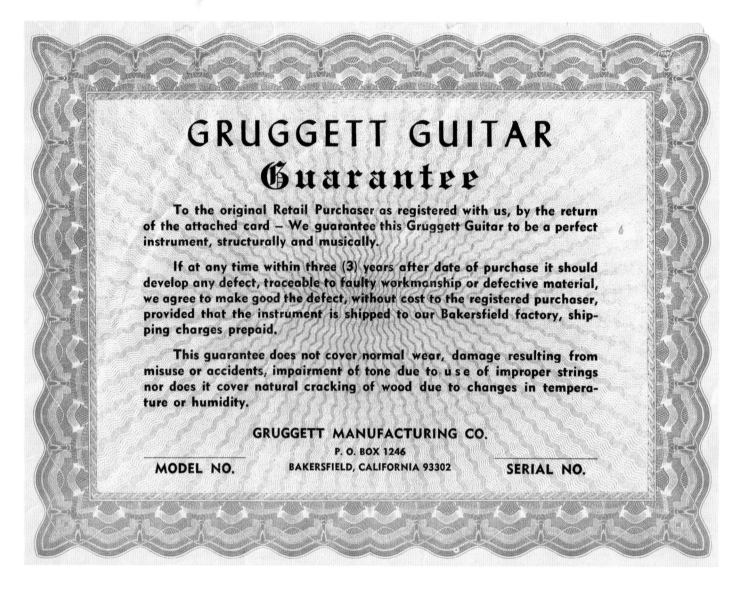

Bodies for the Stradette series, described in company literature as "Semi-acoustic," measured 12¼ inches wide, and 3½ inches deep. They were made from alder, with a laminated arched top and back, and had three-ply binding, front and rear. Necks were made of maple, with a bound rosewood fretboard that had pearloid dot markers.

As for the oddball body silhouette, Gruggett recalled that he was trying for a style that combined a classical, violin-like shape with a modern, double-cutaway guitar. The, er, unique/hybrid look of Stradettes is probably their most endearing feature to guitar enthusiasts.

Scale for the bass was 30½ inches. The tuning keys were Klusons, while other hardware, such as the strap buttons and the handrest, were also seen on other Bakersfield area companies' instruments.

The Stradette bass was available in one-pickup and two-pickup models, priced at $349 and $379, respectively. The "Hi-Fi" pickups were hand-wound, and covered with a tortoiseshell-colored plastic.

Advertised finishes were Goldenburst and Cherryburst, but this instrument is in a rare Cardinal Red finish, as were other instruments that were displayed at the 1967 NAMM show in Chicago. Accordingly, it may have been the instrument displayed at that exposition, and may be one of a kind.

As was the case with other electric instrument lines, Gruggett's Stradette series never really got off the ground, and the company closed its doors in 1968.

Only a few Stradette basses were ever made. Gruggett recalled that they were built early in the company's brief history, and ended up as promotional/catalog display items, since orders weren't forthcoming.

This particular bass had reportedly been in the possession of the owner of a bar and restaurant in Bakersfield for decades. The restaurateur passed it on to his son, who sold it to the present owner.

Gruggett later worked as a builder and consultant to the present-day incarnation of Hallmark Guitars, which is located in Maryland. He died on October 6, 2012, at the age of seventy-five.

GUILD

Guild instruments are often unfairly portrayed in the vintage guitar market as less-desirable copies of Gibson guitars and basses. While numerous cosmetic similarities between certain models do exist, Gibson had its ups and downs regarding quality control, while Guild maintained a steady reputation for manufacturing well-made instruments in the decades since the company was founded in 1952, in the greater New York City area by accordion retailer/distributor Al Dronge (1911–1972) . . . and Guild ultimately went through more than one owner as well.

Many of Dronge's craftsmen were former Epiphone company employees who had opted not to move to Philadelphia with that builder (Epiphone was in a downward spiral anyway, and, as noted earlier, would be purchased by Gibson in 1957).

In 1956, Guild found a suitable production space on the top floor of the Neumann Leathers building in Hoboken, New Jersey, and would remain in that facility for a decade. In 1966, Guild was purchased by the Avnet company, and while Dronge remained as president, production was soon moved to a Westerly, Rhode Island, factory.

Dronge was more of a jazz fan and oriented his company more towards that style of music, so it shouldn't come as any surprise that Guild endorsers were also usually associated with that genre.

Guild began making solid body electric guitars and basses in the early 1960s, but its best-selling bass model over the decades would be the Starfire Bass, a thinline, double-cutaway semi-hollow model that was similar to a Gibson EB-2. The Starfire series of guitars had been introduced in 1960, as thinline, hollow body instruments, and had morphed to a semi-hollow style when the Starfire Bass was introduced in 1965. While the model did indeed fit the "Gibson copy" stereotype, it also happened to have its own intriguing features.

There was at least one significant difference between the Starfire and the EB-2 when the Guild bass debuted—originally, Starfire Basses had a Hagström Bi-Sonic pickup that was centered in the middle of the body (Hagström was a Swedish company), as seen the Cherry-finished mid-1960s example shown here. Some bass enthusiasts have pointed out that sonically, such a location might be preferable, as it would allow the top to vibrate more evenly.

Guild Starfire Bass, late 1960s. *Heritage Auctions*

Guild Starfire Bass, mid-1960s. *John Fell*

Chesterfield cigarette pack logo.

From the top down, the Starfire has a standard Guild center-hump headstock with 2+2 tuners, "peaked" logo, "Chesterfield" decorative inlay (so named because of its resemblance to the logo representing Chesterfield cigarettes), and a shield-shaped truss rod cover.

The neck is made from Peruvian mahogany and has a rosewood fingerboard with twenty-one frets. Scale of the instrument is 30½ inches.

The semi-hollow body was the same as used on Starfire guitars. It measured 16½ inches wide and 1⅞ inches deep (but was catalogued as being two inches deep). The body wood varied with the finish—Sunburst instruments had maple bodies, while Cherry-finished Starfires had laminated mahogany bodies (some natural-finish Starfires with maple bodies were also made). A typical Guild sunburst finish had more of an orange-ish tint to its lighter portion thaa a comparable Gibson.

Body edge binding on the Starfire Bass was three-layer, white/black/white, and the model sported two fingerrests (one of which is missing from the mid-1960s example on page 121).

The bridge/tailpiece unit was also made by Hagström and had rosewood saddles that could be intonated individually.

The Starfire Bass is touted in Guild's 1966 catalog as having, " . . . the acoustical advantages of a hollow body guitar in a double cutaway bass with famous Starfire features. Aided by the resonance of its arched top, this guitar propels your group with the tight, strong sound that keeps the other instruments rocking right along." (Sharp-eyed vintage buffs need to know that the catalog's text does indeed refer to the instrument as a "guitar" instead of as a "bass").

Around the advent of the 1970s, the Starfire Bass had seen its pickup moved to a neck position, and a Guild humbucker ultimately replaced the Hagstrom Bi-Sonic unit (although Starfire Basses with a Bi-Sonic located near the neck were in production for some time). An asymmetrical, slightly harp-shaped bridge/tailpiece plate also became standard.

A two-pickup Starfire Bass was introduced in 1967, and would be popularized during the psychedelic music movement by such San Francisco bassists as Jack Cassady of the Jefferson Airplane and Phil Lesh of the Grateful Dead (although such examples were often modified by the up-and-coming Alembic company). Berry Oakley of the Allman Brothers Band played a two-pickup Starfire before cannibalizing it.

The single-pickup Starfire Bass was discontinued in 1975, and while it may not have the historical significance of the Gibson EB-2 and/or its two-pickup Guild sibling (which was terminated in 1978, before being reintroduced in 1997), it's a unique example of why original Guild models from the 1960s are usually considered as underrated instruments for players and collectors.

In 1970, Guild introduced a new solid body series of guitars and basses that borrowed heavily from the silhouette of Gibson's SG-style body. The cutaways on Guild instruments were a bit more offset, but the comparison was obvious to any guitar enthusiast.

The silhouette and cosmetics of the new basses' headstocks and mahogany necks were the same as found on the Starfire Bass, as was the scale.

One-pickup (JS-I) and two-pickup (JS-II) models, which had mahogany bodies, were introduced at the same time. Unlike the two-pickup Gibson EB-3, which had two different pickups, the two Guild-made humbucking pickups on the JS-II were similar units. Moreover, the controls on the JS-II were laid out like a two-pickup guitar, with a separate volume and tone control for each pickup and a three-way pickup toggle switch. A mini-toggle phase switch was also included on the JS-II, although some JS-II examples without this feature may be encountered.

JS basses became available full-scale models beginning in 1972.

This 1973 natural-finish JS-II lefty may technically be a "JS-2," as 1973 was the annum in which the suffixes of the model numbers switched from Roman numerals to Arabic numerals.

The JS-1 was discontinued in 1976, and the JS-2 was outta there the next year, as Guild cleared the way for a new series of guitars and basses that didn't resemble Gibsons.

As noted earlier, Guild had been sold to the Avnet company in 1966. Founder Al Dronge was killed in a plane crash in 1972, and in the ensuing years the company would go through several owners and managers in what seemed to be fairly quick succession.

Considering Dronge's traditionalist attitude regarding guitar styles and guitar music, as well as the "looks-like-a-Gibson" stereotype of many Guild instruments, it may not have come as a surprise that the first major

Guild JS-II, 1973. *Heritage Auctions*

Guild B-302. *Heritage Auctions*

Guild B-302A. *Willie G. Moseley*

series of electric guitars and basses introduced after Dronge's death was a solid body aggregation that didn't resemble Gibson models.

Aesthetically, the new series (introduced in 1976) looked like nothing else (Gibson or any other brand). The unique body silhouette alluded to traditionally solid body cutaways on its upper bout (although the treble side horn was somewhat stunted), but the lower bout, with its rounded bottom edge that came to a point on opposite sides, was definitely different. Some individuals have referred to the lower half of the body as "bell-shaped," but to others it may have recalled Edgar Allen Poe's *The Pit and the Pendulum*. The basses in this lineup were the one-pickup B-301 and the two-pickup B-302.

Dimensions for the body (guitars and basses) was 14¼ inches wide, 17¾ inches long, and 1⅜ inches depth. The body also featured a belly cut on the back side.

The B-301 and B-302 had a three-piece mahogany neck and mahogany body, but alternate versions with maple necks and ash bodies were also marketed. Those variants were designated by the letter "A" following the model number.

Scale for the B-301 and B-302 was a new-from-the-outset thirty-four inches, and they had a rosewood fingerboard with mother-of-pearl dot markers on a twenty-fret neck that joined the body at the eighteenth fret. The entire series of guitars and basses had set-neck construction.

The width of the neck at the nut was 1⅝ inches. Fretless versions were available at no extra charge, according to a Guild catalog, which, interestingly, also listed all of the dimensions and other measurements in metric numbers.

The electronics for the basses consisted of one or two made-by-Guild single-coil pickups, with two polepieces for each string, and a separate volume and tone control for each pickup. The B-302 had a three-way toggle switch for pickup selection.

Hardware included Schaller tuning keys and a "newly engineered, fully adjustable, solid brass bridge/tailpiece," according to the catalog (the part was known as the BT-4). It, too, was also German-made, and was indeed quite hefty.

The catalog also touted the "white-edged laminated black pickguard."

The 300 bass series was discontinued in 1981, but some apparently leftover instruments were marketed with active electronics as the 400 series until circa 1983.

While unsuccessful, the basses in this slightly-weird-looking Guild lineup paved the way for other instruments that did not resemble Gibsons, including one of Guild's most popular bass series.

As interest in Guild's bell-shaped B-series instruments began to wane, the company opted to introduce the SB-200 series of basses in 1982, which had a body silhouette that was definitely more traditional/Fender-like.

The SB-200 series differed from Fender basses in more than one facet, however. The headstock was Guild's standard-for-the-times center-hump style with two tuners on each side, unlike Fender's four-on-a-side layout. The peghead also had a standard peaked Guild pearloid logo as well as the company's "Chesterfield" inlay.

Moreover, the neck of the SB-200 series was set-in instead of Fender's bolt-on style. The rosewood fretboard had dot inlay, was unbound, and had twenty frets. Scale was an industry standard thirty-four inches, and the neck width at the nut was 1⅝ inches.

The body width of this series was 13⅞ inches. While the cutaway horns were offset, they joined the neck within a half-fret's distance from each other. The bass side cutaway hooked up just past the seventeenth fret, while the treble cutaway met the neck at the eighteenth fret.

When the SB-200 series was introduced in 1982, the basic one-pickup SB-201 and two-pickup SB-202 were seen with the same "soapbar"-type Guild pickups that were found on the B-300/B-400 series models. Controls were, as expected, a volume and tone for the one-pick bass, and two volume controls and a master tone control for the two-pickup instrument. The SB-202 also had a phase switch.

The new series sported Guild's brass BT-4 bridge, also seen on the B-300/B-400 series. The pickguard (debuting in a single-layer white configuration) had an uninspiring oval shape, but had a notched angle at the bridge. The pickups had a somewhat generic layout on the pickguards of each model.

Guild SB-201, early 1980s. *Willie G. Moseley*

GUILD BASSES

Over the last few years, every guitar company has made an issue of the fact that contemporary bass players have more visibility in a band than at any time since the late 60s. We agree with this. More importantly, we did something about it.

Our SB-201, SB-202, and SB-203 models cut through to let players showcase their talents to the fullest. All these models offer exceptional balance and feel, plus quality hardware like our adjustable BT-4 bridge and Guild deluxe machine heads with a 22:1 gear ratio. The differences between models are in electronics. The SB-201 has one Guild split pickup with volume and tone controls. The SB-202 has two split pickups, phase switch, pickup selector switch, two volume controls and master tone control. The SB-203 has three pickups, which as far as we know, is an industry first for bass guitars. This offers the bassist 13 different tonal combinations.

For the more electronic oriented player who requires an extremely wide range of tonal potentials, we created our SB-502E model. Features active, on board equalization, two Guild special design pickups, two volume controls, bass EQ, treble EQ, pickup selector & phase switch, pre-amp on/off switch. Complete instructions, schematics and recommended setting are provided.

10

Catalog page, SB-201, SB-202.

By the next year, two other models had joined the 200 series, and Guild's 1983 catalog hyped the quartet by proclaiming, "Over the last few years, every guitar company has made an issue of the fact that contemporary bass players have more visibility in a band than at any time since the late 1960s. We agree with this. More importantly, we did something about it."

The catalog displayed an SB-201 and two SB-202s that now had black pickguards with a slightly different silhouette, as well as different pickup configurations—the SB-201's pickup was an offset, split unit, while the SB-202 had what would become known as a P/J layout.

The new three-pickup SB-203 was shown as having two offset P-type pickups with a third pickup, this one a "soapbar," in between; however, examples with three "soapbars" have also been seen.

The 1983 catalog proclaimed that the three pickups were, " . . . as far as we know, an industry first for bass guitars. This offers the bassist thirteen different tonal combinations."

Catalog page, SB-203, SB-502-E.

Well, apparently the folks at Guild were a bit more isolated than they should have been, information-wise, because Fender's three-pickup Bass VI had been released more than twenty years earlier (1961), and Gibson's G-3 bass had debuted with a trio of pickups in 1975.

The ultimate example of this bass series actually had a model number that did not begin with "2," thus emphasizing its uniqueness.

The SB-502E had active circuitry; the company had begun exploring that facet of stringed instrument innovation a bit earlier with models such as the B-401A. The SB-502E lacked a pickguard, probably due to the number of and/or placement of controls and switches on the body. The 1983 catalog noted the bass's capabilities as " . . . Bass EQ: +/- 13 dB, Treble EQ: + 15 dB/-20 dB." Both tone knobs had center detent.

In their brief history, the SB-200 series and the SB-502E were offered in sunburst, purple, white, black, candy apple red, black sparkle, and metallic blue finishes. Interestingly, "sunburst" may have meant more than one option; while numerous examples had a dark brown-orange-yellow finish (à la Fender), the earlier-style SB-201 shown here has a black-to-red finish.

All Guild bass models with this silhouette were outta there by 1984, with the exception of the SB-502E, which lasted one more annum. Accordingly, such instruments are relatively rare, since they were short-lived.

It's also not surprising that some unique variants of this series also exist, as exemplified by the close-up photo of the body of a candy apple red SB-202 with a newer-style, five-layer (black/white/black/white/black) pickguard. It most likely dates from early 1983, and its body is routed underneath the pickguard for three pickups; i.e., it appears that at one point the same bass body was used on SB-201s, 202s, and 203s, and this example has two soapbar pickups in the middle and bridge positions instead of the original/standard middle and neck locations.

A previous owner of this unusual SB-202 noted that the bass sounded " . . . a lot like a (Music Man) Sting Ray, only a little bit 'darker', because of the mahogany body."

Like almost all Guild basses, the instruments in this series were well-made and durable and are probably undervalued in the vintage guitar market.

SB-202 with different pickup layout, early 1980s. *Mike Ramos*

Guild would introduce its new SB/Pilot series of solid body basses in 1983, and they had a somewhat traditional (if slightly-elongated) solid body silhouette, which meant that the models' slightly body-heavy balance was quite comfortable for many players. More than one Pilot model would ultimately sport active electronics, and the series would also include one-pickup models and five-string versions.

The frontline instrument for the series was initially known as the SB-602 when it was introduced in 1983. It had a maple bolt-on neck and maple fretboard. Pickups were in a P/J configuration.

The next year, the model became known as the Pilot and acquired EMG active pickups and a rosewood fingerboard. The example seen here can still be pegged as an earlier example, however, as it has a nearly full-front matching pickguard, which wasn't around too long. Nor were the slightly oversized control knobs (two volume, master tone), which were replaced by Fender P-Bass/Telecaster-style knobs. The tuners and bridge/tailpiece are by Schaller.

Endorsers for the Pilot series included legendary bassist Jaco Pastorius, as well as Tom Hamilton of Aerosmith and Alec John Such of Bon Jovi. The Cars' Ben Orr played a Pilot that looked exactly like this black one at Live Aid (July 13, 1985).

Pilots went through four different headstock silhouettes during their time in the marketplace. Some earlier models were available with a Kahler bass vibrato.

The four-string Pilot became known as the Pro4 Pilot in 1993, and acquired a different control layout on a thinner, maple body (some examples of which had outstanding "flame" figuring).

A five-string model called the SB-605 Pilot had been introduced in 1986, and in 1993, became the Pro5 Pilot at the same time the four-string model changed monikers. Shown here is a Pro5 Pilot with the latter-day thinner body and standard gold hardware . . . and it'd make a very cool acquisition for a Green Bay Packers fan.

In spite of the better-than-usual success of Guild Pilots in the bass marketplace, the entire series was discontinued in 1995.

Guild Pro5 Pilot, mid-1990s. *Willie G. Moseley*

Guild SB-602 Pilot, mid-1980s. *Heritage Auctions*

Ad for the original Pilot bass w/ maple fretboard.

HALLMARK

Perhaps the most intriguing and striking design to emerge from the aforementioned short-lived and murky history of guitar building in Bakersfield in the 1960s was the appropriately-monikered Hallmark Swept Wing.

The founder of the original Hallmark company was former Mosrite employee Joe Hall, and this rare semi-hollow two-pickup Hallmark bass is owned by modern-day Hallmark builder Bob Shade of Maryland. Decades after the original Hallmark brand quickly flamed out, Shade's love of "the originals" inspired him to resurrect the brand, and Hall was a consultant for the new Hallmark line.

Hall had founded his company in 1965, and set up shop in Arvin, just down the road from Bakersfield. Hallmark marketed the Swept Wing as a solid body instrument (guitars and basses) in 1966. As it turned out, the modernistic style of the Swept Wing didn't fly—pun intended—with most musicians and musical instrument retailers. The lack of success by the Golden State company was somewhat reminiscent of the failure of Gibson's original Flying V and Explorer guitars almost a decade earlier.

Moreover, West Coast musicians may have been getting more oriented towards semi-hollow electric guitars around that time, in an effort to generate more feedback and sustain, as psychedelic music began to emanate from its musical womb in San Francisco.

Accordingly, in 1967, Hallmark decided to make semi-hollow Swept Wing instruments. He began the process by simply routing out sections out of the alder bodies of solid body examples of the same model to create a skeleton-like frame. A lift was then glued to the center of the front and back of the frame to support the arch of the top and back, which was constructed of marine grade laminated wood. The top veneer on such plywood was birch or a similar wood that had a decent grain pattern and was capable of having a quality finish applied to it. The completed semi-hollow body was 12½ inches wide and two inches deep.

The bolt-on neck on the bass was two-piece maple and had a rosewood fingerwood with twenty-one frets plus a zero fret, which was a mainstay of most, if not all, Bakersfield-area guitars. The neck's slim profile and thirty-inch scale made it extraordinarily fast and easy to play.

The two pickups are covered in cool tortoiseshell plastic. Note the angled neck pickup, à la Mosrite and Gruggett. Each pickup has four exposed non-adjustable Alnico rods, and although later Hallmark Swept Wing guitars had slightly different pickups with adjustable polepieces on their pickups, bass pickups didn't change.

Controls consist of a three-way pickup toggle switch on the treble cutaway, master volume and tone knobs, and a top-mounted jack.

The bridge cover, nickel-plated brass bridge saddles, and strap buttons, among other parts on this bass, came from Mosrite. However, Hallmark made their own bridge deck from stainless steel, while Mosrite used brass on the same part, and Hall recalled that his company made its own tailpieces.

Hallmark Swept Wing semi-hollow bass, 1967. *Michael G. Stewart*

The three-tone sunburst finish was also finished in the same process as Mosrite guitars and basses.

Asymmetrical oddities on the semi-hollow Swept Wings included a three-layer, white/black/white pickguard with a silhouette that looked like the blade of a battleaxe, as well as a small and slightly weird-looking f-hole.

The serial number is found on the neck mounting plate and the back, and Hall reported that his instruments' serial numbers did have a "code," which was somewhat like the Electronic Institute of America's code on potentiometers.

On this bass, "003127" indicates that it was the third instrument ("003") made in the twelfth week ("12") of 1967 ("7").

A 1967 Hallmark order form shows the semi-hollow line marketed as an "electric acoustic" series. On that form, the single pickup "Acoustic I" bass listed for $289.95, while the two-pickup "Acoustic II" listed for $312.95. The "Acoustic" series was only available in Sunburst or Cherry burst finishes.

In a 2004 interview, Hall recalled that he and Bill Gruggett split a booth at the 1967 NAMM show, displaying both brands and clearing off two of their tables at night to sleep on them, in order to save on hotel expenses.

Frugal practices by the founders aside, however, both lines folded soon afterwards.

Most Hallmark basses (solid and semi-hollow) were indeed one-pickup instruments. Two-pickup models were quite rare, so much so that Shade recounted that Hall seemed to think this bass was a one-off and was perhaps a special-order instrument.

"However, you just never know," Shade detailed. "There were a few more hollow-style basses made but not many at all. It was an attempt to satisfy all of the guys who were switching to 'hollows' during the psychedelic period."

Shade states that this instrument has, " . . . a very mellow, clear, and resonant sound. It really sounds quite amazing considering its small body. These are really cool instruments that have a rich, unique sound, and a look all to themselves."

Joe Hall died on February 11, 2011, at the age of seventy-two.

This photo from the 1967 NAMM exhibition shows the Hallmark and Gruggett brands on display in the same space.

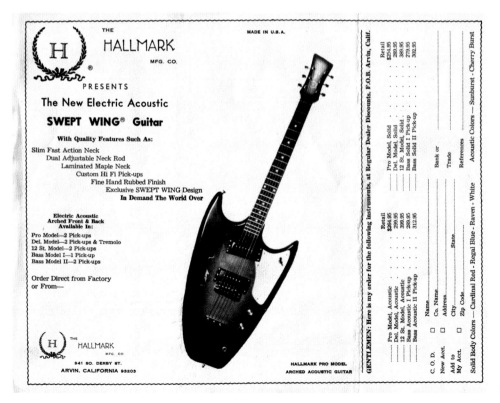

Order form.

"Dude, that is soooo 1980s!" exclaimed the music store owner when the case containing this instrument was opened for his perusal of the contents.

To longtime observers of the evolution of guitar aesthetics (particularly electric solid bodies), truer words may never have been spoken. This bass epitomizes the decade in which the "flash factor" was, to some cynics, at its zenith, as popularized by Spandex-clad "hair bands" playing such angular instruments, many of which also had unique and/or gaudy finishes.

And members of bands such as Judas Priest, Ratt, Motley Crue, and Def Leppard played Hamers.

The upstart manufacturer was founded in Palatine, Illinois, and later relocated to Arlington Heights in the same state. Hamer was at the forefront of designing, building, and marketing instruments with unique silhouettes ever since it introduced its zig-zag-shaped, Gibson Explorer-style Standard model guitar in the mid-1970s, and the company would go on to develop innovations such as the twelve-string bass and the DuoTone, a hybrid electric/acoustic instrument.

Like the Standard, Hamer's Blitz series of guitars and basses were also Explorer/zig-zag-shaped, and while the body dimensions of both series were the same, there were several construction variations between the models.

Differences between the Blitz series and the earlier Standard include edges of the body—Blitzes had a forty-five-degree, 3/8" bevel front and back, while Standards had a rounded back edge and usually had a bound, figured maple cap.

This Blitz Bass conforms to the construction stereotype of Hamer's 1980s "assembly line" (such as they were) instruments, with a Honduras mahogany body and neck with a mortis-and-tenon attachment juncture. Blitz fretboards were rosewood with pearl dot position markers.

Interestingly, the headstocks on many 1980s Hamers weren't particularly "pointy" (even if the body was angular), as exemplified by the one on this example—its profile is relatively close to a typical four-on-a-side, semi-Fenderish style as found on many a solid body bass.

The black Schaller tuners and bridge, which have the Hamer brand name embossed thereon, are also requisite 1980s items. This is a passive instrument; its pickups are by OBL and are in a P/J configuration. The not-particularly-inspiring three plastic control knobs, which look like they could also be found on the vent over a stove in a suburban home, operate two volume pots and a master tone pot.

Obviously, the most striking feature of this Blitz Bass is its finish, which is an example of Hamer's "Day-Glo Zulu" series. The company marketed instruments in three basic black-striped patterns called Zebra, Tiger, and Zulu, which were meant to evoke an African/tribal look. Any color—standard or Day-Glo—could be combined with such striped patterns, and sometimes, more than one color was applied. Accordingly, many unique variants of this concept will be encountered. Among the Day-Glo colors combined

Hamer Blitz Bass, 1980s. *Bill Ingalls Jr.*

with black-striped patterns were orange, pink, and lime, as well as combinations of such bright pigments.

This bass started out with the Zulu pattern on an orange base, with hot pink "splotches" randomly applied. The pattern is even found on the back of the neck, so sussing out the side dots on the fretboard might be a bit more of a chore.

One intriguing "Cracker Jack"/"case candy" relic inside this bass's case pocket is its never-filled-out warranty card, pre-addressed to Hamer's (now-non-viable) West University Blvd. location in Arlington Heights.

The original Hamer company was acquired by the builders of Ovation instruments, Kaman Music Corporation, in 1988. Ovation had been a major factor in the acoustic market for years, but had been unsuccessful in its electric solid body offerings, so the addition of Hamer provided a much-needed quality line in an important niche for Kaman. The Arlington Heights facility remained open until 1997, when production of Hamers was moved to Kaman's home turf in Connecticut.

Regardless of the brand on an instrument's headstock, an Explorer-inspired body silhouette is usually more comfortable to play than might be expected, and that's the case for this Blitz. Moreover, its OBLs provide a crisp and loud "thonk" that was usually compatible with the type of music with which it was stereotypically associated.

One wiseguy who saw this instrument (before its official color designation had been ascertained) observed that its frenetic finish should be called "Blushing Tiger on Amphetamines." True, it's a wild-looking example of a musical era that begat a plethora of such instruments, but its high-quality construction has insured that it's held up well, regardless of how much headbanging its owner(s) may have done.

The other Hamer bass shown here is a more-historically-important instrument from the same era and exemplifies the company's orientation towards innovation, as opposed to the "flash factor" of basses such as the Blitz with the Zulu color scheme.

There's a moment of stage banter heard on Cheap Trick's twenty-fifth anniversary live album, *Silver*, in which guitarist Rick Nielsen refers to bassist Tom Petersson as "the inventor of the twelve-string bass," and such a pronouncement is right on the money.

Petersson had indeed begun working with Hamer in the late 1970s regarding his ideas for a unique low-end instrument that would produce unique sounds, recalling in a 2007 interview: "I wondered what it would

sound like to have an instrument that could kind of be a bass and a twelve-string guitar at the same time. I wanted to have that 'orchestral' kind of sound pretty much for performance, since we didn't have a keyboard player, and there were and are times when Robin (Zander) just sings and doesn't play guitar. I actually only use a twelve-string bass for recording when I think it's needed, which turns out to be about a quarter of the time. Originally, I'd tried using an octave divider with my Fender electric twelve-string guitar, but that didn't work, so I started working with Paul Hamer and Jol Dantzig at Hamer on a bass that would do the same thing."

The basic premise of Petersson's invention is three strings per position—one standard bass string and two unison strings that are tuned an octave higher; i.e., in guitar range. The first Hamer effort was actually a ten-string bass, with E and A strings that had a single unison string and D and G strings that had two unison strings ("At Hamer, they were certain the twelve-string bass wouldn't work," said Petersson). Moreover, the earliest twelve-string bass efforts, with a second unison string in the E and A string positions, had a short scale, but it was ultimately decided that the innovative new bass needed to have a standard long-scale, as Petersson noted: "It took me ten years to convince Hamer to make me a long-scale twelve-string bass. Everybody knows that any long-scale bass is going to resonate better, and that's true for twelve-string basses as well."

Dantzig also weighed in on the development of a full-scale twelve-string bass.

"Mainly, the struggle was two-fold," he recalled. "First, the balance issues encountered with the small double-cutaway B-12 short-scale had to be overcome with a new shape. The increased tension of the longer scale was also proving to be a serious obstacle."

"The Cheap Trick boys came to the rescue on the first item by giving me a drawing submitted by a Japanese fan for a 'design a Cheap Trick guitar' competition," Dantzig remembered. "A Japanese company had already manufactured a guitar for (Cheap Trick guitarist) Rick (Nielsen), so it was a matter of adapting it for bass."

And this 1987 bass is the first instrument that fulfilled Petersson's (long-scale) quest. It has three pickups—one P-Bass type in a pseudo-soundhole for lower frequencies, and two OBL pickups for guitar tones, with a separate jack for each (Petersson would be able to utilize three amplifiers if desired). The controls were also unique—three volume knobs (no tone controls), with separate pickup off/on switches.

"The basic idea was to make it look like an acoustic guitar with a fake soundhole," said Dantzig. "The body was kept very thin to reduce the weight; even so, it weighed a ton! The top was made of spruce veneer to emulate the look of a flat-top acoustic."

This bass was used on the *Lap of Luxury* album, and was first seen in the video of "The Flame" when it was in its original blonde color. It also played the killer bass riff heard on Cheap Trick's cover of "Don't Be Cruel," but a checkered-finish bass, shown in an upright position on a peg, was "played" by Petersson in the video for that song.

"The checkerboard one was made after the recording, specifically for that video," Tom remembered. "I had checkerboard boots on, too. The blonde one was the only twelve-string on that record. In fact, it was the only twelve-string bass I owned at that time."

Petersson later returned the bass to Hamer to have it refinished in its current blue color, and subsequently place planet stickers on the top.

"I should have just had them make me a different one," he observed, "but they were kind of expensive."

Note that there are three sets of different tuners on the headstock—such an array would make for simplified tuning.

"The three different-size tuners just seemed to make sense to me," Dantzig said. "It was hard to keep track of which string you were tuning, otherwise. It also reduced headstock weight."

There's also the 1994 autograph by rockabilly legend Carl Perkins (1932–1998).

"I got the Carl Perkins autograph I got when we worked together for an Elvis tribute in Memphis," Tom remembered. "He was standing backstage, and I got it before (Cheap Trick) went on to play 'All Shook Up' with a bagpipe player."

More than two decades after Tom Petersson received the first full-scale Hamer twelve-string bass, it's still holding up just fine.

"Tom was always driving forward with the 'big vision' ideas," Dantzig remembered. "It was just my job to figure out the details to make it work."

"So far, so good," Peteresson said of his unique, first-of-its-kind instrument.

Hamer twelve-string bass, 1987, owned by Tom Petersson. *Willie G. Moseley*

HARMONY

To many guitar enthusiasts who pay attention to the history of US-built instruments, Chicago used to be to the American guitar manufacturing industry what Detroit used to be to the American automobile manufacturing industry. Huge Windy City-area companies like Harmony, Kay, and Valco cranked out truckloads of stringed instruments for many years. Such guitars and basses were usually student and/or budget-oriented, and had the companies' own brands emblazoned on their headstocks as well as dozens of house brands (some of which were so obscure that, unlike Sears' "Silvertone" brand or Montgomery Ward's "Airline," the lesser-known house brands are sometimes difficult to identify).

Harmony may well have been the "General Motors of guitar builders," as it has been proclaimed that at one point, that company was making more stringed instruments than all other US guitar makers combined (it helps, however, to note

that such production included banjos, mandolins, ukeleles, etc.). Yet the giant manufacturer, which went into business in the late 1800s, closed its doors in 1976, one of the latter-day examples of US budget guitar manufacturers biting the dust due to imported instruments.

As humungous as Harmony was, it seems to be inexplicable that its participation in the burgeoning electric bass market didn't come about until a decade after Fender introduced the Precision Bass in 1951.

Introduced in 1961, the H22 was a hollow body, single-cutaway, thinline instrument. The body, which featured a flat top and back (not arched) was constructed

Harmony H22, mid-1960s.
Heritage Auctions

Harmony H22/1, 1972, signed by B.B. King and ZZ Top.
Willie G. Moseley

of maple veneer. It was finished in a standard Harmony yellow-to-dark-brown two-tone sunburst finish, and had unbound f-holes. It also featured a bolt-on neck with an unbound, rosewood fingerboard, and had a thirty-inch scale. Interestingly, the four tuners were standard-size (instead of larger bass tuning keys), and the pair on each side of the headstock were mounted on metal strips that appear to have also been suitable for three-on-a-side guitar tuners, enhancing the Harmony assembly-line/standardization stereotype.

The H22's pickup was a Rowe-DeArmond unit, made in Toledo, Ohio. The volume and tone controls had "cupcake" knobs, so named because they had a cylindrical shape and serrated edges, resembling the paper containers in which cupcakes were baked.

The 1961 Harmony catalog touted the H22's two-position flip-switch, noting: "Finger tip switch provides a choice of full bass or lighter baritone registers." The switch was actually a tone bypass that generated full treble when activated, offering two

immediate tone choices on a single-pickup instrument. This feature was found on Harmony's first solid body electric guitar, the H44 (introduced in 1953), and other subsequent single-pickup electric guitar models.

Other items on the top of the body included a height-adjustable, non-compensating wood bridge, a fingerrest, and a tailpiece that looks like it covers something but doesn't—the strings simply load through holes in the end.

However, it was the large, triangular single-ply pickguard that was the obvious, kitschy 1960s attention-getter. Re-

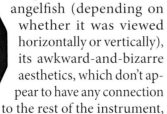

sembling a stealth bomber or angelfish (depending on whether it was viewed horizontally or vertically), its awkward-and-bizarre aesthetics, which don't appear to have any connection to the rest of the instrument,

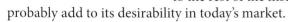

probably add to its desirability in today's market.

The H22 was ultimately supplanted by the double-cutaway H22/1, which debuted in the 1969 catalog. The revised bass featured a thumbrest as well as a fingerrest, set at opposing angles to each other, as well as a three-tone sunburst finish instead of a two-tone (Shades of 1950s Fender instruments!). The H22/1 last appeared in the 1971 catalog.

While initial examples of the H22 had unbound necks, it appears that most H22/1s had bound necks. Of course, as prolific as the Harmony company was, so-called "transitional" basses (H22s with bound necks, H22/1s with unbound necks) will probably be encountered, but such an in-between status won't necessarily enhance such an instrument's desirability or value.

The H22/1 seen here has been autographed by B.B. King (1925–2015) and all three members of ZZ Top (Billy F Gibbons, Frank Beard, Dusty Hill). Signed instruments are a separate and sometimes-nebulous facet of guitar collecting, with specific guidelines about provenance. Ideally, a photo of a celebrity actually autographing the instrument is the definitive type of validation.

Lightweight and easy to play, these Harmony basses were still a bit neck-heavy, as might be expected for any hollow body instrument. However, the H22 and H22/1 are fun to plunk and can sound pretty funky when roundwound strings and a pick get into the act. They're relatively affordable in today's market and can offer a nice time warp experience . . . musically and otherwise.

𝄢

During the "guitar boom" of the 1960s, Harmony not only struggled to keep up with the demand for instruments, but also sought to combat its image as a "cheapo" manufacturer. Its fanciest production lineup from that era was a series of thinline hollow body electrics that included four models of guitars and one bass.

The body for all five instruments had an arched top and back, and was made from laminated maple. It measured 15¾ inches wide and two inches deep, and the top sported two segmented f-holes. The bolt-on neck was maple with an "ovalled rosewood fingerboard," according to 1966 Harmony catalog text describing the guitars as well as the bass.

Cosmetic amenities abounded in this series, including multiple binding (six-layer on the top body edge, for example) and tortoiseshell celluloid overlays all over the instruments, including the headstocks, of all things.

The differences in the guitar lineup were relatively simple: The H75 had a distinctive harp-shaped tailpiece and was described as having " . . . rich brown mahogany shading with sunburst effect," but many vintage guitar aficionados would probably use the term "ice tea sunburst" to describe its finish, just as the same term applies to similar-looking Gibson instruments.

The H76 was an H75 with a Bigsby vibrato. The H77 also had a harp-shaped tailpiece, and its finish was pronounced to be a " . . . warm cherry red tone, lightly shaded." Perhaps not surprisingly, the H78 was an H77 with a Bigsby.

House brand versions of such guitars were also seen, the most prominent of which was a single-cutaway Silvertone model in a cherry finish.

The H27, the solitary bass in Harmony's fanciest series, debuted in the 1966 catalog and went in different directions from not only the logical lineup of its six-string siblings, but the H22 and H22/1 bass models as well.

While the H22 and H22/1 were single-pickup basses with a full-treble/tone bypass switch, the H27 had two DeArmond Golden Tone pickups with intriguing pairs of offset polepieces (eight per pickup) that were unique to this model (as well as a so-called successor—more about that later).

Harmony H76 and H27, mid-1960s. *Bill Ingalls Jr.*

As for the H27's cosmetics, it was only marketed in the light sunburst finish, and while its headstock was also laminated in tortoiseshell, it had a slightly oversized Fenderish four-on-a-side tuner profile, unlike the 3+3 headstocks of the guitars in the series.

Moreover, the H27 didn't have a tortoiseshell pickguard like the guitars, but its three-way pickup toggle switch, thumbrest, and fingerrest were tortoise-topped.

The guitars in this series had block fretboard inlays, but the H27 had dot position markers.

One bit of 1966 Harmony catalog hype is off-the-mark, as the H27 was described as having an "Ultra-Slim maple neck" that was, " . . . full scale, 30 inches from nut to adjustable bridge, Torque-Lok reinforced." As noted in the lexicon, thirty inches means "short-scale" in bass parlance, while "full scale" is considered to be thirty-four inches.

Like its pickups, the H27's bridge and tailpiece were also unique. Touted as "precision 6-way adjustable," the bridge, which had a snap-on cover, was similar to Gretsch's "Space Control" bridge; i.e., the six-way adjustment was for spacing between the four strings and height on either side, but no intonation was possible. The tailpiece, hidden under a cover that screwed onto the body, was a metal block with string grooves.

The H27 had separate volume and tone controls for each pickup; the knobs were cylindrical and silver-topped. This more-modern style of knob was also found on the H72 six-string model and the H79 twelve-string model.

Occasionally, notable flame-maple figuring could be found on the bodies of the H27 and corresponding guitars, enhancing their status as the fanciest Harmonys of their time.

However, the design of the H27 meant that it suffered from the same fate as other hollow body basses such as the Fender Coronado series—it was quite neck-heavy, and its lack of balance seems to be validated in a somewhat subliminal manner by the oversized headstock.

Harmony would later attempt to market a less fancy version of the H27. In the early 1970s, as the company was in its terminal decline, the H420 appeared on the bass scene, in an uninspiring wine/burgundy color. It sported cheaper parts such as a wood fingerrest and thumbrest, a white pickup toggle switch plate, and white control knobs.

The Harmony H27 has a decent sound and a very slim neck, which can make for easy plunking on its short scale. It also helps to remember that when it comes to the history of the Chicago manufacturer, this bass was the fanciest production item of its type that Harmony ever made.

🎼

As it turned out, Harmony was not only behind the timeline regarding electric basses, the gargantuan Windy City company also waited until the 1966 catalog to present a solid body bass.

Under the heading of "Silhouette Solid Body De Luxe Multi-Voice Bass," the H25 was indeed touted as part of the Silhouette series (guitars in that solid body lineup had debuted a couple of years earlier), and the 1966 catalog even advocated interpolating the H25 into the "matching instruments" concept for combos ("Available now to match the appearance of Harmony's renowned No. H19 De Luxe 6-string electric guitar. Permits your group to present look-alike instrumentation to your audiences.").

The H25, a short-scale instrument with a bolt-on twenty-fret neck, a rosewood fingerboard, and pearl dot markers, sported a silhouette (no pun intended) that seemed to hint at an exaggerated/caricature-like Fender shape. Like the H27 (introduced in the same catalog) the H25 sported a slightly oversized four-on-a-side headstock, and its double-cutaway body had parallel waists. Catalog text noted the model's, " . . . free form profile to give the player comfort and ease of handling."

Harmony's solid body bass did indeed match the H19 with which it was associated, as it was offered as a red-to-black sunburst, dubbed Cherry Red by the company, and its multiple-laminated pickguard had a tortoiseshell top.

Electronics consisted of a solitary DeArmond Golden Tone pickup (with adjustable polepieces) set at an angle, and a volume and tone control. The two rocker switches on the upper cutaway might cause some observers to scratch their heads, but their functions offered more tonal versatility—one is for "pre-set tone value," according to the catalog, while the other switch proffered "...multi-voicing from concert bass to baritone."

The bridge had a flip-up string mute (dubbed an "efficient string damper" by Harmony).

The H25 came with flatwound strings and listed for $174.50.

The same 1966 catalog page that had announced the debut of the H25 and H27 basses also introduced the H79 twelve-string electric guitar, so Harmony was indicating that it was determined to remain a player in the rapidly-evolving guitar market.

However, it was also intriguing to note another facet of the 1966 catalog hype, which emphasized that such products were American-made.

🎼

The display of instruments on the bass page of the 1972 Harmony catalog changed abruptly from the previous year's layout. The H22/1, H27, and H25 were all outta there in one fell swoop, and were replaced by the H420 thinline bass and the H426 solid body bass.

Harmony H25, mid-1960s.
Heritage Auctions

As noted earlier, the H420 was a cheaper version of the H27, with cheaper knobs and a nondescript burgundy finish that was much darker in person than the catalog image indicated. Its ad copy was still erroneously referring to the thiry-inch scale as "full bass scale."

The H426 solid body had two pickups. In addition to knobs controlling volume and tone, its rocker switches were now described as controlling "pickup selection and multi-voicing."

Such instruments weren't particularly inspiring when they were introduced, but Harmony was in decline anyway.

Like an aging, arthritic giant, Harmony's domestic production managed to limp along until finally giving up the ghost, as noted earlier, in the mid-1970s.

Harmony H420, early 1970s.
Willie G. Moseley

Harmony Electric Basses

H426. Solid Body Multi-Voice Electric Bass. GoldenTone bass double pickup, has adjustable magnetic polepieces under each string. Rotary controls for overall volume and varying tone; pivot switches for pickup selection and multi-voicing. Metal 4-way adjustable bridge has efficient string damper. Ultra-Slim adjustable reinforced neck. Rosewood fingerboard with 9 inlaid position dots and side dots. 30-inch scale. Flat wound strings. Handsomely polished cherry red sunburst finish.
Size 1½ x 13 x 44¾ in. $179.95

H0426. Carrying Case, Keratol, plush lined $26.50

H420. Thin Hollow Body Electric Bass. Double Cutaway with GoldenTone Double Pickup. Arched auditorium size. In rich polished burgundy finish, with bound top and back edges. Adjustable magnetic polepieces under each string. Individually covered tuning keys. Ultra-Slim adjustable reinforced neck is full bass scale, 30 inches from nut to bridge. Ovalled rosewood fingerboard with 9 inlaid position dots and side dots. 4-way adjustable bridge. Rosewood finger rest. Flat wound strings.
Size 2 x 15¾ x 45½ in. $199.95

H0420. Carrying Case, Keratol, plush lined $29.50

H426

H420

19

1972 Harmony catalog showing the all-new H426 and H420 models.

IBANEZ

The early-to-mid-1970s might be described as the, er, "glory days" for imported instruments that were blatant copies of classic American-made guitars and basses. In such times, the "vintage is cool" vibe concerning older US electric guitars was still in its infancy, and as is certainly the case these days, average players couldn't afford the original American items.

Accordingly, brands such as Ibanez, Aria, and Electra proffered guitars and basses that were cosmetically very close to all sorts of Gibson and Fender models that were new in the 1950s and 1960s. Not surprisingly, some copy guitars from the 1970s have been hyped in the used/vintage market as "lawsuit models," as litigation ultimately ensued.

Another facet of the early-to-mid-1970s copy market was the advent of bogus "replacement" Fender and Gibson headstock decals being offered for sale. Such items would often be seen on imported copies of historic instruments.

Usually, the Asian-made instruments that were copies of Gibsons had bolt-on necks, where the original American models had set-in necks. Sometimes, the copy guitars melded cosmetics from more than one classic model.

Emboldened by the sales of such instruments, importers began concentrating on emulating even more classic models in greater detail. Their retro-creations even included copies of guitars that were originally made in the US in minute quantities.

Ibanez went after the ultimately collectible original American rarities in the mid-1970s when the company presented cosmetically close copies of Gibson's "modernistic" trio of electric guitars from the late 1950s—the "Rocket Roll" was a copy of the original-style Flying V, the "Destroyer" visually channeled the rarer, zig-zag shaped Explorer, and the "Futura" was a nod to the patented-but-never-produced (except as a possible prototype) Moderne.

Ibanez Destroyer, 1977. *Vintage Guitar Magazine* archive

Such instruments attempted to reproduce the yellow see-through finish of the original Gibson modernistic guitars' "korina" bodies, which had been made from limba, an African mahogany-type of wood. To many observers, the bodies on most Ibanez copies looked like they were made of ash, but they were actually sen, another type of mahogany.

The success of the Ibanez retro-trio motivated the company to create two "retro" basses that gave a serious nod to late 1950s Gibson "modernistic" instruments, but weren't copies of previously-existing instruments.

In the case of the Rocket Roll Bass, a Gibson Flying V bass from almost a half-century ago never existed (or at least, has never been documented), so Ibanez's tribute instrument was actually a first-of-its-kind regarding retro cool.

On the other hand, Gibson did make at least one korina-bodied Explorer bass as a custom-order instrument around the dawn of the 1960s. It utilized bass parts found on other Gibson models and went through various modifications (and owners) after it was made. The solitary Explorer bass was a single-pickup instrument; a stereotypical large Gibson bass humbucker was mounted near the neck joint. In its history, it was reportedly refinished more than once, and at last report, had been restored to its original color and configuration.

The Ibanez Destroyer Bass is also relatively rare and has its own curious chronology regarding its marketing. While the model appears on a 1977 Ibanez price list of US-marketed models as "2459B Destroyer Bass, Long Scale . . . $450," a search of available American catalogs from the same era in Ibanez's history by more than one enthusiast hasn't revealed a photo of the model. The vintage store that was marketing this example hyped it as "never catalogued," and such a pronouncement appears to be true, at least within the US.

CHAPTER TWENTY-FOUR

However, an image of the Destroyer Bass was published in a 1977 German catalog, which indicates that certain models were made by the company for Europe, and one vintage authority describes the marketing of different Ibanez models for the US and Europe as "not uncommon."

Yet the Destroyer Bass wasn't a blatant "copy" of the solitary Gibson Explorer bass—the one-of-a-kind Kalamazoo creation had a short scale, and originally had rear-projecting/banjo-style tuners, à la other Gibson basses of the time.

Like its Gibson inspiration, the Ibanez model does have the scimitar/banana-shaped headstock, and the serial number embossed on the back of the headstock on this example indicates a manufacturing date of August 1977. Its #303 "Artist Bass" machine heads were standard configuration. It has a twenty-fret rosewood fretboard with dot markers on a set-in neck, and its scale was 33½ inches.

The yellowish-tinted sen body does indeed recall Gibson's "korina" finish. Like an Explorer, this instrument has a single-ply white pickguard.

Electronics include a 2365-50 "Super Bass" bridge pickup and a 2365-60 "Super Bass" neck pickup. What's interesting is that this P/J pickup configuration preceded Fender's own implementation of the P/J system by about a decade.

The three gold, barrel-shaped control knobs are, as expected, two volume and one master tone. Note the #203 three-point suspension bass bridge, which matches Gibson bass bridges on some of the Kalamazoo company's own 1970s basses, such as the RD Artist.

The Destroyer Bass is relatively balanced for its silhouette; i.e., if you like "reverse" Gibson Thunderbird basses, this one will probably feel somewhat similar. It's a unique example of the better-grade imported copy instruments that flooded the United States in the 1970s.

KALAMAZOO

In the guitar war that ensued between Gibson and Fender for market dominance in the 1960s, it's probably fair to opine that Gibson may have, er, "blinked" first. Gibson's Melody Maker line of budget guitars was making inroads, but those instruments still had set-neck construction, whereas part of a Fender guitar's appeal to many musicians was its bolt-on neck, which could easily be replaced if necessary. For that matter, the manufacturing process for a solid body electric guitar with a bolt-on neck was simpler and more efficient, which helps to explain why Fender had been coming on strongly in the guitar market early in the second half of the twentieth century.

Accordingly, Gibson opted to market an even-more-budget-oriented line of instruments and amplifiers in the middle of the decade, resurrecting the "Kalamazoo" brand name that had been used for budget guitars from the Thirties through the early 1940s.

Aimed directly at students/beginners (stereotypically a teenage male who had seen the Beatles on "The Ed Sullivan Show" in early 1964), the new Kalamazoo line was a solid body series with bolt-on necks, a first for the staid Gibson company. The solitary Kalamazoo bass was known simply as the KB.

The KB's maple neck had an un-Gibson-like four-on-a-side headstock with a vaguely-Fenderish shape (not a first for Gibson, as that style had already been introduced on Firebird guitars, Thunderbird basses, and the Trini Lopez signature model guitar). The Kalamazoo logo appeared to be "branded" into the headstock, and there was also a "USA" embossed beneath the name (probably an allusion to the encroachment of foreign-made budget instruments).

The rosewood fretboard had twenty frets, and the neck joined the body at the sixteenth fret on the bass side and the eighteenth fret on the treble side. Not surprisingly, the KB was a short-scale instrument.

The bodies of Kalamazoo instruments had one of the more unique, if ultimately cheap, innovations in the guitar business (at the time)—they were made of composition board, a.k.a. particle board, a.k.a. chipboard. Such material is common in the furniture manufacturing business, where its primary components of fine-grain

GUITARS

AMPLIFIERS

1966 catalog page.

sawdust and a bonding compound have resulted in the sarcastic term "glit" (a combined moniker derived from "glue" and "s**t").

Such bodies were dense and could be easily painted in a solid color, although their surface wasn't particularly smooth. Kalamazoo instruments were available in three finishes—Flame Red, Las Vegas Blue, and Glacier White.

Hardware for the KB included a handrest (missing from this example) and Gibson's longtime combination bridge/tailpiece with the angled saddle piece.

Kalamazoo guitars and basses shared the same white pickguard, which had a top-mounted jack, and compass-like markings by white molded plastic volume

Kalamazoo KB, 1965 (missing handrest).
Willie G. Moseley

and tone knobs (each of which had a pointer). The pickguard also had a rosewood fingerrest and a top-mounted jack.

As noted earlier, the KB also shared its pickguard, controls, and pickup with the Gibson Melody Maker Bass of the same era.

Gibson's new budget line started out with an offset body that had an obvious Fender vibe to most observers, but it quickly changed to a classic Gibson SG silhouette.

A 1966 Kalamazoo brochure contained a photo of the KB bass in a Glacier White finish (and already in the SG body style), with ad copy that read: "Modern styling in a solid-body four-string bass that offers full, true bass tones in a sleek, rugged, economically priced instrument. With one pickup of extremely powerful design and full volume and tone control, the Kalamazoo Bass creates the full driving bass sound that sells a combo."

It's doubtful that Gibson actively pursued endorsers for the Kalamazoo line, since the company usually sought professional musicians—and not necessarily rock and roll players—to endorse the high-quality instruments in its primary line.

That being said, the advent of Kalamazoo electric guitars, basses, and amplifiers indicated Gibson also recognized that the 1960s guitar boom was for real, and this budget line was one way for the venerable manufacturer to reach for its share of the lower-priced instrument market. One can only guess at how many budding Baby Boomer bassists started out on this brand and model.

And as a bonus, here's a Kalamazoo KG-2 guitar in the same body style and color, averring that even youngsters playing their very first instruments in their very first bands had access to the "matching instruments" concept (and such a notion may have actually been more proportionally important to adolescent musicians). It has a more-recent aftermarket (and intonatable) bridge/tailpiece unit, and was signed on October 25, 2002, by guitarist Steve Howe and guitarist Chris Squire (1948–2015) of Yes, during that band's "Full Circle" tour, which was the last concert tour that featured the classic Yes lineup of Jon Anderson, Rick Wakeman, Alan White, Howe, and Squire. Passes from that particular concert are displayed in the strings.

Kalamazoo KG-2, 1965.

KAY

The Merriam-Webster online dictionary defines "kitsch" as "something that appeals to popular or lowbrow taste and is often of poor quality," and that term, or similar derogatory invective, will sometimes be heard or read when a legendary brand in the pantheon of vintage electric guitars and basses, Kay, is being discussed.

The Chicago-based manufacturer had actually made some very early contributions to attempts to amplify guitars, as in 1929, the Stromberg-Voisinet company, which later evolved into the Kay enterprise, announced electric instruments in an ad, but the marketing attempt was unsuccessful. What's more, Kay was also a large manufacturer of upright/"doghouse" basses.

But many knowledgeable collectors tend to stereotype Kay guitars and electric basses as tacky or homely inexpensive instruments from the 1950s and 1960s. In their time, Harmony and Kay were considered to be the "Big Two" of American budget/cheapo guitar manufacturers, and that generalization is fair, compared to what other guitar manufacturers were accomplishing in the same era.

Kay's first efforts with fretted electric basses came about in the early 1950s, soon after the Fender Precision Bass abruptly changed the low-end facet of contemporary music.

The initial electric bass offered by Kay was the K162, a sibling of the K161 "Thin Twin" electric guitar. The body dimensions were the same for both instruments—15¼ inches wide, 2⅞ inches deep at the end pin (slightly thinner at the neck joint). Construction was all maple with a flat top and a primitive type of semi-hollow configuration—there was a center block running the length of the body.

So, Kay Thin Twins and K162 basses were, technically, forerunners to the innovative semi-hollow series from Gibson that debuted in 1958. However, such Kay instruments didn't have soundholes, and it appears that the main function of the center block was to support the massive magnet(s) of the pickup(s)—that's just the top blade of the pickup poking out on the top of several earlier Kay basses on display here.

The K162's headstock had individual tuners, and its set-in maple neck had a rosewood fingerboard. The scale was 30¼ inches. The neck binding had dot side markers that were ⅛-inch in diameter.

Interestingly, a side-by-side comparison of a K161 guitar with this K162 revealed that the guitar has a flat back, while the bass has an arched back.

The single-pickup was controlled by a volume and tone control, and a two-way toggle switch that bypassed the tone control for a full-on bass sound was also found on the control plate. The configuration of the two knobs was the reverse of most electric instruments from other manufacturers; the tone knob was closer to the toggle switch (and Kay would continue the backwards alignment on other models).

Kay K162, 1950s. *Bill Ingalls Jr.*

ment with different-colored trim. However, there were intriguing differences in its configuration as well as its cosmetics. In addition to the off-white control plate and trim around the pickup, the K5965 had four-ply, white/black/white/black edge binding, and the side dots on the neck binding were now 3/16-inch in diameter. A slightly-different-but-still-primitive bridge was found on the top.

Construction-wise, the pickup on the K5965 was located elsewhere on the top; the center of its "blade" was now 1 5/16-inch from the end of the fretboard. Moreover, the bottom of the neck joint was located ¼-inch above the bottom edge of the body.

By 1961, the K5965 had acquired a "Pro" nickname in the Kay catalog, but in 1964, a "Pro" model with a different model number and configuration would appear.

In their time, such basses simply did their job for many players and held up reasonably well—no muss, no fuss.

More recently, vintage examples of the earliest Kay electric basses have been associated with Sheryl Crow, and as noted earlier, re-issues have been created by noted luthier Roger Fritz. As of this writing, imported versions (with historically-inaccurate but cool-looking "keystone" headstocks) are also being marketed, so apparently there has been enough interest in the original Kays' looks and sound to merit the creation of a new generation of such instruments.

Binding on the edges of the K162's body is five-ply white/black/white/black/white. The garish tortoiseshell plates around the pickup and controls are obvious examples of why Kay instruments figure into the aforementioned "kitsch" category. There's a primitive wooden bridge, and the bottom edge of the neck joint is flush with the bottom edge of the body. On the top, the center of the pickup "blade" is 2⅛ inches from the end of the neck.

The catalog fanfare that announced the K162 included the phrase "Not a guitar . . . it's a big bass viol!," and proclaimed that the new electric bass was " . . . a product of nearly ten years' research." Bassist Chubby Jackson, who had also endorsed Kay upright instruments, was pictured trying out the newfangled Kay bass that looked like a guitar.

"Although the 'guitar stance' is a bit unfamiliar to Chubby, he is among the many famous musicians who say this instrument opens the door to an entirely unexplored field of performance," the ad text trumpeted.

The new K615 bass amplifier, with six tubes and a single fifteen-inch Jensen speaker, was also proffered on the same catalog page.

A similar-looking, slightly-lower-priced bass called the K160 briefly joined the K162 in the mid-1950s, and by the end of the decade the K162 had been supplanted by the K5965, an instrument that, at first glance, might have been thought to be the same instru-

Quite possibly the epitome of aesthetic excess in the history of Kay electric basses (and one of the wackiest/gaudiest instruments in the entire history of electric basses, for that matter), the double-cutaway K5970 "Jazz Special" first appeared in Kay's 1960 catalog. It was priced at $195 and would maintain that price point for the duration of its existence (around three years).

An apparent attempt to, er, jazz up the K5965, the Jazz Special came in two finishes, Jet Black (K5970J) and Natural Blond (K5970B).

Catalogs during the K5970's time dubbed it "our finest model," and touted its construction features: "Beautiful select curly maple body, hard 'rock' maple neck, genuine rosewood fingerboard. Beautifully hand-rubbed and polished to a rich deep luster." Like the K5965, the body was bound front and rear.

The "K" on the oversized headstock has sometimes been called the "Kelvinator" logo, as it reminded some observers of an appliance company symbol. The fingerboard had twenty frets, no markers, and joined the body at the fifteenth fret.

The pickup, bridge, and tailpiece were the same as found on the K5965; note that the pickup is angled on this model, however. There's also an odd, modernistic-shaped pickguard that contains the volume and tone controls. There's no tone switch, and the knobs are inexplicably close to each other.

On the pages of the Kay catalogs in which the Jazz Special appeared, the K5965 (now nicknamed the "Pro") was priced at $150, while two other bass models, which also debuted in the 1960, were priced at only $79.95 (and like the K5970, would retain that price for the entire time they were in the line).

Part of Kay's "Value Leader" series, the K5961 (four-string model) and K5962 (six-string bass guitar—not shown in catalogs) were simply guitars with bass parts on them.

Kay K5961, early 1960s. *Heritage Auctions*

The striking impression you make on your audience—
that's impact! You want your impact to be "Great performance! Great performer!" So head for a Kay. **Each Kay—in its looks, tone, response—is designed to help you make the most sensational impact ever!**

KAY ELECTRIC BASSES—Now every combo can feature the "bass sound" . . . because on these easy-to-play electric basses, any guitarist can double on bass! The electric bass has exactly the same range and tone as the big bass viol—tuned E-A-D-G, like the last four guitar strings, but one octave lower. Ideal for sustained tones and lightning fast action.

KAY "JAZZ SPECIAL" ELECTRIC BASS: our finest model features a double cutaway for greatest playing ease. Large, easy-tuning machine heads. Beautiful select curly maple body, hard "rock" maple neck, genuine rosewood fingerboard. Beautifully hand-rubbed and polished to a rich deep luster. Powerful magnetic bass pickup, fully adjustable for perfect string balance. Separate tone and volume controls.
K5970J (shown) Jet black. **$195.00**
K5970B Gleaming natural blond. **$195.00**

KAY "PRO" MODEL ELECTRIC BASS: a real swinging bass! Laminated curly maple body, arched back—44" long, 15" wide. Heavy celluloid-bound edges. Individual geared machine heads. Rosewood fingerboard, hard maple neck. Adjustable rosewood bridge. Top quality special electric bass strings. Adjustable magnetic bass pickup unit with separate tone and volume controls. Hand-rubbed and polished shaded brown finish.
K5965 (shown) "Pro" Model Electric Bass. **$150.00**
170C Deluxe padded carrying bag. Made of long-wearing, water-repellent plastic that looks like fine leather. Two large pockets, zipper closing. To fit K5970 or K5965. **$37.50**

KAY "VALUE LEADER" ELECTRIC BASS: a tremendous value! Small and compact, yet it has the "big" bass tone. Laminated maple body with celluloid-bound edges. Steel-reinforced neck. Magnetic pickup unit with separate tone and volume controls. Detachable cord.
K5961 (shown) Four-string model (E,A,D,G) **$79.95**
K5962 As above, but 6 strings (E,A,D,G,B,E). Same as Spanish guitar, but one octave lower in tone like the bass. **$84.95**
9619 Carrying case for K5961 and K5962. **$10.50**

$195⁰⁰
K5970

$150⁰⁰
K5965

$79⁹⁵
K5961

KAY STEEL GUITARS are designed to produce true Hawaiian tones . . . and jazz licks, too! They're terrific-looking models, with powerful pickup units.
K1560 Pro model. A classic black-and-white model, with powerful unit that has tone and volume controls. Detachable cord. Musically inspected. Guitar only, **$99.50**
155C Carrying case for K1560. **$12.00**

555L Adjustable nickel-plated legs for K1560. Adjust from 24½ to 45". Fit into sockets in guitar body. Set of 3, **$19.50**

$99⁵⁰
K1560

$229⁵⁰
K515

KAY HEAVY-DUTY BASS AMP has been designed specifically to reproduce the true bass tone. Powerful 7-tube circuit delivers 15-watt undistorted output. Specially-designed 15-inch heavy-duty speaker. Vibrato circuit with separate intensity and amplitude controls. 4 inputs. Stand-by switch; on-off switch with pilot light. The cabinet measures 20 x 24".
K515 Kay Heavy-Duty Bass Amp. **$229.50**
9652 Heavy, clear plastic cover to fit K515 amp. **$6.50**

K157 Student Special. Powerful magnetic pickup. Hardwood body with modern black-and-white finish. **$49.50**
157C Case for K157. **$9.00**

$49⁵⁰
K157

The Jazz Special and Value Leader basses both appeared for the first time in the 1960 catalog.

The hollow body was maple, as was the neck, which was a first-for-Kay-basses bolt-on item. The fingerboard, which usually had red tortoiseshell fret markers, was also maple, as was the bridge.

In the 1960 catalog, the headstock logo was shown as a 1950s-style Kay script inside an oval, but the 1961 edition showed a new tin logo with a "Kelvinator" K. The bottom attachment hole of the logo plate lined up with the top hole of the white, bell-shaped truss rod cover.

The pickguard was a textured aluminum parallelogram, with small volume and tone control knobs installed thereon. The flat, nondescript pickup, which mounted on the top, wasn't particularly inspiring regarding its sonic abilities.

The fact that catalogs in which the Value Leader appeared showed it with the aforementioned maple fretboard and tortoiseshell markers means that the example on page 143 is an aberration, as it has a rosewood 'board. What's more, many Kay instruments had double-dot inlay on other frets besides the (usual) twelfth fret.

The Jazz Special and the hollow body, guitar-scale Value Leader basses were outta there by 1964, as was the K5965. The "Value Leader" term showed up circa 1966–1968 on a series of single-pickup, solid body basses with a 30⅞-inch scale.

𝄢

This inexpensive model K5915 bass is noteworthy for what it—and similar house brand models—*didn't* have.

Such basses did have typical Kay features such as a hollow, single-Florentine (pointed)-cutaway body (with a flat top and back made of maple), checkered binding (not seen on all Kay hollow body instruments or house brands), and a single, anemic-sounding "Kleenex box" pickup (so named because the cover resembled plastic cosmetic covers for tissue boxes during the same era; it has also been dubbed the "speed bump" pickup, also for aesthetic reasons).

But what the instruments don't have is any type of fret/position markers—no dots on the fretboard or on the side of the neck. The same had been the scenario for other Kays on the fretboard only, but the 1960s "guitar boom" was well underway when these instruments debuted, and if this was supposed to be some kind of cost-cutting procedure for Kay, it seems to have been an erroneous ploy, considering that instruments such as these were

primarily aimed at novices. Almost any beginner would surely have appreciated some kind of visual reference on his/her instrument.

Moreover, a 1964 Kay catalog referred to the K5915's "full 30⅞-inch bass scale," when such a measurement would actually be considered short-scale among most bassists . . . or maybe Kay was comparing the scale of the K5915 to the guitar-like scale of the K5961 and K5962 Value Leader basses.

𝄢

While Kay had gotten into the electric bass market in the early 1950s with its technically semi-hollow K162 model, the company would also wait, like Harmony, until the mid-1960s to enter the solid body bass arena.

Appearing alongside two hollow body basses in the aforementioned 1964 catalog, Kay's K5930 "Deluxe Solid Body Bass" was touted as, " . . . our finest model. The sound you've been waiting for—crisp, clean, full."

The K5930's maple body was finished in " . . . shaded brown walnut, hand-rubbed and polished to a lustrous finish," and there seemed to be a vague Mosrite reference in its silhouette (but there probably wasn't an intentional connection). The bolt-on neck had an upside-down style headstock (tuners pointing towards the floor) and a rosewood fretboard. Compared to its hollow body compatriots of the same era, the K5930 has no position markers on the fretboard, but there are dot markers on the side of the neck. Like the K5915, the catalog erroneously referred to the K5930's 30⅞-inch scale as "long."

The new solid body had a Kleenex box/speed bump pickup, and its cheap-looking volume and tone control knobs, as well as an input jack, were mounted on a blob-shaped tortoiseshell plate.

The K5930 apparently went through a couple of refinements in its brief history, as the example seen here has a more traditional headstock, sporting a triangular logo that was seen on other Kay instruments later in the 1960s. By the time the 1966 catalog was released, the model had been replaced by other solid body basses.

𝄢

The 1966 Kay catalog presented no less than a dozen different solid body basses, of which this instrument was an example . . . or was it?

The least expensive series of Kay basses offered in that annum was the déja-vu-monikered Value Leader lineup, which included the

Kay K5915, mid-1960s.
Willie G. Moseley

145

K5917 ("Striking red finish"), K5918 ("Soft Teal blue finish"), and K5919 ("Shaded Walnut finish, golden highlights"). Each instrument listed for $79.50, with a "sturdy chipboard carrying case" available for $16.50.

The silhouette of the Value Leader solid body bass lineup was a bit more "pointy" than Kay's other bass profiles, and the headstock style seen here has been dubbed as the "bush axe" by many vintage enthusiasts (and there's also the ubiquitous bell-shaped truss rod cover). The neck bolted on with three large wood screws. Pearl dot markers on the rosewood fingerboard were offset to better facilitate visibility to a player—Kay had apparently learned its lesson regarding fretboard markers. The slightly asymmetrical body style bears a mild resemblance to (imported) Electra MPC basses of the mid-1970s, but it's doubtful that Electra got its inspiration here.

Electronics consisted of a single Kleenex box/speed bump pickup. As expected, the knobs looked cheapo, and the, er, extremely-no-frills bridge and tailpiece were hidden under a chrome cover that was installed with a single screw.

K5930, mid-1960s.
Michael Law

Kay K5918 (variant?),
1966. *Dean Moody*

This particular bass happens to be finished in an original leaf green color; i.e., it's not a K5918 that has yellowed due to age. The finish on this instrument was possibly an experiment, or maybe it was assembled from leftover parts and then finished in a unique color. Note that the cover for the bridge and tailpiece is missing.

The solid body Value Leader series came along around the time Kay was beginning to go into a tailspin due to the influx of imports, and following a merger with what remained of the Valco company, some instruments were seen sporting parts from both manufacturers.

So it stands to reason that this bass may have been some kind of "after-the-fact" item, built—or at least painted—in the final days of Kay, or even after its demise.

Kay's merger with the remnants of Valco proved unsuccessful, and the once-humungous Chicago-area manufacturers were history by the end of the 1960s. Kay's assembly-line products weren't necessarily of the highest quality, nor were they particularly innovative, but an untold number of aspiring musicians, some of whom went on to become professionals, played their first licks on a cheap Kay guitar or bass.

KRAMER

One American guitar company that made a big splash when it entered the instrument marketplace in mid-1976 was Kramer. The enterprise was originally a partnership between Dennis Berardi, former Gibson vice-president Peter LaPlaca (see Barrington), financial backer Henry Vaccaro, and Gary Kramer, who had been one of the financial backers of Travis Bean's slightly-earlier venture in building solid body electric guitars and basses with aluminum necks (see Travis Bean).

While Gary Kramer left the company that produced instruments bearing his surname within a year after the brand was introduced, Kramer guitars and basses were marketed aggressively during the brand's early days, and catalogs from that era were full of photos of noted players.

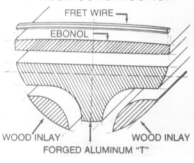

"T" NECK CONSTRUCTION

FRET WIRE
EBONOL
WOOD INLAY   WOOD INLAY
FORGED ALUMINUM "T"

Kramer neck cross-section.

The aluminum necks on Kramer instruments differed from those on Travis Bean instruments in several ways— Kramers had a type of bolt-on neck, while Travis Beans had a neck that ran all the way to the bridge. Moreover, the aluminum portion of Kramer necks actually had a "T" shape, with two wood inserts added to (a) reduce weight and (b) provide a more natural feel to players. The fretboard on Kramer instruments was made of Ebonol, a synthetic substance similar to bowling ball material.

Another distinctive (cosmetic) feature of the aluminum neck was the "tuning fork" headstock.

The initial Kramer lineup consisted of two guitars and two basses, displayed in a four-page brochure in 1976. The fancier bass was the 450B, which had two pickups that were adjusted for height from the rear of the body, and Schaller M-4 tuners. The neck was 1⅝ inches wide at the (aluminum) nut, and the fretboard had twenty frets, joining the body at the seventeenth fret on the bass side and the nineteenth fret on the treble side. The 450B had block-shaped markers starting on the first fret. Catalog hype noted "tropical imported body woods," including Shedua, Bubinga, Afrormosia, and Swetenia, and stated that the 450B weighed approximately ten pounds. Controls were guitar-like, with separate volume and tone controls for each pickup, and a three-way toggle switch.

The next year, the 450 guitar and bass had their own "Deluxe Series" brochure, as Kramer quickly added new models in other series ("Special," "Standard," and "Artist"). The 450B was shown in the configuration seen here; it appeared to be a walnut body with a maple-and-walnut center stripe (but the brochure made no mention of body woods, tropical or otherwise).

The fretboard now had aluminum dot markers, starting on the first fret.

By the 1978 catalog, the bodies and pickup rings of the 450 Deluxe series were identified as being made of "select American black walnut and maple." For the first time, the text noted that the pickups were single-coil.

The year 1978 also heralded the introduction of Kramer's new DMZ series, which had "specially designed" pickups made by DiMarzio.

"Conceived and designed by Kramer with the input from selected top recording artists, these models

Kramer 450B, 1977. *Heritage Auctions*

CHAPTER TWENTY-SEVEN

Kramer DMZ 4001, circa 1979.
Heritage Auctions

deliver exactly what the artist needs when performing today's style of music, both live and in the recording studio," the catalog trumpeted.

The exemplary DMZ 4000 model had a DiMarzio "P bass" offset pickup with active circuitry. It had two mini-switches for power and tone. The neck was the same as found on the 450B and other models, and the catalog touted three body finishes—maple with walnut stripes, walnut with maple stripes, and black.

The next year, 1979, saw the introduction of the DMZ 4001, a passive version of the 4000, which meant that the model had only one mini-toggle for tone. "It offers the bassist all the innovative features Kramer is known for at a modest price," said the 1979 catalog. Body finishes were listed as maple, walnut, or black; there was no citation of alternate wood "stripes" on this model.

Which means that the DMZ 4001 shown here may be a bit unique, in that its body does indeed have inlaid walnut striping.

Usually, black pickups on the DMZ 4000 and the DMZ 4001 were surrounded by a small black plate shaped like an elongated hexagon, while crème-colored pickups usually didn't have a surrounding plate.

Soon after the 1980s began, Kramer began orienting itself towards manufacturing guitars and basses with wooden necks. Aluminum T-necks went the way of Beta video recorders,

Kramer Duke Deluxe, early 1980s. *Bill Ingalls Jr.*

and the last series of Kramer basses that had such metal parts was the unique headless Duke lineup.

Some bass aficionados might presume that the Duke was a less-fancy copy of the innovative Steinberger headless bass, but the actual chronology of its evolution is somewhat different.

Kramer's TL-8 model, a short-scale eight-string bass that had four tuning pegs on the headstock and four tuning pegs anchored to the end of the body, was experiencing production problems, and when an employee happened to chop off the wood "wings" on either side of a TL-8 body, he noticed that the center section of the body, with those four tuners on its end, now had a semi-Steinberger look. Chopping off the tuning fork headstock added to the Steinberger vibe even more.

Accordingly, the first one hundred or so Dukes were made from bodies that were originally intended to be on TL-8 basses.

Duke basses had a short scale of 30⅜ inches, and the Ebonol fretboard had twenty-four frets. While the necks still had wood inserts, they were painted over to match the body of the instrument. Dukes used regular bass strings (unlike Steinbergers, which were normally fitted with a double-ball string). The ball end of the standard string

attached to the headless end of the neck and the standard tuners on the end of the body were made by Schaller.

The Duke Standard usually had a DiMarzio pickup and a standard Schaller bridge, while the Duke Deluxe (shown here) had a Schaller "Double J" or JBX pickup, an upgraded Schaller bridge, and a three-way mini-toggle for series, parallel, or phase pickup coil selection.

The bottom edge of the Deluxe sports a textured pad to allow the instrument to be played in a more stable manner in a seated position. And while the jack is on the same bottom edge of the Deluxe, it's on the top of the Standard's body, but some variants (a Standard with a bottom edge jack, for example) may be encountered.

Dukes may be somewhat sonically-challenged due to their small bodies and short scales, but are extremely lightweight and easy to play, and their pickups provide a decent sound.

Kramer eventually switched exclusively to wooden neck/traditional solid body instruments. The company encountered financial problems in the ensuing years, and the brand was ultimately acquired by Gibson.

CHAPTER TWENTY-EIGHT

Sometimes, certain retail establishments will get into a different facet of business because (a) they feel like they may be missing a particular segment of a potential market, and/or (b) they feel like they have to get into such a segment to keep up with the times, even if said new segment (for the company) may not be perceived (in advance) as vital to the company.

Musical examples, at retail, include instrument stores whose "bread and butter" customers are high school marching bands, yet the stores (sometimes grudgingly) stock electric guitars. Ditto for pawn shops—the "Big Three" for those establishments are gold, diamonds, and guns. Many hock shops take in musical instruments simply because they feel like they have to.

And the musical instrument manufacturing business is also replete with examples of companies venturing into alternate and extraneous territory, and all too often such efforts "bomb." Fender's failed acoustic series from the early 1960s is exemplary, but one of the most notable chronologies in guitar lore was that of C.F. Martin's electric guitars and basses.

The first electric efforts by the venerable Nazareth, Pennsylvania, acoustic guitar company came about in the late 1950s, when Martin simply installed DeArmond pickups on flat-tops such as the 00-18, D-18, and D-28. Said guitars had an "E" added to their model name to designate their electric status and were discontinued by the mid-1960s.

However, Martin undertook production of specific archtop electric guitar models during the 1960s "guitar boom" as well. The company made and marketed the "F" and "GT" series of thinline electrics, but that effort was abandoned in 1968.

The company did begin to install tranducers on its acoustics in the mid-1970s (and still does), but it's interesting to note that even during the 1960s, Martin didn't pursue solid body instruments . . . or electric basses.

In 1979, Martin re-entered the electric guitar market, marketing the solid body "E" series, which consisted of the E-18 and EM-18 guitars, and the EB-18 bass. As the company's first venture into the electric bass market, however, the EB-18 didn't exactly set the world on fire ... or even ignite a huge amount of interest. It was well-made but didn't seem to have anything particularly innovative going for it, and that perception seems to have been applicable to the entire solid body line.

From the top down, the EB-18 had what was termed as a "modified Viennese" headstock shape with a rosewood veneer overlay. One might wonder how enthusiastic Martin was about promoting the solid body series, as only "CFM" appears on the headstock of such guitars and basses, although a standard "C.F. Martin & Co." logo was woodburned into the neck joint in back on most instruments (the earliest examples being the exceptions).

As for the silhouette of the headstock itself, cynics have pronounced it to look like everything from a, er, "deflated condom" to the head of one of Casper the Friendly Ghost's uncles ("Fatso," "Fusso," and "Lazo," a.k.a. "The Ghostly Trio"). It may have been designed to evoke a European/Stauffer reference (i.e., Martin's "roots"), but to many observers, it was just plain homely.

Tuners were originally Grover Titans, later supplanted by Schallers, and in a sonic nod to the times, the EB-18 had a brass nut.

The mahogany set-in neck had an adjustable truss rod, and its feel might be described as "beefy but not uncomfortable." The rosewood fretboard had twenty-two frets and a 33.825-inch scale. Note that the pearl dot position markers feature two dots on the seventh fret, as often seen on many Martin acoustic models.

Martin EB-18, c. 1979. *Vintage Guitar Magazine* archives

The satin-finished maple body had laminated strips of rosewood or walnut. The body silhouette was double-cutaway and "uncomplicated"—not visually striking (which may have been why the inlay stripes were included), but not offensive or radical, either. It also featured standard locking strap buttons to secure the bass strap.

(Passive) electronics consisted of a DiMarzio Model One pickup on the earlier examples of the EB-18, and a DiMarzio "G" pickup on later ones. Controls included a two-position dual-sound switch and master volume and tone controls, which were capped by chrome, P-Bass-type knobs.

The chrome-plated bridge was a Leo Quan "Badass," and the rear cover plate for the control cavity was brass-plated steel on early examples, supplanted by a black plastic variant on later basses.

The EB-18 balanced fairly well and usually weighed in at a little more than nine pounds. It offered a dependable, utilitarian sound for bassists.

Magnum with an all-Martin solid body lineup.

An endorsement deal for Martin's solid body series was part of the lineup's promotion; a factory brochure showed two guitars and a bass being played by a band called Magnum.

The "E" series of instruments remained in production until 1983, and Martin even tried a fancier series, consisting of one guitar and one two-pickup bass (the E-28) with different body styles, neck-through construction, and active circuitry, among other upgrades. That latter series is rarer, but none of the solid body Martins were a smash hit with musicians.

Factory records indicate that at least 874 EB-18s were made from 1979–1983. Two examples of an apparently-fancier "EMB-18" were also listed, but ninety-eight solid body instruments are listed as "unidentified" (and for what it's worth, 217 EB-28 basses were made).

As noted earlier, the body of the EB-18 may not have had a "radical" silhouette, but perhaps it's fair to say that the entire solid body series was probably considered too "radical" for a staid, traditional acoustic company like Martin. After all, the company had been making guitars since 1833, whereas viable solid body guitars and basses had only been around for fewer than thirty years when the Martin models were introduced. What's more, the fact that a lot of the hardware on Martin solid body instruments, as well as pickups, came from outside suppliers may have fomented a subtle or subliminal "parts guitars" stereotype.

They're fairly rare birds built by a legendary American manufacturer, but Martin EB-18s aren't particularly collectible, due in no small part to Martin's reputation as a builder of acoustic instruments.

And for that matter, Fender isn't cited for its acoustic guitars too often.

METROPOLITAN

Houston's Alamo Music Products was primarily known for creating the Robin brand of guitars and basses, but the company also went out on a creative tangent beginning in the mid-to-late 1990s with its Metropolitan brand, which was inspired by the kitschy overkill of some National products of the early 1960s (see Valco), including "map"-shaped guitars and basses.

Among the most unique and rare Metropolitan instruments were no more than a half-dozen Tanglewood basses. As might be expected, the quality of the wood-bodied Tanglewoods was light years beyond their progenitors. According to Alamo president David Wintz, his company had given some preliminary thought to experimenting with a Tanglewood bass, but the go-ahead came at the behest of Tom Petersson, who special-ordered the first example.

The headstock of the basses had a "Gumby"-shaped profile (as did National models), and most basses came with maple necks, bound rosewood fingerboards, and "butterfly" fret inlay, also found on some earlier National guitars (but not on National map-shaped basses). Tanglewood basses also had a full thirty-four-inch scale.

The body dimensions and control layout of Tanglewood basses and guitars were the same, and bass bodies were made of poplar or African fakimba.

The pickups were a new Rio Grande model called the Pitbull, which was developed specifically for the Tanglewood bass. The Pitbull was a bass humbucking pickup designed to fit in guitar pickup-sized routing.

Company records indicate that the few Tanglewood basses made were finished in standard Metropolitan colors—Shell Pink, Pearl Aqua Blue, Pearl Mint Green (seen here), and Basic Black.

Wintz acknowledged that for the Tanglewood bass to have gone into standard production, there would have had to have been a large demand for the model, which didn't happen, but the company had an interesting time creating such retro-vibe rarities.

"We enjoyed makin' 'em," he said, "and they're cool to look at!"

Metropolitan Tanglewood, mid-1990s. *Tom Callin*

MOSRITE

It's a bit of a paradox that the Ventures have been perpetually associated with Mosrite guitars and basses, since the actual official affiliation only lasted a half-decade, in the middle of the 1960s. In a 1997 interview, Ventures bassist Bob Bogle (1934–2009) laughingly noted that the brand, " . . . will probably follow us around for the rest of our lives . . . we can't seem to shake the connection."

The Ventures have often been associated with the early-1960s surf music phenomenon, and although the band did record surf instrumentals during the height of the movement, they also preceded the genre, first charting with "Walk Don't Run" in 1960. And while electric guitarists and bassists generally considered custom-color Fenders to be definitive surf music instruments, Mosrite Ventures Model guitars and basses were pigeonholed with the band; i.e., the Ventures and Mosrite are the first band/brand association many budding guitarists may remember.

However, the brief and ill-fated association also resulted in the production of other unique Mosrite instruments any Baby Boomer guitarist or bassist would probably have loved to own. The mid-1960s were definitely the glory days for the Mosrite brand.

The chronology of the Ventures Model bass was roughly 1963–1965 for the single pickup version, and 1966–1968 for the two-pickup version, although the Ventures' endorsement would be terminated circa 1967.

This single-pickup example is in a sky blue color, as also seen on the cover of the 1965 album The Ventures *Knock Me Out!* The body has the classic Mosrite solid body profile, which has been likened to a flipped-over Fender. Other standard Mosrite appointments include the M-notch headstock, planaria-head truss rod cover, metal string guide, zero fret, hyper-thin bolt-on neck with twenty frets (it joins the body at the eighteenth fret), tiny fretboard markers, 30¼-

Mosrite Ventures,
two-pickup, circa 1967.
Heritage Auctions

Mosrite Ventures, one
pickup, circa 1964.
Jim Page

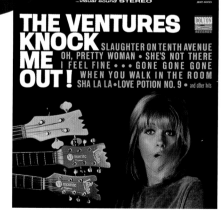

The Ventures *Knock Me Out!* album cover

inch scale, adjustable/intonatable bridge with large silo-shaped saddles (covered by a standard handrest), "German carve" around a portion of its body (as found on almost all Mosrite solid body models), and a unique wood-trimmed tailpiece. Bodies of Mosrite Ventures Models were basswood, the necks were maple, and the fretboards were rosewood.

Like many Fenders and Mosrites of that era, the white celluloid pickguard often acquired a slight greenish tinge due to aging, and its patina is known as "mint green" in guitar jargon.

Mosrite pickups offered a unique, loud sound, and the units on the two-pickup basses shown here are in the normal configuration for matching guitars. Around the time the two-pickup Ventures models were introduced, the company switched to unique "duckfoot" tuners on its basses.

One two-pickup Ventures Model bass shown here may be a one-of-a-kind item. The size (and legibility) of the headstock logos of both the band and the brand aver why, on at least one set of three instruments (two guitars and a bass), the Mosrite factory installed the brand name and a gold medallion logo on a tortoise-

shell pickguard affixed to a white body. Bogle recalled these instruments being made specifically for the Ventures by Mosrite, in an effort to promote the brand the band was playing, and a mid-1960s concert photo shows him playing what is possibly this instrument.

Mid-1960s Mosrite promo material introduced the Ventures Model with a bold-faced proclamation, "THE FINEST PERFORMANCE DEMANDS THE FINEST INSTRUMENT!!," and showed the smiling quartet of Don Wilson, Nokie Edwards, Mel Taylor, and Bogle in matching outfits with matching instruments. Other copy on the page is on the money concerning the lust many players had for Mosrite guitars and basses: "A quality instrument, designed especially for the demanding professional musician and the amateur who desires the finest."

When the Ventures' affiliation with Mosrite ended in a controversial flameout, the guitar and bass models were continued as the "Mark" series (the bass was the Mark X, Model 103). Other basses in other subsequent Mosrite series also acquired a "Mark X" designation as part of their respective model numbers.

Mosrite hooked up with another notable guitarist, Joe Maphis, for his own signature series of instruments, and the bass in that aggregation was known as the Mark X Model 502. Maphis series basses had the same basic neck, short scale, and other features as Ventures Model basses, but their slightly-larger bodies were an unusual combination of a

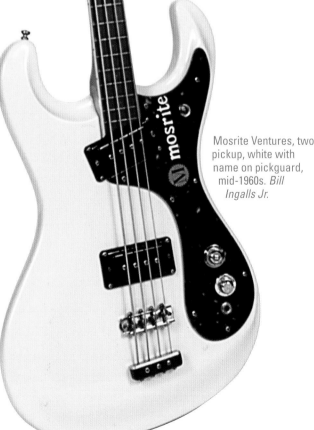

Mosrite Ventures, two pickup, white with name on pickguard, mid-1960s. *Bill Ingalls Jr.*

The Ventures perform onstage in the 1960s, playing their matching Mosrite instruments with the company name and a medallion installed on the pickguards. Left to right: Mel Taylor, Don Wilson, Nokie Edwards, and Bob Bogle.

Mosrite Joe Maphis Mark X Model 502, 1967. *Bill Ingalls Jr.*

Mosrite Joe Maphis Mark X Model 502, 1967, custom sparkle blue finish. *Michael G. Stewart*

Mosrite Combo CO Mark X Model 301, late 1960s. *Heritage Auctions*

Mosrite Celebrity CE II Mark X Model 212, ca. 1967. *Heritage Auctions*

hollowed-out walnut base (depth = 1½ inches) with a "music grade" (to quote factory literature) spruce top. The bass had body binding (called "purfling" in the 1967 catalog) where the spruce top and walnut base joined.

𝄢

The Maphis silhouette was also found on the Combo series of instruments, but the CO Mark X Model 301 was hollow, although a Mosrite catalog referred to this style as "Semi-Acoustic." Combos usually had a maple back and sides with a thick hardwood top (note the bound f-hole). Like the Maphis model, they also had a depth of 1½ inches, but had "purfling" front and rear. The handrest has been removed on this example.

Note the similar pickguard silhouettes on the Venture Models, Maphis, and Combo basses.

Mosrite's Celebrity models seemed to have been the odd series out, as they looked more commonplace. While their symmetrical double-cutaway silhouettes resembled Gibson's thinline series that had debuted in the late 1950s, Celebrity guitars and basses still had bolt-on necks and were promoted as "Acoustic Arch-Top Guitars." The series also had multiple binding front and back, as well as bound f-holes.

The pickguard for Celebrity models was a blob-shaped item, and the controls (master volume and tone, three-way pickup toggle switch, and jack) were all top-mounted in another piece of white plastic shaped like a painter's palette.

Another curiosity regarding the basses in the Celebrity series was found on the specifications list of a 1967 catalog, which listed three different variants. The CE I Mark X Model 203 had a body depth of 2¾ inches, twenty-two frets on a

30¼-inch scale, and neck binding, whereas the CE II Mark X Model 212 (seen on page 155) had a body depth of 1⅞ inches, with a bound neck of the same scale, but only twenty frets were listed. The CE III Mark X Model 221 also had the thinner body, but it had a scale of only 24½ inches and no neck binding; i.e., the CE III was yet another guitar with bass parts installed, but it wasn't a budget instrument like a Kay or Valco product.

The halcyon days of Mosrite were over by the advent of the 1970s. For all of its brevity, the pairing of the Ventures band with the Mosrite brand may have motivated an untold number of aspiring guitarists to concentrate on their playing and/or seek out Mosrite instruments (of any style), so like the band, the brand has a unique status in the history of American guitar music.

Mosrite had several production facilities that opened and closed in the ensuing decades. Company founder Semie Moseley died in August 1992, soon after his final production facility opened in Booneville, Arkansas. The facility closed the next year.

MUSIC MAN

Around a half-decade after he sold his company to CBS, Leo Fender was growing tired of staying on the sidelines in the electric stringed instrument business, and he had grown increasingly frustrated as his ideas for new products were often ignored by the new owner's "bean counters" and other officials, most of whom weren't musicians.

Mr. Fender re-entered the amplifier business with former pre-CBS Fender associates Forrest White and Tom Walker in the early 1970s. The company built Music Man amplifiers, and in 1975, Music Man's first stringed instruments, the Sting Ray guitar and bass, were introduced. The instruments were manufactured at Leo's CLF Research facility in Fullerton, and while the guitar wasn't a success in the marketplace, the bass was a hit, and ultimately became a classic that is still in production.

Leo was keenly aware that his association with another brand besides the one that bore his surname would mean comparisons of his creations would be inevitable. Therefore, his first new bass that wasn't a Fender looked and sounded different.

Cosmetically, the Sting Ray bass was unique from the top down. Forrest White designed the unique "3+1" headstock and recalled in a 1991 interview: "The '3+1' headstock was my idea. I thought that the four-in-a-row style on Fenders could make some basses tend to be neck-heavy for some players, and the 3+1 style was balanced better. Another reason for the 3+1 design was so its silhouette could be easily recognized; somebody could look across a room and say 'Hey, that's a Music Man bass', knowing the brand by the shape of the headstock."

Silhouette aside, the headstock design also offered a straight/direct pull on the strings from the phenolic nut to the tuners.

The bolt-on one-piece maple neck had twenty-one frets (one more than Fender basses) and joined the body at the twentieth fret on the treble side and the seventeenth fret on the bass side. Body woods were ash, alder, or poplar.

The egg-shaped pickguard was also an obvious aesthetic aberration from Fender basses, but the huge humbucking pickup, with eight large polepieces, probably surprised a number of fans of Leo Fender's previous designs, and its location on the instrument probably raised some eyebrows as well. It was installed in what has been termed a "sweet spot" by many musicians—certain locations along a vibrating string are more resonant, and pickup placement can exploit such a sonic opportunity. The pickup and its placement may have looked different on a Sting Ray (compared to where single pickups were placed on other basses), but it worked.

The control plate started out with cheap-looking knobs (volume, bass, and treble), which were eventually replaced with P-Bass-like knobs. The bridge assembly had stainless steel saddles and individual mutes (but who was particularly using the latter item?), and was mounted into brass inserts, to increase sustain and enhance tone. Strings loaded through the rear of the body.

Music Man Sting Ray, 1978. *Heritage Auctions*

According to the 1975 catalog, an internal preamp was optional, but it eventually became standard.

One of the earliest endorsers of the Sting Ray was funkmeister Louis Johnson of the Brothers Johnson, who played on hundreds of sessions for dozens of artists. He would play a Sting Ray on such monumental albums as Michael Jackson's *Thriller*, and on such monumental songs as "We Are The World." Other enthusiastic users have included Tony Levin (King Crimson), Flea (Red Hot Chili Peppers), and dozens of other bassists. In March of 1978, Aerosmith bassist Tom Hamilton played a Sting Ray at the California Jam 2 music festival, and the monstrous open E-string note he hit near the conclusion of "Draw the Line" was probably still ringing when the Fourth of July rolled around.

Mutes were eliminated on later Sting Rays, and strings were loaded through the end of the bridge.

By the time the two-pickup Sabre bass was introduced in late 1978, Leo Fender was already looking towards potentially-greener manufacturing pastures, due to business differences among the Music Man company's principles.

Obviously, the Sabre offered more sonic options, and it was proffered as an active-only instrument from the get-go. It featured a massive new die cast bridge that beget the same item on G & L basses . . . but the Sabre's bridge had individual string mutes.

This photo display from a 1975 Music Man catalog focuses on the numerous features of Leo Fender's new-to-the-market Sting Ray bass.

The three mini-toggles on the Sabre were a pickup selector switch, a bright switch, and a phase switch.

During the "Leo era" of Music Man, catalogued colors for the instruments included white, black, walnut brown, sunburst, and natural (gloss or satin). Other colors such as silver were also seen.

While the silhouettes of the bodies of the two basses are similar, they're actually slightly different, as the Sabre body is a bit slimmer.

Moreover, the pickups on Sabres and Sting Rays also differed. The coils on Sabre pickups were closer together, and a close examination does indeed reveal that the eight polepieces on Sabre pickups are in a tighter configuration. There's also a very slight difference in the location of the bridge pickup of a Sabre and the Sting Ray's solitary pickup on their respective bodies.

However, the placement of the neck pickup on the Sabre was that model's primary (and perhaps only) problem. According to a longtime employee, the pickup was too close to the strings, and its large and powerful Alnico 5 magnets generated a lot of string pull, causing string vibration and annoying harmonics.

Both basses were remarkably balanced and comfortable, but the single-pickup Sting Ray was always the more popular model. A cliché that was heard among musicians was that the Sting Ray Bass might have had just one pickup, but said pickup was located exactly where it was supposed to be.

The Sabre bass was discontinued in 1991. By that time, Music Man was owned by the Ernie Ball company. CLF Research had actually made both Music Man and G & L instruments in its Fullerton facility while the original Music Man company was being dissolved, and Ernie Ball acquired the Music Man brand in 1984.

Music Man Sabre, 1979. *Heritage Auctions*

PEAVEY

CHAPTER THIRTY-TWO

CT-B/T-40 prototype. *Willie G. Moseley*

The phrase "collectible Peavey" might be considered an oxymoron to many guitar aficionados. However, when the gargantuan Meridian, Mississippi, electronics manufacturer, known primarily for its dependable and durable amplifiers and sound reinforcement gear, got into the electric guitar business in the late 1970s, the company's feisty founder, Hartley Peavey, was bound and determined that Peavey stringed instruments would be products that epitomized his mantra of "quality equipment for working musicians at fair prices."

To that end, Peavey's first guitar, the T-60, and its companion bass, the T-40, had several modern guitar-manufacturing "firsts," some of which ultimately ended up being emulated by numerous other guitar makers. To wit:

1. Peavey bodies were the first to be carved by a computer-controlled CNC machine, along "XYZ" programming that worked in three "dimensions," allowing the body to be contoured. Obviously, the creation of a guitar body using a computer results in consistency and quality.
2. The maple necks of T-60s and T-40s were the first to be created using a patented "bilamination" process to maintain rigidity and straightness. In an early 1990s interview, Hartley explained that a truss rod, being literally a bent piece of steel, pre-tensions the neck, and an artificial force is added if the truss rod is added to a neck after the neck has been carved. Accordingly, Peavey created their necks with truss rods already installed, so the neck's surface would already be pre-tensioned when carved.
3. Peavey's circuitry on their new instruments was unique. The two humbucking pickups could gradually be switched to single coil status by rolling off of their respective tone knobs. A two-position phase switch also added tonal options.

Other new ideas included fret installation and blow-molded cases, but the preceding three innovations were the most revolutionary.

Prototype instruments (two guitars and a bass) were taken to a NAMM show in 1977. The bass, known as the CT-B, was so named after the initials of Chip Todd, who developed the instruments along with Hartley.

While production instruments would debut in 1978, with ash bodies in oiled natural finishes and maple fretboards, the CT-B prototype bass had a rosewood fretboard.

The T-60 and T-40 quickly became popular and became available in other finishes in short order. Alternate body woods such as poplar were used for solid color variants. An August 1979 price list notes the instruments as available in natural, black, white, and sunburst. A maple fretboard was standard, and a rosewood 'board was available as a $25 upgrade.

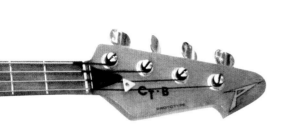

By 1979, Peavey had also lined up endorsers for the T-40, including Ross Vallory of Journey, who brandished one in concert and in a magazine ad.

Other T-series instruments also followed, and the original bass and guitar went through further changes besides even more finishes over the course of their history. "Blades" appeared in the middle of the black oval portion of the humbucking pickups on T-40s and T-60s, the aluminum nut was replaced by a Graphlon variant, and larger toggle switches replaced the original mini-toggles.

The T-40's comfortable neck had a slight radius and twenty frets, and the contoured body had a very slight forearm bevel and belly cut.

The black/white/black pickguard has a large number of screws in it (eighteen), rivaling the count of some of the Bakersfield-made Standel guitars of the late 1960s. One cool and simple idea on some T-40s is the drilled-through-the-black-top-layer-of-the-pickguard-into-the-white-middle-portion foursome of reference dots by each of the "lightning bolt P" control knobs.

The large bridge assembly had four massive saddles to help sustain, and the strings loaded through the rear of the body.

T-40s have a reputation of being heavy, and that's generally true for the ash-bodied variants.

The two 1983 examples seen here were both owned by Paul Goddard (1945–2014), original bassist for the Atlanta Rhythm Section. Usually associated with Rickenbacker basses, Goddard actually used Peavey T-40s extensively in the studio but eschewed live performances due to the weight factor. The differences in the two include finish, fretboard, and toggle switches.

The T-40 was last seen on a March 1987 price list, available only in black. Its tenure in the electric stringed instrument marketplace of more than nine years is impressive, particularly since many manufacturers—including Peavey—have introduced instruments that have come and gone quite quickly, and some came and went quite quickly during the time period that the T-40 was marketed.

Peavey's first foray into the electric bass market did exactly what it was designed to do as an instrument as well as a marketing idea. It was a well-made, affordable, and durable bass that, like all too many other Peavey products,

Peavey T-40 with maple fretboard, owned by Paul Goddard. *Willie G. Moseley*

PEAVEY

161

The Peavey Papers

VOL XXX NO 1

JAN 1982

Paul Goddard of the "Atlanta Rhythm Section"

Paul Goddard on the cover of a 1982 Peavey product periodical.

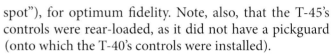

Leon Medica of Louisiana's LeRoux ("New Orleans Ladies") works out onstage with a T-45. *laleroux.com*

didn't get much respect, if any, from guitar snobs (including other manufacturers). Nevertheless, it was a "people's instrument" that sold well for many years, and one can't argue with the bottom line regarding its success.

While the plethora of T-40s around pretty much negates their collectability, they're built like tanks and are still great utility instruments. In other words, they're as much of a value in the used guitar market as they were when new, and to Hartley Peavey, "value" is what it's all about.

🎼

A single-pickup bass known as the T-45 appeared, along with other new Peavey models, in 1982, and this white example dates from 1983. The less-popular T-45 differed from the T-40 in a number of ways besides having one less pickup. While the single humbucker that was on the T-45 was the same as the two pickups on the T-40, and the instrument also had the same roll-off-to-single-coil tone circuit, the T-45's pickup wasn't located where one of the T-40's pickups was found; instead, factory literature pronounced it to be "harmonically-placed" (apparently Peavey's reference to a "sweet

Peavey T-40 with rosewood fretboard, owned by Paul Goddard. *Willie G. Moseley*

spot"), for optimum fidelity. Note, also, that the T-45's controls were rear-loaded, as it did not have a pickguard (onto which the T-40's controls were installed).

The T-40 had a pickup phase switch, while the T-45 didn't . . . but the single-pickup bass had three knobs—volume, tone, and a "special mid-frequency roll-off control for maximum tonal flexibility" (more factory literature text). Curiously, one word was altered on price lists after 1982; the third knob was referred to as a "special *low*-frequency roll-off control." (italics added)

As for necks, the T-45 had a twenty-one-fret version, while the T-40's had twenty frets.

While some early T-45s may have been made with a natural-finish oiled ash body à la the original T-40, that version didn't appear on price lists. Instead, the single-pickup basses were offered in Black, White, Sunburst, Blood Red, and Royal Burgundy at a price of $424.50, with a rosewood fretboard as a $25 upgrade.

And here's the historical rub—throughout the half-decade or so that T-40s and T-45s were both offered, if they had similar options, they always had the same list price, with the exception of a natural-finished T-40 in 1982.

The T-45 last appeared on the November 1986 price list. It did indeed have its own features and capabilities, and any perception that it was a cheaper version of a T-40 was an erroneous stereotype.

🎼

Also introduced in 1982, Peavey's T-20 bass was definitely different from the two other basses then in the Peavey lineup.

The T-20, designed by longtime Peavey luthier Mike Powers, got the Mississippi manufacturer deeper into the bass business in an impressive manner, by offering several new innovations.

Peavy T-45, 1983. *Charlie Bowen*

Peavey T-20, 1983.
Willie G. Moseley

Peavey Fury, 1984.
Bill Ingalls Jr.

Peavey Fury, 1985.
Willie G. Moseley

The neck and body of the new model were, of course, manufactured in the same manner as the T-40 and T-45. When it was first introduced, the April 1, 1982 price list noted that the T-20 was available with a "selected hardwood" body and a twenty-one-fret maple neck.

The body silhouette of the T-20 was different from the other two Peavey basses. To some observers, the T-40/T-45 body looked stodgy, and the T-20's slimmer profile brought it more in line with most contemporary bass body silhouettes. Company literature also touted a laminated cream pickguard.

There were hardware differences as well. The tuning key ratio on the T-20 was described as 24:1, while the tuners on the other basses were 22:1. What's more, the T-20 had a new bridge instead of the die-cast monsters seen on the earlier twosome. The T-20's bridge was a lightweight "triple chrome plated" item, which had fairly large barrel-shaped saddles instead of the rectangular saddles found on the earlier die cast bridge. Strings loaded through the body on the T-40 and T-45 but loaded through the end of the bridge on the T-20.

The new electronics on the T-20 were obvious at first sight. A new, powerful, single-coil Super Ferrite pickup was installed at an angle, and the price list proclaimed that like the T-45's pickup, the T-20's pickup was "harmonically-placed."

The pickup was surrounded by an "integral, mounting ring/thumb rest combination," and the practical, asymmetrical design of this item was another aesthetically intriguing idea that probably caught the eye of many players.

Sporting "lightning bolt-P" knobs like all other Peavey guitars and basses of the time, the T-20 had a (less complicated) "tone compensated volume control" and a "wide-range tone control."

The T-20 had two finishes noted on the April 1982 price list, "Satin Sunburst" and "Gloss Sunburst." There's no mention of an oiled, natural finish, although such instruments were apparently available right at the outset. Suggested retail included a molded, oval-shaped case.

The new, sleeker-looking Peavey bass proved to be popular, possibly because it was a simpler instrument visually and sonically. It was balanced, easy to play, and the potent new pickup was bright and beefy.

The August 1, 1983 price list noted that the T-20 now came in several finishes, including Natural with a maple neck (a rosewood fretboard was a $25 upgrade), as well as what would turn out to be a fairly rare T-20FL fretless version, the rosewood fretboard of which had dot markers and "sissy lines" for reference.

Two new attractive metallic colors, Sunfire Red or Frost Blue, were also cited on the same price list. Curiously, a cream pickguard was also mentioned again, but most Peavey guitars and basses in Frost Blue and Sunfire Red were seen with black pickguards.

By the latter part of 1984, the T-20 was gone . . . or was it? The T-40 and T-45 remained on a November 1984 price list, along with several similar guitars, under a heading titled "Technology Series." There was also a "Contemporary" series of three guitars and an "Impact Series" of seven guitars and three basses.

Included in the Impact Series was the Fury. Not only did the Fury itself look familiar, its description was almost identical to the T-20, but literature also referred to the Fury's "select hardwood Naturalite body design" (details coming up) and "Graphlon top nut" (an alloy). This time, the pickguard was noted as a black/white/black laminate. First edition Furies were proffered in T-20-associated finishes such as Natural, Frost Blue, and Sunfire Red, and even more finishes, including Black, Burgundy, and Inca Gold. The case was now priced separately.

A close perusal of a first edition Fury indicates that differences between that model and a T-20 include the nut, an even sleeker body shape (cutaway horns that are more pointed), a narrower pickguard that conforms to the body silhouette, and a trapezoid-shaped bridge with large, barrel-shaped saddles.

The T-20ish configuration of the Fury would last until sometime in 1986. The Fury moniker would be resurrected in 1987, on an instrument that resembled a Fender Precision Bass.

Peavey Foundation, 1983.
Bill Ingalls Jr.

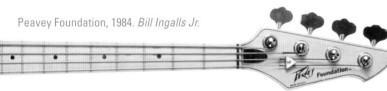

Peavey Foundation, 1984. *Bill Ingalls Jr.*

Even though they were fairly ubiquitous in their time, T-20s and first edition Fury basses were relatively short-lived models from Peavey. They're very playable and sturdy instruments and are usually a bargain in the used/vintage market.

❧

About a half-decade after Peavey began its stringed instrument efforts, the company began transitioning from its "T"-monikered models, introducing the Mystic, Horizon, and Razer guitars, as well as the Foundation Bass, on the aforementioned August 1983 price list.

The new Foundation Bass had Peavey's typical semi-arrowhead, four-on-a-side headstock and a slim, bi-laminated bolt-on maple neck that was 1½ inches wide at the nut.

Fretboards were either the maple top of the neck or a laminated rosewood board. A lined fretless option on the rosewood board was available from the outset.

The first price list on which the Foundation appeared stated that the instrument had a maple body, and it was initially offered in natural, white, black, and sunburst finishes. However, the natural-finish, first-year example seen here has an oiled ash body, as found on original T-series instruments. What's more, it's quite light, weighing in at only eight pounds.

On the other hand, the other Foundation (a 1984) is finished in one of the company's original-style sunburst finishes (sort of a "root beer-ish" tint) and does have a maple body (and weighs a little more than nine pounds).

Hardware for Foundations included the new trapezoid-shaped bridge with barrel-shaped saddles, as found on the Fury.

The Foundation was the first Peavey bass to feature two Super Ferrite pickups, and its controls consisted of two volume knobs and a master tone knob.

The 1983 price list noted that a case was included with the Foundation Bass.

The Foundation's simple efficiency made it a hit among bass players in numerous musical genres, and it would have an opposite duration chronology compared to the T-20/first edition Fury. It would go through numerous configurations during an almost twenty-year history, including variants such as a neck-through model and a five-string model.

The aforementioned Impact series on the November 1984 price list included the Foundation Bass, the case of which was now priced separately.

❧

The November 1984 price list also announced the debut of another one-pickup bass in the Impact series, the Patriot.

Unlike the Foundation or the Fury, the Patriot bass had a matching guitar with the same moniker. It was also cosmetically different, with more pronounced cutaway horns and alternate headstock "pinstriping."

What's more, the Patriot first had a neck width at the nut of 1¾ inches, but the model ultimately also became available with a slimmer 1½-inch neck profile (like the Fury and the Foundation).

Mike Powers notes: "It started as a wide neck, then we did an in-process change to a narrower neck because people seemed to prefer it on entry level models."

Peavey Patriot, 1987.
Willie G. Moseley

Peavey Patriot,
1984. *Bill Ingalls Jr.*

The Patriot's single Super Ferrite pickup was located closer to the bridge and was perpendicular to the strings instead of angled. The Patriot also had a different (and more standard-style) bridge/tailpiece unit.

Note also the differences in the logos and pinstriping on the headstocks of the two Patriots on display here.

The Fury, Foundation, and Patriot basses were touted in the late 1984 price list for their "Naturalite" body style, and according to Powers, the weight of the earlier T-model basses had prompted the company to strive for lighter instruments. The designer recounted that the company began using hackberry instead of northern ash, as well as gum, walnut, light mahogany (on Patriot guitars and basses), and even cottonwood. Solid color bodies were usually made from poplar.

"Hackberry is a form of swamp ash," Powers explained, "and it had more grey streaks and knots, but it sure was lighter and easier to work with."

Considering Peavey's cutting-edge use of CNC computers to construct guitar bodies, it shouldn't come as any surprise that the bodies on the instruments seen here are made from multiple laminates ... and the number of pieces in each body can be counted on the natural-finish and sunburst examples displayed here. For the record, the 1984 Fury body is made from six separate pieces, the 1983 Foundation has a four-piece body, the 1984 Foundation has a two-piece body, and the 1984 Patriot body has four pieces ... but an observer has to look very closely to find the seam lines on any of these instruments.

Peavey's mid-1980s basses continued to forge a viable path for working musicians as the company headed towards its second decade of producing guitars and basses.

In 1985, Peavey introduced the Dyna-Bass, its first production bass with active circuitry. Named after the company's first bass amplifier (i.e., the company had already registered the name many years earlier), the instrument listed for $729.50, including a deluxe hardshell case.

Peavey Dyna-Bass, mid-1980s.
Bill Ingalls Jr.

To many observers, the initial version resembled a step-up version of Peavey's popular Foundation bass, but the active circuitry of the Dyna-Bass offered a greater range of sonic options, and the model would ultimately offer numerous configurations during its time in the marketplace.

Hartley Peavey recalled that several of his company's mid-1980s instruments were an attempt to move beyond his company's no-frills instruments, regarding guitar and bass aesthetics as well as features.

"When we did the 'T' series, it was fashionable to have big, heavy bodies," said Peavey. "Then, there seemed to be a shortage of basses that were not P-Bass or J-Bass copies. While I would be the first to admit that our T-40 was kinda clunky, I believe our Dyna-Bass was a step in the right direction."

The original Dyna-Bass configuration, of which the blue bass shown here is an example, had a bolt-on maple neck that was offered in two neck widths, "Wide" (1¹¹⁄₁₆ inches at the nut) or "Narrow" (1½ inches at the nut); this one has the Narrow neck width. The nut is made from Peavey's trademarked "Graphlon" alloy.

The rosewood fingerboard had pearl dot markers, an eight-inch radius, and twenty-one frets. The neck joined the body cutaways just past the sixteenth fret on the bass side and at the twentieth fret on the treble side.

The body was usually made of alder or poplar. This instrument weighs in at nine pounds.

In addition to active circuitry, earlier examples of the Dyna-Bass differed from the Foundations of the same era regarding Super Ferrite pickup placement, and the Dyna-Bass body had deeper contouring.

Original colors offered for the Dyna-Bass were Gloss Black, Metallic Charcoal, Pearl White, Sunfire Red, Bermuda Coral, and Teal Blue. It appears that Dyna-Basses had matching headstocks from the get-go.

Lynyrd Skynyrd bassist Leon Wilkeson onstage with his Peavey Dyna-Bass.

All models came with black chrome hardware (including a standard Schaller bridge), except for basses finished in Pearl White and Sunfire Red, which had gold hardware.

A five-string Dyna-Bass (list = $799.50, including case) debuted at the same time, as did a four-string model with a Kahler bass vibrato ($929.50 list, including case); the four-string with vibrato was available in the narrow neck width only. 1980s price lists on which this model appears refer to the Kahler item as a "tremolo" instead of "vibrato" (another modern version of the historic Fender reversal of the same terms in the 1950s and 1960s).

Power for the active circuitry came from a nine-volt battery, which installed in the rear of the body.

Peavey TL-5, circa 1990.
Willie G. Moseley

The controls on the Dyna-Bass were laid out in a simple and logical manner—the first large knob (nearest the space between the two pickups) is a master volume control and the other large knob is a blend-pan control, which has a center detent to indicate that the output of both pickups is equal.

The three smaller knobs are, as might be expected, equalization controls, and they, too, have center detent.

The knob nearest the master volume is the "Low" frequency control. The middle control is, not surprisingly, the "Mid Control" knob, and the High equalization knob is furthest to the rear.

The small, two-way mini-toggle switch is an active/passive switch to conserve the battery . . . or, according to the owner's manual, " . . . to allow the player to conveniently switch to the passive mode in the event of battery malfunction or failure."

In its time in the Peavey lineup, the Dyna-Bass would become available in numerous variants, including a five-string version, models with different pickup configurations, and/or a scooped-out headstock configuration, as well as a "Unity" neck-through version.

Over the years, several endorsers would sign up for different models of the Dyna-Bass, and one of the earliest notable players was Leon Wilkeson of Lynyrd Skynyrd, who was seen not only in a Peavey ad touting the model, but also onstage with a Pearl White Dyna-Bass when the band reunited in 1987. Photos of Wilkeson with his Dyna-Bass can also be seen in photos accompanying the live *Southern by the Grace of God* album, which was recorded during the reunion tour.

As the 1980s ended, Peavey opted to get into signature model basses (or instruments that were created with the input of notable bassists), and their first model in this category was perhaps their most innovative bass up to that point in the company's history.

The TL-5 debuted in 1988, and was Peavey's first bass that was created and marketed as a five-string instrument from its inception. Veteran session bassist Tim Landers lent his expertise to the development of the model, which had, as expected, a low B string, making the TL-5 exemplary of the trend regarding the burgeoning five-string bass market.

Listed at the top of the basses proffered on the October 1988 price list, the TL-5 had a neck-through design and was touted as having a matched eastern flame maple "four way contoured solid body." Its ebony fretboard had a twelve-inch radius, twenty-four frets, and oval, mother-of-pearl inlays. The side position markers were also mother-of-pearl.

The active circuitry included hum-canceling Super Ferrite pickups, and the controls included a rotary pickup selector/pan pot, an active/passive switch, and three-band tone equalization (EQ) controls.

Initial colors were Transparent Blue, Transparent Black, and Transparent Red. List price in 1988 was $1,200, with an optional hardshell case for $110.

Refinements over the history of the TL-5 would include a transition to a fifteen-inch radius, different EQ controls, and other finishes, including Transparent Emerald, seen on this example. The list price of the TL-5 eventually went up to $1,499.99, and a TL-6 contrabass (with a high C string) was introduced in the early 1990s (at a beginning list price of $1,799).

The TL-5 and TL-6 were out of Peavey's lineup by mid-1997, but their high quality and state-of-the-art features construction signified that Peavey was determined to be a factor in the professional-grade bass market.

Peavey RJ-IV, ca. 1991.
Bill Ingalls Jr.

To say that his weekly appearance on "American Idol" was just the tip of the iceberg in the decades-long career of the ubiquitous Randy Jackson is an understatement.

The veteran bassist has played with and/or recorded with and/or produced musicians ranging from violinist Jean Luc-Ponty to Bob Dylan to Jerry Garcia to Mariah Carey to Bruce Springsteen to Charlie Daniels . . . for starters (and the Daniels gig was at the Grand Ole Opry, no less . . .).

However, many music fans probably recall a 1986 performance video of Journey's "Girl Can't Help It" as their first encounter with Randy Jackson, who had played on that band's *Raised on Radio* album (also released in 1986) and was invited to tour with the band.

And a few years later, Jackson collaborated with Peavey on a bass with logical utilitarian appointments.

When it was introduced, Randy Jackson's Peavey model had a list price of $1,099.99 plus $119.00 for a hardshell case. Curiously, more than one Peavey spec sheet referred to the model as the "RJ4" while "RJ-IV" is found on the headstock and the instruction manual.

The RJ-IV had several intriguing "what you don't see" facets. For example, its original stock finishes—Black Pearl Burst, Blue Pearl Burst, Purple Pearl Burst, and Red Pearl Burst—made it impossible to tell that it was an all-maple instrument and had neck-through construction, but company literature noted its configuration and touted its "select maple body" and "eastern maple bilaminated neck construction with graphite reinforcement."

The headstock profile was similar to other upgraded Peaveys of the time, with a recessed/scooped-out portion beneath the tuners. Note that the tuners and the intonatable "milled bridge with individual saddle tracks" (spec sheet description) are in a popular-for-that-era black color.

The RJ-IV also came equipped with a Hipshot D-tuner flip lever for the E string. A separate set of instructions for setting up the tuner, signed by Hipshot's David Borisoff, was included.

The nut of the RJ-IV was made of Graphlon, and the width of the neck at the nut was 1.6 inches.

Its fingerboard was made of macassar ebony and had a ten-inch radius and twenty-one frets. Some observers/cynics might opine that the mother-of-pearl fretboard inlay (unique to this model) looks like a line of golf tees, but to others, the inlay may resemble icicles.

Company literature also hyped the " . . . reduced body size with four-way radial contour." The body is eighteen inches long and thirteen inches wide.

As for its electronics and controls, the RJ-IV came off as practical and simple to operate . . . on the surface. Its P/J pickup configuration is active, powered by a 9-volt battery that installs on the back of the body, in a small compartment separate from the rear control cavity. The control knobs are labeled "V" (volume), "B" (bass), "M" (midrange), and "T" (treble), and each of the three tone knobs has a center detent. Pickup selection is accomplished by a three-position mini-toggle switch. Equalization adjustments could be made by accessing the rear control area.

Cosmetically, the RJ-IV's Red Pearl Burst finish might evoke a brief initial comparison to Rickenbacker's Fireglo finish, which is also a pink-to-red color (albeit a see-through/sunburst-type).

Peavey Forum, mid-1990s. *Bill Ingalls Jr.*

Those fret markers may also have a subliminal Rickenbacker vibe as well, perhaps resembling, um, "atrophied" wedge-shaped markers as found on upgrade Rickenbacker models.

In addition to the original Pearl Burst finishes, the RJ-IV was later proffered in Pearl Black, Pearl White, Pearl Blue, and Sunfire Red. A natural finish koa RJ-IV eventually became available, as did a budget/fewer-frills version called the RJ-B.

When Randy Jackson appeared in his instructional video, "Mastering the Groove," in 1992, he appeared on the cover brandishing an RJ-IV in Red Pearl Burst.

The RJ-IV bass was in the Peavey lineup for approximately four years. While it's debatable to what extent Jackson's high profile in recent times might increase interest in this model (as well as its selling price), it remains—as is the case for almost every other Peavey bass—a well-built and practical value in the used instrument marketplace.

In the 2003 book *American Basses* (Backbeat Books), author Jim Roberts noted that for all of the Peavey Electronics Corporation's innovations in the mid-1990s, such as the Cyberbass (a MIDI controller bass), ". . . the company hadn't forgotten their regular customers," whereupon Roberts cited Peavey's Forum model as a "good old meat-and-potatoes bass" of that era.

The Forum series did indeed exemplify the Mississippi manufacturer's ongoing efforts to adhere to founder Hartley Peavey's aforementioned mantra. The lineup was only around for about four years, but Forums went through some noteworthy changes during their existence.

Debuting in 1993, the Forum bass looked like a lot of other instruments—basic P-Bass silhouette, "P/J" pickup configuration, etc.

The neck of the original Forum was made of eastern maple and was 1½ inches wide at the Graphlon nut. The fretboard was rosewood, and had twenty-one eighteen-percent nickel-silver frets. The neck joined the body at the sixteenth fret on the bass side and the nineteenth fret on the treble side.

The body was made ". . . from the finest western poplar," according to Peavey literature, and came in polyester/urethane finishes. The pickguard, bridge, etc. were also generic-looking, and controls consisted of two volume knobs and a master tone knob. Overall, the Forum exemplified simple Peavey dependability.

An active circuitry variant known as the Forum Plus was also available and was powered by a 9-volt battery.

Within two years, however, the Forum series underwent a noticeable makeover, perhaps to differentiate it from other basses in the market . . . including other Peaveys.

In 1995, the basic Forum became a one-pickup active instrument (page 169). The neck was now 1.7 inches wide at the nut, and the body was now touted as ". . . constructed from the finest Swamp ash or Alder," and underwent a slight modification that saw the cutaway horns lengthened to add an even more balanced feel.

The large, rectangular pickup was Peavey's new and powerful VFL Plus active unit, and was, like earlier Peavey models, "harmonically placed."

"I used the old T-40 design to start with," said Mike Powers, "then changed it to an active type for VFLs."

The three knobs on the second-generation Forum controlled volume, treble, and bass; the two tone knobs had center detent.

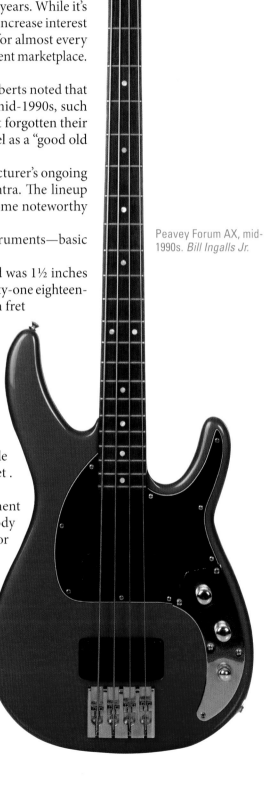

Peavey Forum AX, mid-1990s. *Bill Ingalls Jr.*

The new two-pickup model, the Forum AX, was a sonic monster, with two harmonically-placed VFL Plus pickups and appropriate controls—master volume, a rotary pickup blend control with center detent, and concentric bass and treble controls, each with center detent.

Note the differences in the control layouts on the Forum and Forum AX shown here—the one-pickup bass still has its knobs mounted on the "tail" of the pickguard, while the two-pickup model's controls are mounted in a chrome plate. Pickguards on both models were usually three-layer, black/white/black.

The circuitry in the revised Forum basses was analog, according to Powers. It was powered by two 9-volt batteries and was described in owner manuals as "an active high/low pass shelving circuit." Centering the tone controls meant that the pickup response was flat. Rotating the treble control clockwise from its centered position increased all frequencies 255 Hz and above, while counterclockwise rotation decreased the same frequency range. The same principle applied to the bass control—clockwise rotation increased frequencies 96 Hz and below; counterclockwise rotation decreased frequencies in that range. The owner's manual summarized that the use of such circuitry " . . . translates into an audible cut/boost of twelve decibels."

Interestingly, the bridges on the second edition Forum and the Forum AX were different—the single-pickup bass still had a standard-looking bridge, while the two-pickup model's bridge was a hefty and aesthetically sharp item.

"The massive ABM bridge on the Forum AX is machined from a solid block of brass for maximum sustain and offers the ultimate in adjustability. String height, intonation, and spacing may be adjusted to fit literally any playing style," the owner's manual stated.

A five-string model with a low B string, the Forum 5, was also offered in the new configuration. It had a 4+1 headstock silhouette and was otherwise a five-string version of the Forum AX.

Peavey had other basses in mind for the late 1990s and beyond, so the Forum series was discontinued a little after the middle of the decade. The Forum lineup epitomized the Peavey manufacturing credo, and some of them—particularly the Forum AX—are potent-sounding instruments that can hold down the low end in almost any musical scenario.

Mike Powers died on April 29, 2013.

PEDULLA

One of the more enduring styles in higher-end basses—particularly lined fretless variants—has been the M.V. Pedulla Buzz Bass. It was introduced in 1980, by luthier Michael Pedulla's company, located in Brockton, MA, and was created with the input of two notable bassists who also claimed Brockton as their hometown.

Tim Landers recommended Pedulla to Mark Egan of the Pat Metheny Group when, seeking to emulate Jaco Pastorius, Egan had removed the frets from his 1964 Fender Jazz Bass.

"I had attempted to brush on an epoxy finish on the rosewood fingerboard," Egan recalled. "I botched the job and it came out uneven and unplayable. Michael was able to spray on an epoxy finish and it came to life as a fretless, which I then took out on tour with Pat Metheny."

Both Egan and Landers were interested in a fretless version of the basses Pedulla was creating and ultimately provided a lot of input to the luthier. Egan cited the neck dimensions as an example.

"I was interested in a Fender Jazz Bass neck profile," he detailed, "but an even thinner neck from front to back and less of a radius on the fingerboard. I also wanted a fretless that had great sustain and a growl, more like a bass sitar."

The unique maple body silhouette (available with quilted, flame, or bird's-eye maple options) was refined from Pedulla's original style. The two cutaways on the body resemble amoeba pseudopods.

"My input included ideas to make the cutaway extend enough to be able to play up to the twenty-fourth fret comfortably," Egan detailed, "and to extend the upper horn for a better body fit."

The neck-through design is described in early 1980s factory literature as a "capillary" style made with two or three pieces of maple. It measures 1.55 inches wide at the nut. Scale on the instrument is thirty-four inches.

The lined fretless ebony fretboard, marked with white inlay for twenty-four frets, was the obvious focal point in the design.

"Michael developed this coating," Egan recounted. "It was a very hard finish and long-lasting, while at the same time it created great sustain. His fretless fingerboard finishes are the finest and a very important feature for the Buzz Bass, giving it the growl much like a great upright bass sound."

The finishing process, now applied to the entire Buzz Bass instrument (not just the fretboard), is now known as Diamondkote.

M.V. Pedulla Buzz Bass, 1987. *Heritage Auctions*

THREE

The Buzz Bass was available with Bartolini active pickups or DiMarzio passive units. The selections included the JL (two Jazz-type Dimarzio pickups), JB (two Bartolini Jazz-type active pickups), PJL (DiMarzio pickups in a "P/J" array), or PJB (active Bartolinis in a P/J array, as seen on this 1987 example).

As for pickup brand choices, Egan detailed, "The Bartolinis were attractive to me, more so than the DiMarzios for a few reasons. I preferred their warmth and punchiness, and they produced less hum, which was caused by stage light interference. I had first replaced the pickups in my 1958 Precision Bass with Bartolini pickups while in Chicago on the road with the Pat Metheny Group. For fretless, I prefer a P/J combination for punchy mids and a warm bottom end, usually favoring the J bass bridge pickup."

Hardware is the Schaller brand and includes tuners, bridge/tailpiece, and security strap buttons.

Another unique feature is found on the back—the compartment for control access is actually a removable part of the body.

"The lid on the back of the body is Michael's design," Egan said, "and another example of his fine woodwork detail. It gives complete access to the wiring and makes changing batteries a very simple process."

The controls on this example with PJB pickup array are separate volume knobs, master tone, a pre-amp/active circuitry gain knob, and a three-position pickup toggle switch. The mini-toggle switch is a pre-amp/active on-off switch with an LED to indicate that the circuitry is on.

The Buzz Bass would evolve to become available in five-string and fretted models. Among the noted players of M.V. Pedulla's enduring bass over the years are David Hungate, Kip Winger, Timothy B. Schmidt, Jimmy Haslip, Chuck Rainey, Will Lee, and Gene Simmons.

Mark Egan received the first example of the Buzz Bass, and his affiliation with M.V. Pedulla would continue over the decades to include the first doubleneck M.V. Pedulla bass the company ever produced.

"After I left the Pat Metheny Group, I started a group with (drummer) Danny Gottlieb called Elements," the bassist explained, "and I would write things where I heard a different sound in the bridge of the song or some other part, and when we played live I wanted to have an instrument where I could go back and forth instead of having to put an instrument down and pick something else up. I asked Mike how he felt about making a doubleneck that included an eight-string neck; in the 1970s, I'd had an Ibanez eight-string. So I asked Mike to make me a doubleneck with a Buzz Bass fretless neck and an eight-string fretted neck."

Egan averred that there was never a time when any facet of the doubleneck was scrapped when the instrument was being developed, noting "We did a lot of homework beforehand. We talked a lot, going back and forth about the concept and design. And it worked!"

The original doubleneck, like the Buzz Bass, is all maple, and both necks have a neck-through configuration.

The upper neck is indeed a lined fretless item exactly as found on the original Buzz Bass, and it has side and fingerboard dot markers. The lower neck is fretted, and all eight of its string tuners are on the headstock. Subsequent examples of Egan's doublenecks would have four tuners on the headstock of the eight-string neck and four tuners on the end of the body, not unlike some early Kramer aluminum neck eight-string basses from the late 1970s and early 1980s. According to Egan, mounting half of the tuners on the body made for better balance.

Each neck has a brass nut as well as a brass Badass bridge ("Mike and I thought that 'brass-to-brass' would add to the sustain," reports Egan).

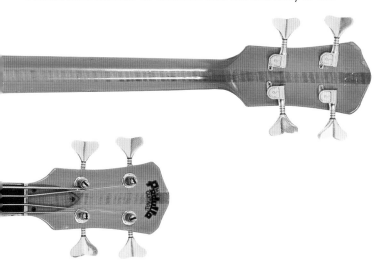

Sharp-eyed observers will note that the two necks are not quite parallel. "We thought the upper neck would resemble the neck angle of normal position," Egan explained. "Also, there was room to move the left hand around between necks by having a slightly-angled-out position, and another reason was to leave room for the tuners on each neck. If the necks were parallel it would be difficult to tune."

The long, narrow strips of wood on the bass side of the pickups are another incongruity. According to Egan, they're ebony thumbrests that he custom-ordered on all of his Buzz Basses, and he detailed: "I like to be able to rest my thumb in a variety of areas for different sounds. I play closer to the neck for a rounder and warmer sound and closer to the bridge for more punch and attack."

Both necks utilize active Bartolini pickups, as was the case on the original active version of the Buzz Bass.

Egan's color choice for the first doubleneck was white, because he didn't have an instrument that color.

The controls include a master toggle switch for pickup selection on the neck(s) being utilized. As was the case on the Buzz Bass, a mini-toggle switch triggers the pre-amp, and a small LED indicates that the pre-amp is on, as well as separate volume knobs for each pickup, a master tone knob, and a pre-amp volume knob.

An obvious and necessary extra control is a three-position rotary knob for neck selection (either or both). Curiously, the output on the instrument is mono, but Egan advised that such a configuration makes sense since " . . . I only play one neck at a time."

Interestingly, Egan noted that this first doubleneck, which weighs fourteen pounds, is not as heavy as later examples created by Pedulla.

"I wrote *Mosaic* (Egan's 1985 debut solo album) using this doubleneck," the bassist enthused, "and I was going back and forth so much that it opened up a whole new 'door' of possibilities regarding composing. And to be honest, the fretless neck on that bass is one of my favorites; I've used it in the studio on certain Elements records."

Egan's comment about playing one neck at a time not withstanding, a unique example of his capabilities on a Pedulla doubleneck was seen in the mid-1980s, when he hosted "New Visions," a show on VH-1 that specialized in light jazz and New Age videos. Egan was seen (and heard) in the studio, playing a solo version of "Ocean Views" (from *Mosaic*), on both necks, playing the anchor riff on the eight-string neck with one hand while performing the plaintive melody with his other hand on the fretless neck.

Now several decades old, Mark Egan's affiliation with M.V. Pedulla is still active.

Pedulla doubleneck, first one made, early 1980s.
Judith Schiller

Mosaic cover artwork.

RICKENBACKER

Model 4000 Bass

This Rickenbacker Electric Bass is made from the finest mahogany and maple available, hand polished to natural finish. The instrument has a separate rosewood 20-fret fingerboard attached to the one piece, solid mahogany neck running the full length of the instrument. The extreme "cut-away" body assists in playing higher notes, and also adds to the attractive appearance of the instrument as a whole. The full length neck with two double metal adjusting rods, and the fact that the tailpiece, bridge, nut, and patent heads are mounted on the same piece of wood, assures the player of maintaining a straight neck. The bridge cover, pickup assembly, tailpiece, and patent heads are chrome plated and add to the beauty of the instrument. The full length neck, adjustable heighth strings, and individual adjustments for string length assures the player of perfect pitch and intonation for each string. This instrument has the famous Rickenbacker pickup unit combined with separate volume and tone controls. The physical size of the electric bass makes it more portable than the conventional acoustical bass, and still it produces more volume.

Rickenbacker

Model 4000 Bass

The catalog debut of the Rickenbacker 4000 bass showed the instrument in its original thicker-bodied configuration.

For all of the "icon" accolades afforded to Rickenbacker's two-pickup model 4001 bass (and its association with such famous players as Paul McCartney, Chris Squire of Yes [1948–2015], and Motorhead's Lemmy [1945–2015]), it's sometimes easy to forget that the 4001 wasn't that company's original entry into the new field of solid body electric fretted basses. What's more, the earliest Fender Precision Basses were actually sold by the company that would later own Rickenbacker.

F.C. Hall's Radio-Tel company of Santa Ana, California, was the distributor for Leo Fender's products when Hall bought Adolph Rickenbacker's Electro String company in late 1953. Taking stock of the burgeoning electric guitar market (much of which was indeed being pioneered by Fender innovations), Hall began to steer his newly-acquired

company in a direction towards Spanish type electrics, and in the mid-1950s, enlisted Roger Rossmeisl, a German-born luthier, to create a new line of electric guitars and basses that would turn out to be the aesthetic antithesis of Fender's somewhat plain-looking instruments.

Rickenbacker's first solid body bass was the single-pickup 4000, and it differed from Fender's Precision Bass not only visually but in its construction features as well.

The 4000 prototype was first photographed in April of 1957, and production began in June. The body and headstock silhouettes were stunning—the style of the body has come to be known as a "cresting wave," and the semi-fishtail design of the 2+2 headstock was also eye-catching.

Construction-wise, the 4000 differed radically from the P-Bass. While the Fender product had a bolt-on neck, the new Rickenbacker bass was the first production instrument of its kind to feature "neck-through" construction. A solid piece of wood ran the full length of the instrument, all the way from the edge of the headstock to the butt end of the body, and maple "wings" were placed on either side of the center section to complete the silhouette.

The pickup, tailpiece, and bridge were all mounted on the center piece of wood, which helped to evoke the legendary piano-like tone for which Rickenbacker basses are noted.

"You'd have to call it a 'high fidelity bass' sound," said Rickenbacker Chairman/CEO John Hall (F.C. Hall's son) in an October 1993 interview, "in that it produces a more-defined, sharper, and more precise sound than almost any other bass on the market. It certainly was the first bass in that genre; it was the first bass to depart from the thumping, thudding Precision-type sound."

Rickenbacker 4000, 1961, owned by Tom Petersson. *Willie G. Moseley*

CHAPTER THIRTY-FOUR

Unique tone aside, Rickenbacker nevertheless added a sliding string mute system to the bridge cover in late 1957, to facilitate an upright bass-type sound, if desired.

Another unique and practical facet of the 4000's design was the fingerboard, all twenty frets of which were clear of the body. The instrument's scale was 33½ inches.

The 4000 would evolve considerably during the first few years of its existence. The prototype and earliest production examples had a mahogany center section. Walnut neck-through portions soon followed, and in 1960, maple became the standard for the 4000's neck-through section. Some earlier 4000s have a maple center section, but also have small walnut "wings" on the headstock.

Electronics on earlier 4000s was a "horseshoe"-type pickup (as pioneered by Rickenbacker in the 1930s). Controls were a simple volume and tone knobs.

The overall body thickness was slimmed down considerably circa 1961.

A new "Hi-Gain" pickup was introduced in the 1960s, and the 4000 also acquired a new bridge/tailpiece assembly, which included a muting system that ran under the strings.

Other changes to the 4000 during its time included a different pickguard style and the relocation of the jack from the top of the instrument to the side. A clear fingerrest that had been originally installed at an angle ultimately ended up parallel to the strings.

And this very clean 1972 example, in a Mapleglo (natural) finish, exhibits all of the features that the 4000 eventually acquired over its life in the marketplace. Note the all-maple construction, including the headstock "wings." The walnut center stripe runs the full length of the instrument on both front and back.

The handrest over the Hi-Gain pickup is also still in place; such items are often removed.

The 4000's cosmetics conformed to the guidelines for Rickenbacker's standard models—pearl dot fret markers, and no binding on the neck or top body edge. However, the factory made at least one 4000 circa 1960, in a Fireglo

finish that had "Deluxe" features (triangular crushed-pearl fret markers, neck binding, and top edge body binding).

Rickenbacker's frontline double-pickup solid body bass proved to be more popular than their single pickup model, and for all of its historic innovations, the original 4000 bass was discontinued in 1985. It appeared that the "classic Rickenbacker sound" was easier to acquire via the company's two-pickup 4001, which was introduced in 1961.

The earlier example seen here is a 1973 model with "Deluxe" features, which became the, um, standard for the two-pickup bass, even though there was a less-frills 4001S bass exported to England in the 1960s ("S" implying "Standard," as the bass had dot fretboard markers and no neck binding). The 1978 model also has Deluxe features.

The brown sunburst finish on these examples was dubbed Autumnglo and is now discontinued.

The handrest/cover has been removed from the pickup near the bridge on both of these 4001s, which shows the Hi-Gain unit that replaced "horseshoe"-type pickups. The "chrome bar" neck pickup on the 1973 4001 has also been called a "toaster top" pickup by some guitar buffs, as it resembles an overhead view of that particular kitchen appliance. It, too, would later be replaced by a Hi-Gain pickup, which is seen on the 1978 model; the newer 4001 also has the better-grade tuners that the model acquired.

In 1980, the 4001 was supplanted by the 4003, which had a superior truss rod system, according to Rickenbacker. Some re-issues by the company still have a 4001 moniker.

Rickenbacker 4000, 1972. Olivia's Vintage

Rickenbacker 4001, 1973.
Heritage Auctions

Rickenbacker 4001, 1978.
Heritage Auctions

It shouldn't have come as any surprise that Rickenbacker would ultimately attempt to meld their successful hollow body electric guitar style with an electric bass, and such a model, the 4005, was introduced in 1965.

Rickenbacker's original 360-375 "Capri" hollow body electric guitars were double-bound, but those models underwent a noticeable change in 1964, when the top edge was rounded and only the rear edge was bound. Accordingly, when the company opted to introduce a hollow body bass the next year, its body had a similar style, albeit with a longer cutaway horn on the upper side. The 4005 was first introduced in the company's Fireglo and Mapleglo finishes, and was later offered in Rickenbacker's standard Colorglo finishes.

The 4005's headstock had the same "semi-fishtail" silhouette as solid body Rickenbacker basses. The maple neck had a twenty-one-fret rosewood fretboard and "Deluxe" appointments.

Rickenbacker 4005,
1967. *Olivia's Vintage*

Rickenbacker 4005,
1979. *Bill Ingalls Jr.*

Rickenbacker
4005WB, 1967.
Olivia's Vintage

4005s began with two "chrome bar" pickups, as seen on the 1967 examples. They were installed at extreme ends of the body face; i.e., right next to the end of the neck and right next to the bridge.

As was the case with other Rickenbacker guitars and basses, the chrome bar pickups on the 4005 were eventually replaced by the company's Hi-Gain pickups.

The large, flat pickguard houses a three-way toggle switch, two volume controls, two tone controls, and a fifth knob that allows blending the tone of the pickups (as found on "Capri"-style guitars beginning in 1962).

Other standard comparisons to the "Capri" series of guitars on the 4005 bass included a slash-shaped soundhole and an "R" tailpiece (as cited in the Fender Coronado chronology).

The small snap-on cover over the bridge has a foam mute on its underside, which does exactly what its name implies, so to get an optimum "high-fidelity sound" out of this model, the foam (or cover) would need to be removed.

The 4005 was ultimately marketed in several other variants, including the 4005WB, introduced in 1966. This model was bound front and rear (the "WB" stood for "white binding"). Six-string variants (i.e., bass guitars) known as the 4005/6 were also made.

As was the case with the 4001 solid body bass, some plainer-looking 4005S models were exported from 1965–1969 to the Rose-Morris & Co. in England.

The Rickenbacker 4005 was a unique idea but was ultimately unsuccessful. The 4005/6 was discontinued in 1977, the 4005WB was outta there by 1983, and the original 4005 was last marketed in 1984. They all have the legendary cool look that is standard on Rickenbacker guitars and basses, but their status as a sonically-important instrument is dubious.

At various times in its history, Rickenbacker has dabbled in the lesser-frills/budget market with both short-scale and full-scale bass models being offered, but their efforts weren't as successful as Fender's Mustang Bass or the Kalamazoo KB.

Nevertheless, their lower-priced models were well-made, and some featured parts that were also found on Rickenbacker's frontline basses. Made from 1975–1984 (i.e., after the 1960s guitar boom), the 3000 was a short-scale, single pickup bass with a bolt-on neck. Its looks were somewhat nondescript, although its headstock silhouette was that of Rickenbacker guitars, instead of the semi-fishtail look on the company's frontline basses.

A full-scale model, the 3001, was proffered during the same time frame as the 3000's existence.

Rickenbacker is still owned by Hall family members and is still occupying a niche in the electric bass marketplace that is both sonically and aesthetically unique.

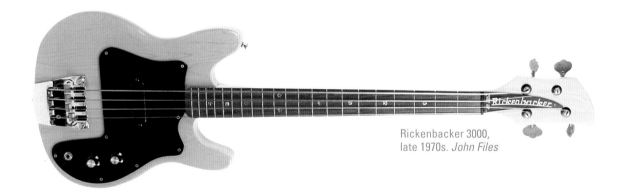

Rickenbacker 3000, late 1970s. *John Files*

ROBIN

CHAPTER THIRTY-FIVE

RIVAL
· Hard rock maple or maple with rosewood fingerboard neck construction
· Stylistic body design in the Robin
  tradition
· Distinctive new headstock design
· Low radius fingerboard with 22 jumbo
  frets for sustain and easy bending
· Barrel string tree for smooth transition
  of strings
· Powerful vintage wound single coil
  pickups
· 5-way pickup selector switch with
  standard and "out of phase" pickup
  combinations
· One volume and one tone control
· Standard vintage type tremelo
· LTS — fine tunable and locking tremelo
  system optional
· Sky blue, all black, metallic red, pink,
  pearlescent white

"LTS"
Fine tunable and locking tremelo system
optional on all Robin guitars with
standard tremelo.

RL-1 HUMBUCKING
Same distinctive body styling as Rival,
but with:
· One Hot Humbucking pickup
· One volume and one tone control
· No pickguard
· Rear loaded electronics
· Locking tremelo system optional

RL-2 HUMBUCKING
Same as RL-1 with:
· Two Hot Humbucking pickups
· Two volume and one tone control
· 3-way pickup selector switch
· Locking tremelo system optional

FREEDOM BASS
· Hard rock maple or maple with rose-
  wood fingerboard neck construction
· Vintage style neck with fast low action
· Neck pitch adjustment
· Full 34" long scale
· Distinctive Robin headstock
· Modern contoured body styling
· Powerful Humbucking pickup and active
  electronics. Treble and bass boost
  controls, increased frequency response
· Heavy duty chrome plated hardware
  and enclosed machine heads
· White, black, 3-tone sunburst, natural,
  metallic red, old blonde

FREEDOM BASS II
Same features as Freedom Bass except
· 2 powerful Humbucking pickups
· Slim "jazz" type neck
· 3-way pickup selection switch

RANGER BASS
· Hard rock maple neck · 32" medium scale for comfort and playability · Popular
'Ranger' body design with body contour · Heavy duty chrome plated machines and
hardware · Hot vintage "split" pickup · Lightweight and extremely comfortable · Black,
2-tone sunburst, metallic red, old blonde

This page from Robin's 1983 catalog announced the
company's first bass models, the Freedom and the Ranger.

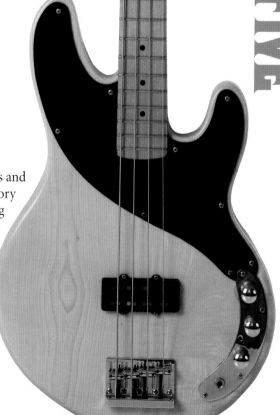

Robin Freedom,
1983. *Bill Ingalls Jr.*

The saga of Houston's Alamo Music Products, builders of Robin guitars and
other brands, is one of both "retro-innovation" (admittedly a contradictory
term, but nevertheless on-the-mark) and an against-the-trend manufacturing
chronology. The company's reverse "imported-then-domestic" story is
an intriguing facet of the vintage guitar phenomenon.

Robin first began its history by importing guitars and basses
made by such Japanese builders as Chushin, ESP, and Tokai. Guitars were first marketed in 1982, and basses (all manufactured by
ESP) followed the next year. The company's 1983 catalog announced
two full-scale basses, the single-pickup Freedom Bass and the two-
pickup Freedom Bass II, as well as the thirty-two-inch (medium)

Robin Ranger, 1993. *Bill Ingalls Jr.*

Robin Medley, 1995. *Bill Ingalls Jr.*

scale Ranger Bass as the company's first entries into the low-end electric stringed instrument marketplace. The Ranger Bass coordinated with a matching Ranger guitar, but the Freedoms did not have a six-string counterpart.

All three models featured maple necks. Fretboards were maple (part of the actual neck) or a rosewood fretboard cap. In spite of the differences in scale length, the fretboards on both models had twenty-one frets.

The headstock vaguely resembled an upside-down Fender headstock and had a 2+2 tuner configuration. It also had an unusual centered string tree to guide the A and D strings.

The body wood was usually ash or alder, and the contours on both models were quite comfortable. The larger-than-usual pickguards gave a retro nod to the original Fender Precision Bass instruments of the early-to-mid-1950s.

The Freedom models featured humbucking pickups and were introduced with active circuitry, although passive versions were later available. The models also featured a "high-mass" bridge/tailpiece combination. Controls were a master volume knob, bass, and treble, and the Freedom II featured a three-way toggle switch for pickup selection.

Initial colors for the Freedom and Freedom II were White, Black, three-tone Sunburst, Natural, Metallic Red, and Old Blonde.

One bit of historical significance regarding the Freedom Bass on page 179 is the fact that it is from the very first shipment of basses that ESP sent to Houston. Such a status is verified by measuring the width of the neck at the nut – it's 1¾ inches wide (à la a P-Bass). The neck also has a walnut "skunk stripe" on the back.

"The very first Freedoms had wide necks," Alamo's Dave Wintz recounted. "*Too* wide, in fact; wider than we had requested. As soon as we got them, we changed (the specifications) for future production."

Wintz estimated that only twenty-five to fifty of the wide-neck Freedom Basses were made in 1983.

Later-model Freedom Basses had a 1½-inch neck width at the nut. Their necks didn't have a skunk stripe, and the headstocks also featured a latter-day bar-type string tree that was installed in Texas after the guitars were received from Japan.

"Once we realized that three strings could use some help, we installed the bars here in Houston," said Wintz, "using the hole from the round 'two-string' tree, and drilling another hole for the bar."

Freedom and Freedom II basses would evolve in yet another way during their short history—they would be seen with black hardware.

Notable players of Robin basses during the 1980s included Tommy Shannon (Double Trouble) and Brad Houser.

Imported Robin basses were only in the marketplace for about a half-decade, but were unique-looking instruments that were finely-crafted and ergonomically comfortable.

The last catalog in which Japanese-made Robin basses appeared was the company's 1988 edition. Robin was already in the initial stages of domestic guitar production, and while the Freedom Basses were discontinued, the Ranger Bass would be held over in name only, as the domestic-made version was a very different instrument.

The Texas-made variant of the Ranger Bass was introduced in 1989. Gone was the thirty-two-inch scale and single pickup; the Ranger Bass now sported a full thirty-four-inch scale on a twenty-fret neck with a ten-inch radius, as well as a P/J pickup configuration with a three-way toggle switch on a larger, contoured body that still had parallel waists. Bodies on US-built Robins were, once again, ash or alder, and maple or rosewood fretboards were available. The large pickguard was still there, but the headstock was now a reverse style like Ranger guitars, with tuning keys aiming at the floor.

Wintz points out that it's actually more comfortable to tune a guitar or bass with keys on the underside of its headstock, as a player's arm assumes a more natural posture and doesn't have to twist. By the time the 1994 catalog came out, however, the Ranger Bass headstock had assumed the, er, "industry standard" silhouette, with tuning keys on the top edge.

The mid-1990s also brought about the corporate change for Wintz's operation to become known as Alamo Music Products, and the company expanded into two more brands, Metropolitan (RE: The experimental Tanglewood bass seen earlier) and Alamo (no bass models).

Pickups on Ranger Basses built in the Lone Star State were originally Seymour Duncans, which were later supplanted by Rio Grande models. While some players might consider three-position toggle switches to be somewhat out of place on a bass, the "potential plus side" is that such instruments offer instant switching to a trio of unique sounds, and in particular, the center position on most Rangers conjures up a plump, sounds-like-it-might-be-slightly-out-of-phase tone that is fat and bright.

According to Wintz, stock colors for the domestic Ranger Bass would have included Pearl Mint Green, Black, Old Blonde, and Transparent Orange, but other custom-order hues were available. This 1993 example is finished in Black Pearl, which has a very faint but cool-looking glitter appearance. The Alamo president noted with a chuckle that Black Pearl " . . . was a popular color during the 'shred years.'"

The Ranger Bass was the longest-running bass model in Robin's chronology, with about fourteen total years of production for imported and domestic models.

The Robin Medley Bass, like many other models from the Texas company, also has the same curious chronology as the Ranger: There was originally a Japanese-made version of this model, followed by a domestic variant.

Introduced in the mid-1980s, the original Medley Bass (made by ESP) had a (usually alder) body with fairly long cutaway horns, a twenty-four-fret bolt-on neck with a thirty-four-inch scale, black hardware, and a "reverse blade" headstock (tuning keys pointing downwards).

One of its pickup configurations was, perhaps surprisingly, a two-single coil/humbucking threesome, complete with a five-way switch, as found on many hard rock-oriented guitars.

The domestic Medley Bass first appeared in the 1990 catalog. The body shape was very similar to its imported predecessor, as was the scale length, number of frets, and hardware. However, the headstock was the "Split-V" style, as popularized on other domestic Robin guitar models such as the Medley Custom TX and the Machete series.

Moreover, the pickups on domestic Medley Basses were in a P/J configuration with a three-way toggle switch. Again, the original pickups were usually Seymour Duncans, which were supplanted by Rio Grandes in the early 1990s.

Bodies were made from ash if the instrument had a see-through finish, or poplar (and sometimes ash) if the bass was a solid color. Fretboards were usually rosewood, but maple fretboards (laminated to the maple neck) were also seen.

The Medley Bass went through yet another cosmetic change to its headstock and was discontinued, along with all other Robin basses, in 1997, when the company made the decision to concentrate solely on guitars.

Accordingly, the 1995 Medley Bass seen here has several incongruities to ponder.

First, its neck and body aesthetics are the first configuration for American-made Medley Bass, but its serial number indicates it was made after Robin had already switched to the final style for this bass.

Its tuners are locking-type Sperzels, but while Sperzels were used on Robin basses, Wintz doesn't recall that his company used locking variants, and noted that they may have been a sample set that the instrument hardware manufacturer supplied to Robin.

The ash body is finished in a transparent rusty brown color known as "Root Beer." The company usually applied it to the backs and necks of instruments that had an alternate finish on the body's top.

"People typically don't like brown guitars," Wintz offered. "Think about those walnut-finished guitars Fender made back in the 1970s; nobody wanted 'em. 'Root Beer' looks great on the back of an instrument that's got something different on the front."

The company president opined that this example may be the only Medley Bass with a Root Beer finish.

So put 'em all together and what do you have? Most likely, a bass that was made with some leftover parts, which Robin (and almost every other guitar manufacturer) would probably consider doing at some point. The folks in Houston apparently had an original US configuration Medley Bass body and neck hanging around the factory or storage area (one wonders if the body was already finished in Root Beer), and the use of atypical tuners on this possibly-created-from-leftovers instrument could have been rationalized.

The ash body is quite lightweight, and those long cutaway horns give the neck a "closer-in" feel. The neck shape has somewhat of a beefy, "vaguely-early-

P-Bass" feel, but it's not so chunky that it would be uncomfortable. It ought to be ergonomically-acceptable for most bass players.

Bottom line, however, includes the fact that it's a brown instrument.

As noted earlier, in 1997 Robin made the decision to exit the bass market, but not before crafting a few unique basses.

In that annum, the company built approximately five four-string and five five-string Freedom Basses in Houston, and the handwritten serial number on this four-string domestic example indicates that it was the first one made.

Interestingly, the slim, tapered necks on the four-string Freedom Basses were imported (maybe somebody found 'em in storage in an out-of-the-way place in the Houston factory), while the five-string necks were made domestically. The neck width at the nut of the four-string was 1½ inches, the rosewood fretboard had pearl dot markers, and the instrument's scale was a standard thirty-four inches.

The US-made body is ash and has mild criss-cross figuring. It's got a typical Robin retro-vibe look with a three-tone sunburst finish and a large white pearloid pickguard.

The crescent-shaped control plate houses two volume controls and a master tone control, as well as a three-way pickup toggle switch. The Houston-assembled Freedoms had the potent and unique-sounding Rio Grande Powerbucker pickups.

It's quite possible that the short run of Freedom Basses was made to use up parts; i.e., like the aforementioned Root Beer-finished Medley, they may have been "floor sweep" instruments.

As for the decision to discontinue basses, " . . . it was an exercise in restraint," Dave Wintz said with a chuckle. "I like too many different things, and it wasn't enough of a genre for us to keep it going. I loved those (late-1990s Freedom Basses), and we've never had any problems or complaints."

In late 2010, Alamo Music Products shut down production of its guitar-making facility, but continued to make and market Rio Grande pickups. As of this writing, Wintz is unsure what the future holds regarding if or when the company will re-enter the guitar-making business.

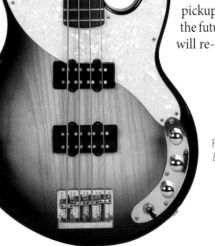

Robin Freedom, 1997.
Bill Ingalls Jr.

STANDEL

In the early history of the California electric guitar and amplifier business, Bob Crooks' Standel company was known for building high-quality amplifiers that were played and praised by top musicians such as Merle Travis and Joe Maphis. In particular, Standel's model 25L15, which utilized a J.B. Lansing D-130 speaker, was a classic, and is now a highly-prized collector's item among amp aficionados.

As was often the case, the "can't-have-one-without-the-other" syndrome concerning amplifiers and electric guitars motivated Standel to get into marketing guitars bearing its distinctive logo (which featured a snake-like "S"). As it turned out, the Standel sojourn through that facet of the musical instrument business was one of the more curious and convoluted tales of the 1960s guitar boom.

Crooks' first dealings regarding Standel-branded guitars were with builders from the Bakersfield area. In the early part of the decade, Semie Moseley of Mosrite would build a small number of instruments bearing the Standel name prior to his fabled affiliation with the Ventures and their Mosrite signature instruments.

1967 catalog cover.

July 1965 ad in *Downbeat* magazine for Hallmark-made Standel instruments

Former Mosrite employee Joe Hall's Hallmark company then built a number of Standel guitars and basses in the mid-1960s. Such instruments were advertised in *Downbeat*, and as if to

exemplify the never-particularly-stable relationship between Standel and the Bakersfield-area builders, double-branded guitars can be found in the vintage instrument marketplace bearing the Hallmark logo on the headstock, while a Standel "snake S" emblem was found on a metal plate that houses the guitars' pickups.

A third builder from that area began proffering Standel instruments circa 1967, but around the same time, Crooks, seeking classier guitars and basses to bear the Standel name, opted to hook up with a builder of higher-grade instruments all the way across the country.

New Jersey's Harptone company had been founded in 1893. In the 1960s, the redoubtable Sam Koontz was Harptone's head designer. Harptone's acoustic instruments featured a headstock profile that was vaguely reminiscent of that of an ultra-desirable D'Angelico archtop acous-

Standel 400S. *Bill Ingalls Jr.*

tic, and they had a unique arched back. Koontz would apply the same features to his designs for a series of Standel instruments.

The 1967 Standel "Professional Acoustic Electric Guitars" catalog cover was replete with a vibrant orange and yellow pattern over a line drawing of a long-haired band wearing matching outfits, playing Standel instruments. Inside, the hype noted that "Standel has carefully categorized its Electric Hollow Body Instruments into three basic lines, the Deluxe Artist Line, Deluxe Line, and Standard Line."

The solitary bass found in the four-page catalog was the model 400, a member of the Standard series. Available in a sunburst finish (400S, seen here) or cherry finish (400C), it had the same double-rounded-cutaway body dimensions (sixteen inches wide, 1¾ inches deep) as the model 420 Standard line guitar. The semi-hollow body has all-maple construction on the outside (including the aforementioned arched back) and an internal block, à la Gibson EB-2, which it resembles. The neck is one-piece mahogany.

While Standel's Standard Line was the only series that had pearl dot position markers (on a rosewood fingerboard), the plethora of cosmetic appointments on the company's lowest-priced series is still commendable—note the bound headstock with large decorative inlay, neck binding, three-ply binding on body edges, and single-ply f-hole binding.

Moreover, the headstock shape and body silhouette of Standel thinline electric-acoustic instruments, with slightly-slimmer double-rounded cutaway horns that flared out a bit more than their Gibson/Epiphone competitors, gave the Harptone-made guitars and basses a distinctive aesthetic.

The Standel 400's scale was 30½ inches, and the nineteen-fret fingerboard joined the body at the sixteenth fret. Note the zero fret by the headstock.

Of particular note on this bass is the neck profile, which is quite unique. The owner of this instrument described such a feel as "hard 'U'/soft 'V.'" Indeed, the sides of the neck are at almost a right angle at the juncture with the fretboard, but taper into a comfortable angle with a slight V-feel.

The pickup is a bass version of a DeArmond DynaSonic. Controls consisted of a volume and tone control, and the catalog noted the instrument's hardware, including its "adjustable compensated roller muted bridge" and "enclosed chrome individual metal machines."

Sam Koontz estimated that Harptone built only a few hundred Standel-branded instruments. While the line may have been short-lived, and the quantities manufactured were miniscule compared to other guitar ventures of the time, there were still some variants that differed from the examples seen in the catalog. For example, the pickup on this 400S is closer to the neck than the DynaSonic seen on the 400C in the 1967 catalog, and this one also has an apparently-original juxtaposed fingerrest and thumbrest in different locations from the same items on the catalog illustration.

For bass players, the Standel 400 represents a unique, well-crafted turn on EB-2-style short-scale, semi-hollow instruments.

STEINBERGER

Arguably the most striking bass instrument of all time, the Steinberger headless bass accomplished—at least, visually—what the Fender Precision Bass had done when it was introduced almost three decades before the black, headless, minimalist-bodied Steinberger item made its debut at the 1980 summer NAMM show.

However, the bizarre-looking bass wasn't furniture designer Ned Steinberger's first venture into instrument-making. In the mid-1970s, he'd collaborated with bass builder Stuart Spector on the creation of the Spector NS model, but Steinberger felt compelled to come up with newer and more radical innovations to reduce the size of basses, facilitate optimum balance, and reduce instrument weight.

Toiling in a Brooklyn woodworking co-op building, Steinberger worked through several different materials and shapes before debuting a headless bass with a smaller, rectangular body made entirely of a graphite, epoxy, and carbon fiber mix. Its black industrial/stealth appearance and radical silhouette added to the perception that this was an instrument that was on the cutting edge of technology.

Steinberger Sound was founded in 1979, and four initial basses were promoted on a 1980 brochure—the H1 had a single DiMarzio high impedance pickup while the H2 had two pickups; the L1 featured a single EMG low-impedance pickup, and the L2 was the two-pickup version. The L2 was also the most popular of the four new models, by far.

The L2's fretboard had twenty-four frets, and cylindrical, knurled tuners were anchored at the end of the body, eliminating the need for a headstock. Strings were to be a new, double-ball style made particularly for Steinbergers, but standard strings could also be used if four small threaded set-screws were inserted into the holes at the end of the neck (where a headstock would normally be) to install the loose/raw end of a bass string.

The new bass's strap configuration was also unique. A swiveling pivot plate was installed on the back of the instrument; the plastic item, which looked somewhat like a boomerang, could be adjusted for tension to allow the bass to be locked into place at a certain angle, or to pivot freely, depending on player preference.

And if a player wanted to sit down instead of playing standing up, a removable plastic leg rest could be installed on the lower edge, using a metal stud plug. This configuration proved to be impractical, so Ned re-designed the leg rest as an attached flip-down mechanism.

Among the earliest proponents of the new Steinberger bass were frontline bassists John Entwistle of The Who, the Dixie Dregs' Andy West, and King Crimson's Tony Levin.

Steinberger's radical new bass was sturdy, had an accurate response, stayed in tune, and was easy to play. However, to some players and listeners, Steinbergers still sounded somewhat "brittle," thus their stereotypical sound may have been an acquired taste.

"They're almost clavinet-like," bassist Leland Sklar, another early Steinberger player, said in a mid-1990s interview. "One thing that's great about them is if you tune them up, you can do a whole tour and not have to re-tune. They're really quite amazing for their properties; they're not my instrument of choice, but when it's the right instrument for a certain track, it's great."

Sklar's use of a Steinberger can be observed and heard in Phil Collins' *No Ticket Required* concert video (recorded in 1984), and his note-for-note riffing with guitarist Daryl Stuermer on a tour-de-force number titled "Hand in Hand" is especially impressive.

The L2 won an award from the Industrial Designers Society of America (IDSA), and *Time* magazine also honored it with one of five best design awards in 1981.

Steinberger L2, early 1980s. *Robert Tompkins*

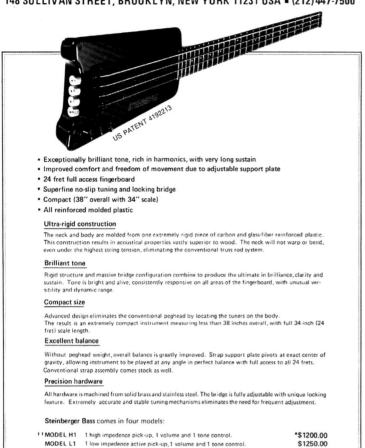

CHAPTER THIRTY-SEVEN

STEINBERGER SOUND

148 SULLIVAN STREET, BROOKLYN, NEW YORK 11231 USA ■ (212)447-7500

US PATENT 4192213

- Exceptionally brilliant tone, rich in harmonics, with very long sustain
- Improved comfort and freedom of movement due to adjustable support plate
- 24 fret full access fingerboard
- Superfine no-slip tuning and locking bridge
- Compact (38" overall with 34" scale)
- All reinforced molded plastic

Ultra-rigid construction

The neck and body are molded from one extremely rigid piece of carbon and glass-fiber reinforced plastic. This construction results in acoustical properties vastly superior to wood. The neck will not warp or bend, even under the highest string tension, eliminating the conventional truss rod system.

Brilliant tone

Rigid structure and massive bridge configuration combine to produce the ultimate in brilliance, clarity and sustain. Tone is bright and alive, consistently responsive on all areas of the fingerboard, with unusual versitility and dynamic range.

Compact size

Advanced design eliminates the conventional peghead by locating the tuners on the body. The result is an extremely compact instrument measuring less than 38 inches overall, with full 34-inch (24 fret) scale length.

Excellent balance

Without peghead weight, overall balance is greatly improved. Strap support plate pivots at exact center of gravity, allowing instrument to be played at any angle in perfect balance with full access to all 24 frets. Conventional strap assembly comes stock as well.

Precision hardware

All hardware is machined from solid brass and stainless steel. The bridge is fully adjustable with unique locking feature. Extremely accurate and stable tuning mechanisms eliminates the need for frequent adjustment.

Steinberger Bass comes in four models:

†† MODEL H1	1 high impedence pick-up, 1 volume and 1 tone control.		*$1200.00
MODEL L1	1 low impedence active pick-up, 1 volume and 1 tone control.		$1250.00
MODEL H2	2 high impedence pick-ups, 2 volume and 1 tone control.		$1350.00
MODEL L2	2 low impedence active pick-ups, 2 volume and 1 tone control.		$1400.00

* Manufacturer's suggested retail price. †† All instruments include special case, cord and strap. (Prices and specifications subject to change without notice.)

1980 product sheet.

As the decade progressed, Steinberger basses won more awards, and subsequent Steinberger converts would include Sting of the Police (circa their *Ghost in the Machine* album), Benjamin Orr of the Cars, and Rush's Geddy Lee. No paid endorsements were given for Steinbergers, but many musicians recognized that the unique basses had their own sonic niche.

Steinberger Sound relocated to Newburgh, New York, in 1983, and the L-series was replaced in 1984 by the XL series. Steinberger would eventually manufacture and market guitars, as well as other basses with wood bodies and composite necks in various shapes and colors. The company would eventually be acquired by the Gibson conglomerate.

And since the "imitation is the sincerest form of flattery" cliché is a huge facet of the guitar business, small-bodied, headless basses marketed by such companies as Kramer, Washburn, Cort, Warwick, and Aria appeared in the instrument marketplace during the "Me Decade."

The instruments seen here are stereotypical examples of the Japanese-made instruments that entered the American market during the 1960s guitar boom, contributing to the demise of the budget American guitar manufacturing industry.

Which means, of course, that an untold number of American teenagers played instruments like these.

The Teisco company of Japan was one of the primary manufacturers of electric instruments in that decade. Teisco instruments were imported by Westheimer Sales, a wholesale distributor, which later changed the brand name to Teisco Del Rey.

Teisco Del Rey
EB-200, mid-1960s.
Willie G. Moseley

Custom Crafted

All Teisco Electric Guitars Come Complete With Amplifier Connecting Cord.

ET-200
Two pick-up electric guitar with tremolo tailpiece. The pick-ups have individual string adjustment screws, and are controlled by separate volume and tone controls. There are individual, noiseless, velvet touch ON/OFF switches for each pick-up. Contoured hardwood body. The rosewood fingerboard is inlaid with 8 position markers. The steel reinforced neck is adjustable. Protective pick guard is satin finished metal. Chromed adjustable bridge. List $90.00

E-200
Same as ET-200 but without tremolo. List $81.00

EB-200
Deluxe two pick-up bass guitar with extended neck. Tone and volume controls, and individual noiseless velvet touch ON/OFF switches. Two ultra high sensitive pick-ups. The detachable and adjustable steel reinforced neck is warp-proof. Chromed metal machine heads and tailpiece. Extended rosewood fingerboard has 10 inlaid position markers. Brushed satin metal plates protect the body finish.
List $150.00

ET-200

EB-200

ET-300
Deluxe three pick-up electric guitar with hinged cover tremolo tailpiece. The extra large double cutaway body is contoured and beveled for proper feel. The detachable and adjustable steel reinforced warp-proof neck has a rosewood fingerboard with 10 inlaid position markers. 22 fret extended neck. There are separate volume controls and noiseless velvet touch switches for each pick-up. Tone is regulated with one control. The chromed bridge is adjustable. A satin finish metal protective plate protects the beautiful lacquered hardwood finish. List $120.00

ET-300

1965 catalog page.

One of the more-often-seen basses that teenagers thumped in garages all across the country during the 1960s was the solid body EB-200 (page 187), a relatively simple short-scale instrument that still had some interesting aesthetic features, some of which were quite practical.

The oversized headstock has a silhouette that exudes a vague Egyptian Pharaoh vibe to some observers, and the crown on the logo plate alludes to the "Del Rey" (Spanish for "of the king") portion of the brand name.

The twenty-one-fret rosewood fretboard (on a bolt-on neck) has commendable fretboard inlay on the bass side for easier reference, with a double marker at the twelfth/octave fret.

The bridge/tailpiece was found under a plate that attached with a single thumbscrew. Underneath the top edge of the plate was a thick chunk of grayish-green foam that muted the strings.

The two rocker switches are described in a 1965 Teisco Del Rey catalog as "individual noiseless velvet touch ON/OFF switches" that controlled "Two ultra high sensitive pickups."

The same catalog description notes that "Brushed satin metal plates protect the body finish," a reference to not only the pickguard, but the plate on the headstock as well.

By the following year, Teisco Del Rey guitars and basses (and associated brands) began appearing with striped brushed metal pickguards; the matte finish on such parts was applied to reflect light in two different directions.

The year 1966 also saw the introduction of a new, cosmetically-unique Teisco Del Rey bass. The EP-200B was a short-scale bass in a series of hollow body instruments that featured offset body waists instead of parallel waists, as well as offset cutaway horns; i.e., sort of a Fender Jazz Bass profile on a thinline-type of body. Moreover, the headstock of Teisco Del Rey basses acquired a "3+1" tuner configuration, while most of the electric guitars in the line acquired a "4+2" tuner layout. Most of the newer models began to exhibit ordinary dot markers on the fretboard, and the EP-200B had twenty-one frets, like its peers and predecessors.

That being said, it's doubtful that the headstock profile of Music Man basses was (directly) inspired by Teisco Del Rey basses that appeared almost a decade earlier. Ditto the offset body profile of Fender's Starcaster, which appeared as a guitar only (no matching bass) in 1976.

The top of the EP-200B's body was quite crowded, as it had two pickups, two f-holes, a thumbrest and fingerrest installed at oddball angles, master volume and tone controls, and a three-way rotary pickup (installed on the treble cutaway). The separate bridge was still covered by a plate that included foam for muting, and the trapeze tailpiece had an oval-shaped portion in which the strings anchored.

The two examples shown here differ not only in finishes, but headstock colors (one natural, one matching), but the model name on their respective neckplates is still the same.

These basses are just token examples of the umpteen imported brands and models that countless Baby Boomers played when they were teenagers. Finding examples as clean as these may be a rarer experience than one might think.

Teisco Del Rey EP-200B, circa 1966. *Willie G. Moseley*

Teisco Del Rey EP-200B, circa 1966. *Willie G. Moseley*

TRAVIS BEAN

Solid body guitars and basses built by Travis Bean (1947–2011) briefly appeared in the electric guitar and bass marketplace during the latter half of the 1970s. What made them unique was their innovative solid metal neck, described in company literature as a "precision-machined rolled billet of Reynolds 6061-T6 aluminum." Running from the headstock to the bridge, the aluminum neck was promoted by the company as being able to extend the vibration of guitar strings significantly, as the same literature trumpeted that the neck, " . . . provides an ideal anchor for each end of the string, allowing it to vibrate absolutely as long as physics will allow."

Further sonic enhancements on Travis Bean instruments included pickups that were mounted directly on the neck. The guitars had humbucking pickups, and the bass had high-gain single-coil units. Originally, the company stated that a Reynolds 6061-T6 nut was also found on the neck, although a later catalog cited a "solid brass nut" in its specifications section.

Travis Bean TB 2000, mid-1970s.
Sid Green

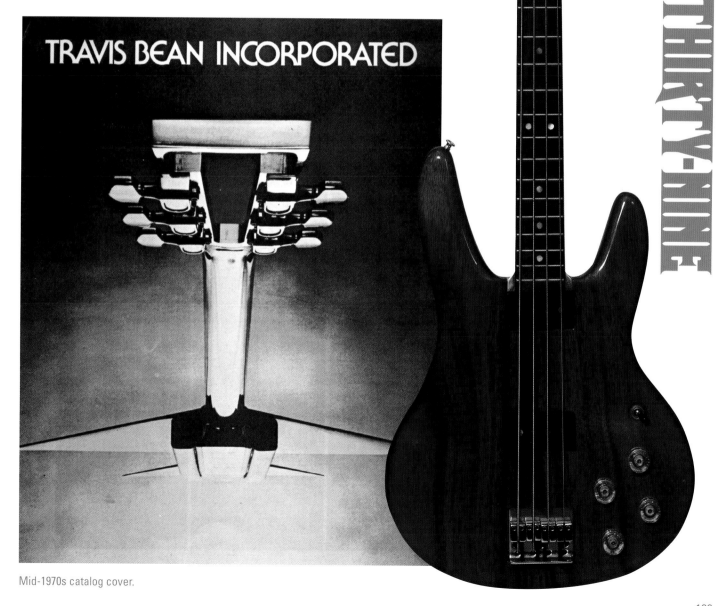

CHAPTER THIRTY-NINE

TRAVIS BEAN INCORPORATED

Mid-1970s catalog cover.

Wood portions of the instruments included double-cutaway koa bodies (although some examples made from other woods were constructed) and rosewood fingerboards. Finishes were usually natural, but red, black, and white pearl instruments were also built.

When the first Travis Bean instruments hit market, their shiny necks (with a "T" silhouette cutout in the headstock), precision-mated into a slot in a gorgeous koa body, commanded immediate attention from guitarists and bass players. The original models included the koa-bodied TB 1000 guitar and the TB 2000 bass.

The TB 2000 was 41⅜ inches long, with a body with offset cutaways that was 14½ inches wide and two inches deep. The fretboard had a 33¼-inch scale with twenty frets that joined the body at the last fret (all Travis Bean instruments offered complete access to all frets). A perusal of a TB 2000 shows not only the distinctive "T" in the headstock, but also the aluminum neck poking out on either side of the body/neck juncture.

Controls were guitar-like, with a volume and tone control for each pickup and a three-way pickup toggle switch.

Noted bassists who played the TB 2000 included Bill Wyman of the Rolling Stones, for whom the company built four to six short-scale instruments (the only short-scale Travis Bean basses produced), and Peter Sweval (1948–1990) of Starz; Sweval had earlier been a member of Looking Glass, of "Brandy" fame.

The Travis Bean company went out on its furthest tangent with the introduction of the modernistic-looking and appropriately named TB 3000 Wedge guitar and the TB 4000 Wedge bass, the rarest production Travis Bean models. They were, respectively, TB 1000s and TB 2000s on different body silhouettes.

Interestingly, the Wedge guitar and bass used the same body (unlike their guitar and bass predecessors).

With its literally wedge-shaped body, the TB 4000 bass was pretty lengthy, measuring 48½ inches long, thirteen inches wide, and two inches deep. Around three dozen Wedge basses were estimated to have been built, and unlike other models it appears that most TB 4000 examples were painted instead of having a natural finish.

While quite innovative, the aluminum necks on Travis Bean guitars and basses probably felt cold to many players, and the brand flopped in the marketplace in fairly short order. One authority noted that their metal necks were " . . . just too strange for people to get used to." Neck heaviness was also a problem.

Business problems also afflicted the company, and the original Travis Bean company ceased production in 1979.

And here's a sardonic afterthought: A nickname for a Wedge guitar or bass back then was "the flying broom."

Travis Bean would attempt a brief comeback in the late 1990s, with an even more radical approach to guitar building, and not surprisingly, the concept still involved aluminum. However, that venture never really got off the ground.

One of the aforementioned collectors of Travis Bean instruments summed up the position of that brand (both its 1970s instruments and the proposed late-1990s line) in the history of American guitar-building by stating "In all, they remain a great idea that was well-executed and just not well-enough received."

Travis Bean TB 4000, mid-1970s.
Vintage Guitar Magazine archives

FORTY

TURNER

Some of the more unique guitars and basses to come out of California in recent decades have been the creations of veteran luthier Rick Turner. His experience in guitar craftsmanship goes all the way back to the early days of the Alembic company and its collaborative efforts with the Grateful Dead, but his time-in-grade as a repairman and musician dates back even further and includes a stint as a backing guitarist for folk singers Ian and Sylvia, as well as employment at Dan Armstrong's guitar shop in New York City.

Turner left Alembic in the late 1970s, and founded his own company in Ignacio, located in Marin County, just north of San Francisco.

The initial offering from Turner Guitars was the Model 1 guitar, the six-string variant of the bass seen here. Turner estimates that during the three years his company was in business the first time around, only 25–30 basses were built, and of those, approximately half were shipped to Japan. Model 1 basses had one pickup, Model 2 basses had two pickups.

Fleetwood Mac guitar Lindsey Buckingham was the primary purveyor of original Turner guitars, but players who used the relatively rare basses included David Hayes with Van Morrison, Dusty Wakeman with Michelle Shocked, and Pete Anderson.

All original Turner basses had a thirty-two-inch scale, and Rick Turner observed: "That's a length that I really like, although it's not done much. I think thirty-two inches is way underappreciated; there's no lack of punchy bottom end."

The headstock features Schaller tuners aligned for a direct-pull on the strings and a walnut veneer.

Interestingly, one design facet that Turner changed (considering the instruments he created at Alembic) was neck-through construction.

"I got away from the neck-through design because I thought it had its own set of limitations," he observed, "particularly (as applied to) the guitar sound I wanted to develop."

Necks were laminated maple and purpleheart, and the fretboard had twenty-four frets, plus a zero fret, on Indian rosewood. The side dot markers for such instruments were made of brass, and Turner detailed that they were actually pieces of 1/16-inch braising rods, installed on black celluloid binding. This Model 1 bass's neck measures 1.6 inches at the nut and 1.9 inches at the

seventeenth fret, where it joins the upper bout of the body.

The bodies of Turner guitars and basses were Honduras mahogany and had what the founder described as " . . . a clamshell construction with the chambers for the optional pickup selector (for Model 2 instruments) and for the electronics. They were routed out before laminating the top and back halves together, and then the shape profile was done on a pin router. The tops and backs were arched by hand."

The bodies also had black celluloid binding, but the black stripe on the bass side of the body of the instrument seen here is simply an incongruity in the mahogany, according to Turner.

Hardware included the aforementioned Schaller tuners and a bridge that " . . . came from Star's Guitars, and was based on the original brass design I'd done at Alembic," said Turner.

The obvious "sonic focal point" of Turner guitars and basses was a rotating pickup on the Model 1 versions. The second pickup found on Model 2 guitars and basses was stationery, located closer to the bridge. As alluded to by Turner, a rotary six-position pickup selector was installed on the upper bout of Model 2s.

The pickups were designed by Turner and built by Bill Bartolini, and Turner had an interesting take on the one that rotated.

"That was never intended to be a major feature," he detailed. "That design allowed me to mount the pickup without springs, and yet still have the height and bass/treble tilt adjustment. There are two screws in the round plate, pulling the pickup up, and a single screw through the back, pulling the pickup down. Removing the pickup mounting plate also gives access to the pickup selector switch cavity in the upper bout, and originally, the truss rod nut was accessed by removing the pickup plate."

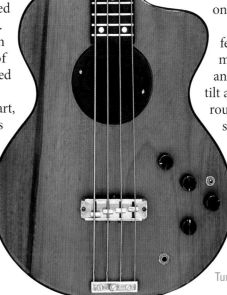

Turner Model 1, 1980. *Mark Ritchie*

Turner basses were active; and their electronics were sophisticated enough to warrant an 18-volt system. The knob closest to the bridge is a master volume control, and the other two knobs in the angled row of three controls consist of a frequency-sweep control in the middle and boost/cut control for the semi-parametic equalizer. The solitary knob closer to the butt of the body is a passive tone control. The mini-switch near the boost/cut knob is an EQ-on/EQ-bypass switch.

"A lot of people thought that was an active/passive switch," Turner said of the EQ switch, "but those instruments were active all the time."

According to this instrument's spec sheet, the frequency of the sweep ranges from 200 Hz to 6 KHz, with a boost or cut of 15 dB available at the selected frequency.

Turner noted that all original guitars and basses were numbered sequentially, in the order that they were completed and shipped, and that the second part of serial numbers was the year the instrument was built. He estimates that approximately 200 instruments total were made during his first go-round as an independent builder. He later supported himself as a cabinetmaker, worked briefly for Gibson, and returned to his own venture in the mid-1990s, as Rick Turner/Renaissance Guitars.

VALCO

The builder of the quirkiest instruments to be shipped out of the Chicago area during the 1960s "guitar boom" was Valco, which had historical and convoluted connections with the National and Dobro companies. Valco's flagship brand was indeed called National, and the company also had a sub-brand/promotional line called Supro. Numerous house brand instruments were also made by Valco, and as exemplified by the two polar-opposite basses shown here, some of their offerings looked downright weird (then and now).

First, there's a 1965 National 85 bass, which has been nicknamed the "map" bass in vintage guitar jargon, as its body silhouette vaguely resembles a map of the United States when viewed horizontally. Its predecessor was the Val-Pro 85, a similar instrument introduced in 1961, which had a rounded treble cutaway.

In addition to its silhouette, the construction style of the body was also unique— it was comprised of two halves of a molded fibreglas/resin substance known as Res-O-Glas, which snapped together with a rubber strip at the center seam.

Other oddball ideas—construction-wise and visual—permeated Valco instruments. Many of their instruments had a 2+2 headstock style called a "Gumby" shape, as seen on this map bass. The scale length on the Val-Pro 85 and National 85 basses was twenty-five inches; i.e., the scale of a standard guitar. Like other basses seen herein, it appeared that Valco simply took guitar necks and added different tuners and nuts to convert such parts into bass necks. The quarter-circle fret markers are sometimes referred to as "quadrant" markers.

The body has a fingerrest and a thumbrest, both made of clear plastic. Those two items, as well as the clear plastic bridge base, have a silvery, foil-like material underneath.

The neck pickup is mounted right next to the neck/body joint, but this is actually a two-pickup instrument. The other pickup is one of Valco's fabled/notorious "Silversound" units, which was built into the bridge assembly, and was a primitive precursor to transducer-type pickups . . . and the cloth wire that runs from the bridge into the body has all of the aesthetic appeal of a worm in an apple.

The two knobs are actually volume controls for each pickup; however, the Silversound unit sounds so bright—or dinky—its volume knob also serves as a type of tone control; i.e., roll back, and a deeper sound is evoked; turn it up and an almost "ticking" sound can be heard anytime a string is plucked.

This National 85 dates from the last year of the model's production. By that time, the incursion of imported guitars and basses into the American marketplace was well underway, and Valco and other budget instrument manufacturers were in serious trouble.

As noted in the profile of the Ampeg see-through bass, St. Louis Music is a longtime wholesale distributor, and at one point in its history, marketed its own house brand products, sporting the Custom Kraft moniker.

National 85, 1965.
Willie G. Moseley

By the time this 12178 "Bone Buzzer" bass appeared in a 1968 Custom Kraft catalog, Valco had merged with Kay, having done so in 1967. However, that marriage only lasted for about a year before manufacturing was shut down, so this bass was marketed around the time Valco and Kay ended. While some products from such times have parts that came from both companies, this thinline bass appears to be all Valco.

The Custom Kraft Bone Buzzer was another definitive example of Valco weirdness, even though its body had now-accepted-in-the-marketplace thinline construction. In the 1968 catalog, it listed for $199.95, and appeared on the same page as two Valco-made thinline hollow body electric guitars, the six-string "Super Zapp" ($175), and the twelve-string "Sound Saturator" ($199.95). All three instruments carried the same finish options—Sunburst, Cherry Sunburst, and Emerald Sunburst.

Despite the body's nod to Gibson's EB-2 and similar instruments, a plethora of typical Valco weirdness abounds on this bass. Note the "dragon snout" headstock, with a brand name, medallion, pinstriping, and "Made in U.S.A." all crowded onto its top surface. The bolt-on, bound neck has a zero fret on a rosewood fingerboard with block markers.

The elevated pickguard, on both sides of the top was referred to as a "Smart new Custom Kraft Butterfly guard plate," and was possibly a St. Louis Music exclusive. Ditto the two lightning bolt-shaped f-holes on the body possibly having been another St. Louis Music exclusive, or at least, a house brand exclusive, as National thinlines of that final era had a different f-hole configuration.

As for electronics, the two pickups are described in the catalog as "super field" (?) units. The volume and tone controls (one for each pickup), as well as the three-position toggle switch, appear to have been laid out in a haphazard configuration.

Many, if not most, Valco-made instruments reportedly had a way-too-strong capacitor on the bridge pickup tone control that caused said pickup to sound terribly thin—so much so that a player might think something is amiss electronically if the tone control is at full treble (shades of the Silversound pickup). When playing this bass (or any similar Valco product), a musician should roll off of the bridge pickup's tone control, and the output of the treble pickup should improve dramatically.

This instrument also has what are possibly original black nylon tapewound strings, as the 1968 catalog noted them as being standard on new Bone Buzzer basses.

Curiously, the same three thinline instruments appeared in the 1969 St. Louis Music catalog, even though the manufacturer had closed its doors. All of the text and pricing were the same as in 1968, except for the case for the bass, which had jumped from $25 to $33.

The Custom Kraft model 12178 Bone Buzzer bass was a "caboose" example of the cosmetic and electronic wackiness of the late Valco company, but it is also an odd-looking representative of an American-made budget instrument. No famous bassist was ever seen plunking on a Bone Buzzer, but it's got enough weirdness and coolness to make it interesting to guitar buffs.

Custom Kraft 12178 Bone Buzzer, 1968. *Steve Evans*

CHAPTER FORTY-TWO

WAL

The Wal company, a respected English builder of basses, began in the mid-1970s as a collaboration between luthier Pete Stevens and Ian Waller, who developed the electronics for their instruments.

The first Wal bass, however, wasn't particularly impressive, as it was a short-scale "Frankenstein" instrument made from an ash body. It had a Gibson bridge and knobs and pickups from a Fender Mustang Bass and a Guild bass. Still, it had an eye-catching hand-tooled leather pickguard that would be seen on numerous other early Wal basses, including the one on display here (serial #JG1128), which was custom-made for The Who's John Entwistle in 1978.

The "JG" in serial numbers of early Wal basses is a reference to veteran English bassist John Gustafson, a respected Liverpool musician who played with the Big Three and the Merseybeats. He had subsequent gigs with Roxy Music (playing on their *Stranded* album) and the Ian Gillan Band. Gustafson was an important advocate for the brand in its infancy.

Also among the earliest Wal purchasers and players were Mick Taylor, Paul Simonon of the Clash, and Bow Wow Wow bassist Leigh Gorman, who can been whomping a Wal in that band's early 1980s "jailbait-on-the-beach" video of "I Want Candy," a rollicking cover of an old Strangeloves hit.

The bass seen here conforms to the early configuration and construction of most J.G. Wals, with a slightly pudgy, somewhat generic-looking body silhouette and a 2+2 headstock that appears to be a bit oversized. Its present owner has done research that indicates it was the eighteenth instrument made.

It has a bolt-on, multi-laminated neck (the number of laminations on Wals have varied, depending on the model), and the neck's truss rod was accessible at the neck joint. This bass's headstock has the company's name in script as well as "J.G. Custom Bass," and two Phillips-screw attachments serve as solitary string trees for the A and D strings.

The body is one-piece ash, finished in a see-through "Salmon" color, and it's contoured with a forearm bevel on the front and a belly cut on the back.

An obvious visually-striking facet of #JG1128 is the aforementioned hand-tooled leather pickguard, a part of most instruments in the J.G. series. Most appear to have been decorated a floral motif as seen here, but some early Wal J.G.s had plain leather scratchplates.

The fretboard on this bass is rosewood and was ordered by Entwistle as a lined fretless item. Notes from the now-deceased Who bassist stated that it was one of his first fretless instruments, and that he could never figure out how to work the controls. The instrument has two volume controls, two tone controls, a master volume control, and a three-way pickup toggle switch on the treble cutaway. The pickups are exclusive Wal products and have eight adjustable polepieces. Sharp-eyed observers may be able to spot slider switches, which offer series/parallel sounds, on each pickup mounting ring.

The beefy intonatable bridge/slotted tailpiece combination, also developed by Wal, is a notable item. In fact, the company takes pride in the fact that almost all of its parts are either made at the manufacturing facility itself, or are manufactured by contracted suppliers.

Entwistle appeared with this instrument in two English magazine advertisements.

It has been reported that the bass line for the seminal English charity single, "Do They Know It's Christmas," was performed on a Wal (John Taylor of Duran Duran was playing one in the video), and that Wal basses were seen onstage at Live Aid in 1984, being played by Martin Kemp (Spandau Ballet) and John Ilsley (Dire Straits).

Other owners of Wal basses over the decades have included Paul McCartney, Geddy Lee (Rush), Sam Rivers (Limp Bizkit), Jeff Ament (Pearl Jam), Jonas Hellborg, Michael Hogan (Cranberries), Flea, Percy Jones (Brand X), and others—quite an across-the-board collection of players from assorted musical genres.

While some custom Wal basses with unique looks or configurations have been made (and continue to be made), most seem to have a fairly common aesthetic to many observers. So-called average looks aside, however, this meticulously-made, not-too-common brand has had a disproportionate share of notable players, indicating that the sound of Wal basses is highly desirable to professional musicians.

Wal J.G. fretless, 1978. *Heritage Auctions*

Founded in the early 1980s, Germany's Warwick bass company produces high-quality, precision-built instruments using unique woods. However, Warwick's history is actually connected by blood lineage to an earlier and well-known German brand, in a time when that nation was still divided following World War II.

"My father was the founder of Framus," Warwick owner Hans-Peter Wilfer recounted. "He started in 1946, with permission from the US Zone, in Nürnberg (Bavaria)."

The younger Wilfer worked at his father's facility, but the original Framus company went out of business in the 1970s. His interest in building stringed instruments was undiminished, however, and in the early 1980s he began his own venture.

"I founded my company on September 13, 1982," Hans-Peter recalled. "The first year, I made guitars and basses, selling out of my tiny workshop—more often, (I made) basses. Players liked them more in the beginning . . . so I decided to concentrate on basses."

The company's first model was one of its more intriguing. The Nobby Meidel model was a headless, small-bodied instrument that appeared to be inspired by the silhouette of the then-cutting-edge Steinberger instrument. However, while the Steinberger was made of composite materials, the Warwick used high-grade woods and had a neck-thru design.

What's more, Wilfer was actually motivated by another headless bass instead of a Steinberger.

"I was inspired by the Washburn Bantam Bass," he recalled. "Later on, (I saw) pictures of the Steinberger. Please remember, in 1982 we didn't have any internet."

Warwick soon began making conventional-looking basses, as the company integrated non-standard woods into their designs. Some of the species were quite hard and/or dense, and were practical for more than one reason.

"In the 1980s, bass players loved graphite necks," Wilfer explained, "but I couldn't get the material, so I thought: 'Which natural wood could I use that is extremely hard?' I found wenge, bubinga, and afzelia."

One of Warwick's most enduring models is the Thumb Bass, originally introduced as the JD Thumb Bass in 1985.

The "JD" designation refers to expatriate American bassist John Davis, a player in Germany whose popping, funk-based style (utilizing the stubbiest digit on his right hand) impressed Wilfer.

"The Thumb Bass was designed specifically for new comfort in slapping and playing in a virtuosic way, and it was the first bass with such a small body design, which gives you a lot of possibilities."

As for the aesthetics of the Thumb Bass design, Wilfer commented, "I was educated a bit as an illustrator, and my mother was a sculptor; I probably inherited that taste from my mom."

1986 Warwick Thumb Bass.
Rob Wheeler

The example shown here is a 1986 example of the original Thumb Bass configuration. It conforms to the earliest construction and finish methods of Warwick.

The seven-laminate, full-length neck is made of alternating sections of wenge and bubinga. The fretboard is also wenge, and has twenty-six frets and a thirty-four-inch scale. Wilfer noted the construction style of the bass allowed more frets to be added, giving a bassist " . . . more virtuosity."

The instrument is a "hidden neck-through" model, and such construction is a proprietary Warwick technique, validating Teutonic technology at its best.

Sharp-eyed observers will note the apparent absence of the neck running the full length through the center portion of the body on the front view of the instrument, as seen on other instruments such as Rickenbackers or Alembics. The neck-through construction is there, albeit underneath the cap of the top. The body isn't merely slotted underneath for the neck to slide in. Instead, the top is composed of three sections—two wings plus a plank-like section that mounts on top of the neck-through portion. All three sections are cut precisely from one block of selected wood. The three sections are installed on the neck in a manner that makes them still look like the original contiguous piece.

"The process is very complicated," Wilfer averred. "This is a question of hundredths of millimeters."

The bass also has a typical-for-the-times oil-and-beeswax natural finish.

The nut is Warwick's own brass "Just-A-Nut" design, and in perhaps an even-more-unique use of an unusual metal, the frets are made of bell bronze.

Other hardware includes Schaller tuners, bridge/tailpiece, and locking strap buttons. Wilfer stated that the bridge was exclusive to Warwick in that era and was his own design.

The installation of the tuners in a non-perpendicular configuration was a pragmatic innovation, Wilfer noted.

"The angled tuners have to do with the angle of your hands," he said. "It is just more natural to turn your tuners in this way."

The Thumb Bass had both active and passive capability. Its treble pickup was angled in order to get a better signal from the D and G strings.

Circa 2001 ad for Jack Bruce's first limited edition Warwick signature bass, based on a Thumb Bass four-string model.

Its controls are appropriate—the one nearest the pickups is a master volume control with push-pull capability for active or passive mode. The middle knob controls a pickup pan potentiometer with center detent, and the concentric knob closest to the bridge offers tone controls (lower knob = bass, upper knob = treble).

Not unexpectedly, the Thumb Bass was available in five- and six-string variants.

The Thumb Bass is still a key model for Warwick, but has undergone changes over the decades.

It now has a separate bridge and tailpiece, and a slightly-different body shape with a shorter upper cutaway horn. Bolt-on models have also been interpolated into the lineup.

One early user and endorser of Warwick basses was Jack Bruce, who was later affiliated with Warwick on two different signature model basses. The first was a limited edition variant of the Thumb four-string model, and the latter was aesthetically reminiscent of his iconic 1960s Gibson EB-3.

Warwick ultimately outgrew its Bavarian facility and relocated to Markneukirchen in Saxony. The company is now considered one of the music industry's most "green" instrument manufacturers regarding its finishing process, according to Wilfer, who is gratified that his effort has been a success in the thirty-five years it's been in business. He's even been able to crank up the Framus brand name again, as well, in a separate venture.

"The company is still family-owned," he said proudly. "Never sold it, never went bankrupt. I love my work as much as I did on the first day. My wonderful wife Florence helps me, my daughter Estelle works in graphics, and my son Nicholas is learning to be a guitar builder.

"I am an honored man in life to be in business with wonderful people and employees . . . I hope I can still continue for the next seven to ten years before I hand it over to my son and daughter."

FORTY-FOUR

WESTONE

The relationship between Japanese instrument builders and US distributors was an important facet of the evolution of guitar sales in the United States, and was a primary factor, if not the most important factor, in the demise of budget American guitar manufacturers in the late 1960s.

Japan's Matsumoku company was a family-owned woodworking enterprise that had been founded around 1900, and first established a relationship with an American firm shortly after World War II, when signing on with Singer to build cabinets for sewing machines.

Matsumoku entered the guitar-building market in the mid-1950s, and over the decades would manufacture parts or instruments for numerous brands, including Yamaha, Aria, Greco, Vantage, Univox, and Westbury, among others. Norlin, an owner of Gibson, contracted with Matsumoku to make imported Epiphone instruments in the 1970s.

The Japanese contract builder also had a longtime relationship with St. Louis Music, which had been in business since 1922. SLM imported and distributed the Matsumoku-made Electra brand with a great deal of success—the early 1970s saw that company selling Electra "copy" instruments, but later in the decade, Electras began to be seen with their own distinct designs.

The Westone brand came along from Matsumoku around the advent of the 1980s, and St. Louis Music distributed that line as well. As might be expected, some Electra models that were being phased out and some Westone models that were being introduced looked quite similar to each other.

As the decade continued, certain Westone models were introduced that were quite unique and innovative in their own right. Among these was the "Genesis" limited edition series, created for St. Louis Music's sixty-fifth anniversary, and marketed circa 1987–88.

The XA6520 was the bass in the Westone "Genesis" lineup. It listed for $569 when it was introduced. It came in three colors—Burgundy Pearl (XA6520BUP) on a poplar body, and Transparent Walnut (XA6520TWA) or Transparent Burgundy (XA6520TBU, seen here) on a Canadian ash body. While similarly named, the Burgundy Pearl and Transparent Burgundy instruments seen in the limited edition series catalog had quite different hues—more of a purple for the former, and cherry for the latter.

The 2+2 headstock features Westone "Trak Wind Deluxe" tuners, and sharp-eyed observers may have noticed that the "W" logo is a silhouette of an eagle. The nut is carbon graphite.

The three-piece neck is made of Canadian hard rock maple, and is 1 9/16 inches wide at the nut. The rosewood fretboard has twenty-four frets. The dot markers are smaller than average, but the neck also has side dot markers.

On the back side, the neck plate was embossed from top to bottom with the Westone logo and name, "A Matsumoku Product," the serial number, and "Made in Japan." As if that wasn't enough information, a sticker on the body just below the neck plate noted the brand and model number, plus the

Westone Genesis XA6520TBU, 1987. *Bill Ingalls Jr.*

fact that it was an "Anniversary Edition." Also included were the St. Louis sixty-fifth anniversary logo and the dates (1922–1987).

The body of the XA6520 had more than one of the facets that made this model interesting. The neck joins the body at the nineteenth fret on the bass side and the twenty-first fret on the treble side.

At first glance, the body might seem to be a bit undersized, considering its slim waist and fairly-offset, slender cutaway horns. At its widest point, the body measures 12¾ inches, and it narrows to 7¾ inches at the waist. Its overall length is 18¼ inches.

Having a body that's a bit more diminutive might imply that a player should expect neck-heaviness when it's strapped on, but that's not the case, possibly because of the density of the Canadian ash—this instrument balances quite nicely and weighs in at 9½ pounds.

The most obvious oddity on the XA6520's body was what Westone hyped as "our exclusive Genesis stepped body." The area of the body face on the treble side from the neck joint to the cutaway horn is recessed by ¼-inch, and such a lower-level contour isn't just cosmetic. The catalog notes that those areas on such bodies are "carved away to allow easy slap technique."

The two pickups on the XA6520 were a "Magnabass III" and "Magnabass IV" (note the difference in polepiece configurations).

Controls include a three-way pickup toggle switch and a three-knob layout: There's a master volume knob (nearest the treble/bridge pickup), tone control for neck/bass pickup (center), and tone control for the treble/bridge pickup (nearest the top-mounted jack). In particular, the knobs on this bass are somewhat unique, as they have serrated sides and are slightly "funnel"-shaped, narrowing at the bottom. Accordingly, they may deserve the "cupcake" cosmetic designation as much, if not more so, than the old Harmony knobs from the 1950s and 1960s that were also described with that term.

The bridge is a "Magnacast" brass item, and has spring-mounted, individually-intonatable string saddles. Another hardware "plus" are the larger-than-average strap buttons, à la G & L.

The XA6520 may have been short-lived (it was, after all, a limited edition), but it was a powerful-sounding passive instrument. The excellent quality of Matsumoku-made instruments may have been somewhat unheralded over the years, and the XA6520 is exemplary of a model with unique facets to consider.

ZEMAITIS

Okay, so this one's not electric. It's such a cool item, however, that the urge to include it in this book is irresistible.

To say that the creations of legendary British luthier Antonio "Tony" Zemaitis (1935–2002) were eye-catching is only a mild description. Known primarily for their metal tops with exquisite engravings, Zemaitis electric instruments were painstakingly handcrafted, and were, for all intents and purposes, works of art with strings.

Originally a cabinetmaker of Lithuanian heritage, Zemaitis began building guitars in the 1950s. One of his most visually-striking and famous instruments from the 1960s was "Ivan the Terrible," an oversized twelve-string acoustic guitar that was special-ordered by Eric Clapton, who used it in 1969, on the *Blind Faith* album. Clapton recalled that the guitar was the first Zemaitis had built with a heart-shaped soundhole. The guitar was also played by George Harrison and Dave Mason in that era.

"Ivan the Terrible" was sold by Clapton at the second Crossroads Centre benefit auction in 2004; its pre-auction estimate was $30,000–$50,000, and its actual realized auction price was $253,900.

Zemaitis's handcrafted electric guitars were also unique. In an effort to cut down on pickup noise, the builder began installing metal tops on guitar bodies. Such items often covered the entire front of the body, but sometimes they were disc-shaped. To give each metal-front instrument its own distinctive look, Zemaitis relied on the skills of gun engraver Danny O'Brien.

A "breakout" of sorts for the Zemaitis name happened in the early 1970s, when guitarist Ron Wood and bassist Ronnie Lane of the Faces toured with metal-front instruments. The "flash" appeal of such instruments was obvious to players and audience alike, and soon, Tony's client list read like a Who's Who of British rock.

Zemaitis continued to make acoustic instruments, however, and around the time his instruments began to garner international notice thanks to Wood and Lane, the luthier began venturing into the acoustic bass realm, which had previously been occupied by instruments such as Mexican guitarrons and the 1930s Gibson Mando-Bass. As noted earlier, American luthier Ernie Ball was beginning to experiment with his Earthwood brand of acoustic basses around the same time.

The British builder would ultimately handcraft special-order acoustic basses for David Gilmour, Ron Wood (a single-cutaway model), Mike Oldfield, and Tony Visconti. It is believed that the fretted acoustic bass made for Oldfield, creator of *Tubular Bells*, was possibly the first one made, and the 1972 fretless instrument seen here may have been the second.

The original owner of this instrument was Jeff Allen, who ran a musical equipment rental company and a recording studio in London. Allen reportedly ordered this instrument due to the increasing number of artists who were seeking an acoustic bass sound.

Zemaitis fretless acoustic bass, 1972.
Vintage Guitar Magazine archives

Construction-wise, the bass has a mahogany neck, fretless rosewood fingerboard, spruce top, and solid mahogany back and sides. The bridge and string retainer are hand-carved rosewood, and abalone inlay is found on the latter part.

The jagged, carved headstock silhouette is fairly common to Zemaitis basses, as is the decorative red wood-stain stripe in its center. The fingerboard may lack frets, but side dots can be found on its edge for reference.

Curiously, this bass doesn't seem to have a truss rod. No truss rod cover is seen (such items are found in photos of the Oldfield and Gilmour instruments).

The overall length of the bass is forty-eight inches. Its upper bout is 12¾ inches wide, and the lower bout is 18½ inches wide. The body depth isn't quite uniform—it's four inches deep at the neck end and four and a half inches deep at the bridge end.

The instrument weighs five pounds, nine ounces, and is nicely-balanced. It has never been fitted with any kind of electronics.

The heart-shaped soundhole is an obvious aesthetic facet, but Zemaitis also crafted acoustic instruments with soundholes that were moon-shaped and harp-shaped. It doesn't appear that Allen ordered any particular woods on this bass.

A comparison of this instrument to David Gilmour's 1978 acoustic bass, seen in Tony Bacon and Paul Day's *The Ultimate Guitar Book*, underlines the individuality of each Zemaitis creation. Like this one, the Pink Floyd guitarist's

bass has a spruce top and a heart-shaped soundhole. However, the later instrument has an ebony fingerboard, which, while fretless, has lines and position markers on its face. Gilmour's bass also has a maple back and sides, and the bridge and string retainer are ebony. There's also the aforementioned truss rod cover, which is engraved with Gilmour's name.

Long before the advent of the "unplugged" genre of popular music, Tony Zemaitis created several rare and unique instruments to explore the lower sonic range of acoustic music. Such acoustic basses were part of the acclaim for Zemaitis instruments, and their reputation now resonates worldwide.

𝄢

During his tenure with the progressive rock juggernaut Emerson, Lake & Palmer, bassist/vocalist Greg Lake owned and played more than one instrument made by Tony Zemaitis.

And few instruments made by "Tony Z" were as unique as this doubleneck.

It's reportedly one of only two doublenecks that Zemaitis ever made. Designed by Lake, this heavy hitter, sporting a body silhouette that looks somewhat like a lopsided Batman logo, has numerous unique features, even for this ultra-high end brand.

Construction-wise, the instrument has a body and necks made from mahogany, with ebony fretboards, and rosewood overlays on the headstocks. The scales of the necks are 25⅝ inches for the guitar and thirty-two inches for the bass. Number of frets = twenty-four on the six-string and, er, 23½ on the low-end neck, as the angle of the fretboard

Greg Lake's Zemaitis double-neck, circa 1980. *Maverick Music*

edge slashes across the would-be twenty-fourth fret. Position markers include the cluster of markers at the twelfth fret, which the luthier referred to as the "snowflake."

The metal portion of this creation is made of Dural, an aircraft alloy. What sets this doubleneck apart from other Zemaitis instruments is the fact that the Dural top has been inlaid rather than installed as a cap over the wood body; note the tiny wood "border" around the metal.

The headstocks contain a diamond-shaped, engraved "Z" logo plate, as well as an engraved truss rod cover that says "CUSTOM."

Engraving on the rest of the body isn't as intricate as what's found on many other Zemaitis instruments. The decorations include Lake's initials, "GSL" on the front, and "Designed by G.S. Lake" on the Dural plate that covers a large portion of the back of the instrument. Lake also autographed the instrument on the rear plate with a marker on October 23, 1981.

The instrument's pickups were made by English builder John Birch (also deceased; Birch also made instruments). Curiously, the bass side is active while the guitar side is passive; the battery is accessed through a panel on the instrument's back.

At initial glance, the assortment of knobs and "chicken-head" pointer switches may be intimidating, but the layout isn't as complicated as it seems: The pointer switches to each side of the respective bridges are three-position rotary controls for pickups. The four cylindrical knobs behind the pickup switches are volume and tone for each pickup. There's also a master volume knob for each side, with a slight aberration in the layout design, in that the master volume knob for the bass side is a knob; the guitar's master volume has a chicken head cap. Each side also has a coil-tap chicken-head switch, and the chicken-head in the center, just below the engraved tailpieces, "turns on" one neck or the other.

The use of the term "heavy" in describing this instrument could not only refer to its impressiveness and/or the bombast of Emerson, Lake & Palmer's music, it's also applicable in a literal context to the doubleneck, as it weighs 17.2 pounds.

This exquisitely built, one-of-a-kind doubleneck guitar/ bass epitomizes the tools of their trade that rock stars who were at the pinnacle of success could design and have created to their specifications. Impressive music is often created onstage by impressive-looking instruments, and they don't get much more impressive-looking (or heavier) than this.

Greg Lake passed away on December 7, 2016.

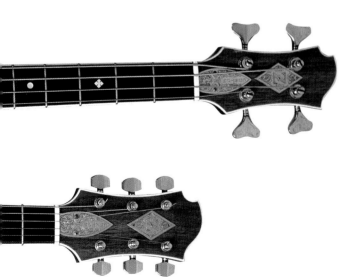

OUTRO

Take a close look at this 2008 Fender Tony Franklin signature model Precision Bass—while it may appear "generic" to some seasoned observers, it validates that while the electric bass has continued to evolve since it first (successfully) appeared in the marketplace more than sixty years ago, the basic lines and function of the progenitor haven't changed.

Franklin is a "player's player"—not particularly famous, but an innovative bassist whose work has included gigs with Jimmy Page and Paul Rodgers in the Firm; i.e., he's respected among his peers to the point that the Fender company opted to market a signature model bass bearing his name.

Franklin has been cited primarily for his work on fretless bass, and his original Fender signature model, which debuted in January of 2006, was indeed in that configuration. The company added a fretted version in 2008.

The neck and fretboard have been shaped to Franklin's specifications. The neck is 1.625 inches wide at the nut (which is made of synthetic bone), and the fretboard has a 9.5-inch radius.

The "specially-voiced" pickups have also been designed with Franklin's input, according to Fender consumer information. They're laid out in a now-considered-generic P/J configuration, and the controls are a three-way pickup toggle switch and master volume and tone knobs. Clean and simple.

While Fender's Tony Franklin signature Precision Bass has some unique features, it's still a relatively basic instrument that gets the job done, and the involvement of the bassist for whom it is named underlines how some signature models are practical instruments that are designed by bona fide musicians, rather than gaudy items with outlandish features and cosmetics demanded by self-indulgent rock stars.

Fender Tony Franklin signature Precision Bass, 2008. *Heritage Auctions*

Don Summers of Texas experienced a brief flirtation with fame in the mid-1960s, as the bassist for the Moving Sidewalks, a Houston-based blues/psychedelic aggregation that is remembered in the pantheon of rock music as guitarist Billy F Gibbons' pre-ZZ Top band.

The Sidewalks toured with Jimi Hendrix in early 1968, and not long afterwards, Summers and the Sidewalks' keyboard player, Tom Moore, were drafted. After serving in Vietnam, Summers returned to US soil; his "day job" for decades was with the Railway Express company.

Following his retirement, Summers, a longtime woodcrafting aficionado, opted to get into the luthiery business. He focused on basses, using the classic single-cutaway Fender Telecaster body shape; which Fender never put into production on its standard basses.

The distinctive feature of Summers' instruments is their laminated tops made of Kirei Board, made from recycled sorghum straw. The environmentally-friendly material is primarily used in furniture, cabinetry, and even as wall board ("*Kirei*" means "beautiful" in Japanese).

Summers currently offers his basses in both full-scale and short-scale configurations. His venture is just one of an untold number of smaller and unheralded companies who are creating unique basses in America.

🎵

Looking somewhat like a prop from a Star Trek movie, this all-aluminum bass is a custom-made twelve-string instrument, created in 2010. It was ordered by Tom Petersson, and he still owned it as of this writing.

All-metal and partially-metal guitars have been around for decades, and Kevin Burkett, founder and owner of the Electrical Guitar Company of Pensacola, Florida, came of age admiring the metallic innovations of companies such as Travis Bean and Kramer and their aluminum-neck instruments, as well as Veleno (all aluminum instruments). His own firm has been manufacturing instruments since 2003, and is currently backlogged on orders.

Petersson was made aware of the Electrical Guitar Company by recording engineer Steve Albini and bassist Bob Weston.

"My idea was to do a 'lefty' body à la Mosrite," the veteran bassist remembered. "I wanted Mike Lull five-string Thunderbird-type pickups because they have a bigger magnetic field."

As for the proximity of the two pickups, Petersson was inspired to place them in close proximity by Höfner basses from the 1950s, and he also wanted a brushed gold pickguard like older Rickenbacker basses, as well as gold hardware.

Summers short-scale bass. *Willie G. Moseley*

Electrical Guitar Company 12-string bass, owned by Tom Petersson. *Willie G. Moseley*

"The neck and body are carved out using a CNC (computer numerical control) machine," Burkett detailed. "It's a neck-through design with a hollow aluminum body. As far as (Petersson's) specs, it was pretty wide open. He wanted the Lull pickups pushed all the way to the neck; it's a bit amazing how much of a difference there is in the two pickups! The body is a hybrid; Tom said he wanted something in an offset asymmetrical-type shape, so I started with my Series One body, flipped it, and just started modifying it until it looked good."

Burkett detailed that the entire instrument is made of T6061 aluminum, except for the fretboard, which is T7075 aluminum. The fretboard has a twelve-inch radius.

The gold pickguard is also aluminum, albeit powder-coated in the color requested by Petersson. The tuners are by Gotoh, and the bridge was made by Schaller. The controls are a standard volume and tone knob for each pickup and a three-way selector switch.

Burkett's company is staying busy making aluminum electric guitars and basses in more conventional styles (including the number of strings).

"I've made some ten-string baritones in the past," the builder said, "but I think the twelve-string (bass) is the most extreme thing we've made at this point."

"I love the bass," Petersson enthused. "It's a heavy metal grand piano!"

While the Tony Franklin signature Precision Bass is an appropriate modern take on a classic instrument and the Summers bass is an exemplary retro-style bass with a contemporary touch, the aluminum Electrical Guitar Company twelve-string bass is perhaps a definitive example of ongoing modern innovations to the electric bass, including its sonic capabilities.

And that all-metal, multiple-stringed bass validates Tim Bogert's statement that the style and sound of the electric bass is still evolving. However, its place in most contemporary music ensembles and modern genres is permanent. Not a bad accomplishment for an instrument that's about two-thirds of a century old as of this writing.

And the (low-end) beat goes on.

BIBLIOGRAPHY AND REFERENCES

In addition to the *Vintage Guitar Magazine* articles by the author from which the bulk of the updated and revised text in this book was culled, the following sources were also used (and are suggested reading as well).

Extensive catalog research in preparing original articles as well as the revised versions herein was also done through the www.vintaxe.com website and other catalog sources.

BOOKS:

Bacon, Tony and Paul Day. *The Ultimate Guitar Book*. New York: Alfred A. Knopf, 1991.

Bacon, Tony and Barry Moorhouse. *The Bass Book*. San Francisco, California: Miller Freeman Books, 1995.

Bechtoldt, Paul. *Leo's Legacy*. Peckville, Pennsylvania: Woof Associates, 1994.

Bechtoldt, Paul. *Guitars From Neptune*. Peckville, Pennsylvania: Backporch, 1995.

Carson, Bill & Willie G. Moseley. *Bill Carson: My Life and Times with Fender Musical Instruments*. Bismarck, North Dakota: Vintage Guitar Books, 1998.

Carter, Walter. *Gibson Guitars: 100 Years of an American Icon*. Los Angeles, California: General Publishing Group, Inc., 1994.

Carter, Walter. *Epiphone: The Complete History*. Milwaukee, Wisconsin: Hal Leonard Corporation, 1995.

Crossroads Guitar Auction: Eric Clapton and Friend for the Crossroads Centre. New York: Christie's, 2004.

Day, Paul. *The Burns Book*. London, England: PP Publishing, 1979.

Duchossoir, A.R. *Gibson Electrics: The Classic Years*. Milwaukee, Wisconsin: Hal Leonard Corporation, 1994.

Gruhn, George and Walter Carter. *Electric Guitars and Basses: A Photographic History*. San Francisco, California: Miller Freeman Books, 1994

Gruhn, George and Walter Carter. *Gruhn's Guide to Vintage Guitars: An Identification Guide For American Fretted Instruments*. Milwaukee: Backbeat Books, 2010.

Hopkins, Gregg and Bill Moore. *Ampeg: The Story Behind The Sound*. Milwaukee: Hal Leonard Corporation, 1999.

Longworth, Mike. *Martin Guitars: A History*. Minisink Hill, Pennsylvania: 4 Maples Press, 1987.

Moseley, Willie G. *Guitar People*. Bismarck, North Dakota: Vintage Guitar Books, 1998.

Moseley, Willie G. *Vintage Electric Guitars: In Praise of Fretted Americana*. Atglen, Pennsylvania: Schiffer Publishing Ltd., 2001.

Moseley, Willie G. *Peavey Guitars: The Authorized American History*. Oxford, Mississippi: Nautilus Publishing Company, 2015.

Moust, Hans. *The Guild Guitar Book*. Breda, the Netherlands: GuitArchives Publications, 1995.

Roberts, Jim. *How the Fender Bass Changed the World*. San Francisco, California: Backbeat Books, 2001.

Roberts, Jim. *American Basses*. San Francisco, California: Backbeat Books, 2003.

Scott, Jay. *Gretsch: The Guitars of the Fred Gretsch Company*. Fullerton, California: Centerstream Publishing, 1992.

Smith, Richard. *The History of Rickenbacker Guitars*. Fullerton, California: Centerstream Publishing, 1987.

Smith, Richard. *Fender: The Sound Heard 'Round the World*. Fullerton, California: Garfish Publishing Co., 1995.

Wheeler, Tom. *American Guitars*. Revised and updated edition. New York: HarperCollins Publishings, 1992.

Wright, Michael. *Guitar Stories*, Vol. 1. Bismarck, North Dakota: Vintage Guitar Books, 1995.

Wright, Michael. *Guitar Stories*, Vol. 2. Bismarck, North Dakota: Vintage Guitar Books, 2000.

ARTICLES:

Blecha, Peter. "Rare pair: The Audiovox 736 electric Bass and 936 amp." *Vintage Guitar Magazine*, February 2017.

Gruhn, George. "Gibson Upright Electric Bass." *Vintage Guitar Classics*, June 1997

Gruhn, George and Walter Carter. "Rickenbacker Electro Bass." *Vintage Guitar Magazine*, February 2007.

Wilson, Riley. "G & L SC-2: When Is a Tele Not a Tele?" *Vintage Guitar Magazine*, February 1997.

Author/columnist/lecturer **WILLIE G. MOSELEY** is the senior writer for *Vintage Guitar Magazine*, and columnist/news editor emeritus for Tallapoosa Publishers, Inc. He resides with his wife Gail and their daughter Elizabeth in "Hank Williams Territory" (central Alabama). This is his tenth book.